From Gold to Code

From Gold to Code

A History of Monetary Evolution

Jahan Vespari

Mindful Pages

Published in 2026

ISBN: 9789374596722 (PB)
ISBN: 9789374594278 (eBook)

Published by

Mindful Pages
Imprint of Alpha Editions LLC
312 W. 2nd St #1834
Casper, WY 82601, USA

This book was developed using advanced writing tools to support the drafting and ideation process. All content has been thoughtfully curated, refined, and reviewed to ensure quality and relevance.

Content

Introduction

The first thing one notices is the sound. In a crowded port where spices, stories, and suspicions all travel on the same wind, a merchant moves his thumb across a string of beads, each bead a record of obligation, settlement, or promise. The rhythm is soft yet decisive, as though every click ratifies a private treaty with the world. Thousands of miles away, beneath humming fans in a converted warehouse, a miner monitors a screen while a block edges towards confirmation. This too is a ritual of trust: the silent wait, the probabilistic finality, the moment when a line of code becomes a settled truth in a global ledger. The two characters share no civilisation, no era, no language. Yet they are bound by something ancient and urgent: the human act of believing in value, then acting upon that belief.

What moves through their hands is not merely currency or computation, but a story—one persuasive enough to mobilise labour, redirect ambition, and shift the balance of power between strangers. A bead on a cord and a digital signature in a dispersed network seem worlds apart. One is tactile, the other ethereal. One belongs to the sphere of craft, the other to the domain of cryptography. Yet both perform the same miraculous transformation. They turn uncertainty into coordination. They convert the messiness of human desire into something that can be counted, transferred, and stored. They make cooperation between people who do not know or trust one another not only possible, but routine.

This book examines how those stories solidify into systems, and how those systems—once entrenched—become rulers in their own right. Money is often described as a medium of exchange or a store of value, but such definitions skim the surface. Money is, at its core, a social technology: a designed solution to the perennial problems of trust, memory, and motivation. It channels collective expectations into predictable behaviour. It organises society by providing the scripts through which economic life unfolds. And because it stands at the intersection of belief and institution, it is at once fragile and formidable. A coin can be debased, a bank can be drained, a peg can crack—yet the underlying human need to compare, to coordinate, to settle, and to preserve persists through every upheaval.

To trace the history of money is therefore to study a succession of designs, each responding to the constraints, anxieties, and aspirations of its age. The port merchant's beads and the miner's block serve as bookends for a vast narrative stretching from early tally sticks and household ledgers to imperial coinage, paper promises, global reserve currencies, electronic payments, and cryptographic protocols. At each stage, the same questions reappear in new guises. Who deserves trust? How is verification performed? What mechanisms enforce honesty when incentives tempt towards deceit? And how do the architecture and governance of a monetary system shape its resilience, reach, and fairness?

This is not merely a historical curiosity. We live in a period when the most basic assumptions about money are being questioned with unusual intensity. For decades, the underlying infrastructure of payments and banking was largely invisible, ignored by all except specialists. Now it sits at the centre of political debate, technological experimentation, and geopolitical competition. The rise of digital wallets, the contest over stablecoins, the debate surrounding central bank digital currencies, the global migration to faster payment rails, and the ideological disputes around cryptographic money have all thrust monetary design back into public view. A growing part of the world now interacts with value through interfaces rather than institutions, tapping screens where once they handled notes or negotiated face to face.

The stakes are unusually high. Monetary systems encode power: who issues, who verifies, who surveils, who bears risk, and who reaps advantage. They shape the incentives of households and the strategies of empires. They determine whether economic shocks cascade into crisis or are quietly absorbed. They influence whether prosperity is broadly shared or narrowly captured. And they define the texture of daily life—whether paying rent is a steady ritual or an anxious calculation, whether wages hold meaning across pay cycles, whether a migrant worker can send savings home cheaply, and whether a small business can access the short-term credit that keeps its shelves stocked.

To make sense of such a landscape, one needs a framework that unites the past and the future without romanticising either. The popular narratives—barter myths, golden ages, villainous bankers, magical algorithms—tend to obscure more than they illuminate. What is needed is a way to compare yesterday's coins and tomorrow's code by the same yardstick; a way to evaluate forms of money not by ideology or fashion, but by design, incentives, and trust structures. This book adopts precisely that approach. It argues that every monetary system, from the humblest tally to the most advanced distributed ledger, can be understood as a combination of tokens, ledgers, and protocols, governed by some mix of trust, verification, and enforcement. This lens cuts through complexity, revealing the trade-offs that every designer—from ancient rulers to modern engineers—must navigate.

The historical arc of monetary evolution is less a straight line than a recurring dance between centralisation and dispersion, between convenience and control, between resilience and efficiency. Early communities relied on memory and reputation; temples and palaces introduced centralised record keeping; empires minted coins to standardise value across vast distances; banks layered credit upon deposits; clearinghouses stabilised private networks; central banks emerged to anchor standards and quell panics; and global markets tied national systems into an intricate web of claims, promises, and exposures. Every innovation solved one problem while creating another. Every breakthrough had its dissenters. Every reform bore the imprint of power struggles lurking beneath the surface.

Yet there is also continuity across this sweep of history. The tally stick and the blockchain both grapple with the same dilemma: how to create durable records of obligations in a world full of uncertainty and opportunism. The stamped coin and the digital token both broadcast assurances backed by some authority, whether a state, a consortium, or a cryptographic guarantee. The goldsmith's receipt and the modern stablecoin both promise convertibility into something deemed more reliable. The clearinghouse and the consensus protocol both attempt to coordinate settlement without exposing participants to undue risk. These parallels suggest not a procession of unrelated inventions, but a long experiment in designing systems to manage cooperative risk at scale.

One motif runs through this book: the choreography of trust. Trust is never static. It shifts, stretches, contracts, and mutates as technologies and institutions change. Sometimes trust is personal, anchored in long-standing relationships. Sometimes it is institutional, resting on courts, auditors, or central banks. At other times it becomes architectural, embedded in code or protocol rules. The balance between these forms determines how widely and swiftly value can move. When trust fails, panic races faster than policy; when trust is abundant, economic life flourishes with surprising ease. Understanding how trust is constructed, signalled, enforced, and repaired is essential for understanding money itself.

This book moves chronologically, but not mechanically. Each chapter takes a pivotal moment or conceptual shift and opens it up, revealing how people solved coordination problems with whatever tools they had. We revisit the exaggerated tale of barter and uncover the subtler reality of early credit economies. We examine why certain commodities became money-like long before coins existed, and why temples and palaces acted as proto-banks. We study the emergence of coinage and explore how empires used monetary standards to consolidate authority. We follow the rise of banking as receipts transformed into circulating promises, and we observe how private clearinghouses created stability long before central banks formalised such roles. We then enter the contemporary world: the plumbing of modern payments, the politics of reserve currencies, and the frictions of global finance that make crises so contagious.

Only then do we arrive at digital innovation—not as an isolated revolution, but as part of this century-spanning continuum. Cryptographic signatures, consensus mechanisms, digital scarcity, and tokenised claims all build on old questions with new methods. Their claims to novelty are legitimate, yet their vulnerabilities and trade-offs echo familiar patterns. Stability, elasticity, surveillance, governance, interoperability—these are not inventions of the digital age; they are perennial design challenges resurfacing under unfamiliar conditions.

The purpose of this introduction is not to persuade the reader that one form of money is superior, more righteous, or more inevitable than another. Rather, it is to prepare the ground for a more discerning conversation. The public debate about money is often dominated by slogans, nostalgia, or technological determinism. Gold enthusiasts speak of timeless value; blockchain advocates promise trustless systems; sceptics warn of illusions built on sand. Yet beneath these claims lie more interesting and more tractable questions. What exactly makes a monetary claim credible? How do rules, incentives, and enforcement interact? When do markets discipline issuers, and when do issuers discipline markets? How do states harness monetary systems to project power or absorb shocks? And how should societies evaluate the trade-offs between privacy, efficiency, inclusiveness, and stability?

Readers may notice that throughout this book, monetary designs are treated less as monuments and more as choices—choices that can be judged, compared, criticised, and improved. A coin can be assessed by the consistency of its weight and purity. A bank can be judged by its liquidity, solvency, and governance. A digital protocol can be evaluated by its consensus rules, economic incentives, and resistance to capture. These criteria apply across centuries and technologies. They offer a way out of the entrenched binary debates—fiat versus crypto, state versus market, centralisation versus decentralisation—and towards a more constructive terrain where design principles matter more than dogma.

As we stand on the threshold of another transformation, the need for such clarity is especially acute. Payments are accelerating. Credit assessment is being reshaped by data trails. Stable tokens aim to anchor digital value. States are experimenting with new forms of digital issuance, each carrying implicit visions of governance and social order. Private platforms increasingly mediate our financial lives, creating tensions between consumer convenience and systemic dependence. And cryptographic systems propose alternatives that challenge familiar assumptions about authority and coordination. The world is not moving towards a single dominant monetary design; it is drifting towards a more plural, contested landscape, where different models coexist, compete, and sometimes collide.

This pluralism demands fluency. It requires citizens, policymakers, engineers, entrepreneurs, and scholars to speak a common analytical language, even when they hold opposing preferences. The goal is not agreement but understanding—an ability to see the architecture beneath the rhetoric, the incentives beneath the claims, and the governance structures beneath the interface. Without such understanding, societies risk either clinging defensively to legacy systems or surrendering too readily to seductive but unexamined innovations.

At this point, a reader may reasonably ask: where does this story lead? What vision of the future is implied? The honest answer is that the future of money is not predetermined. It depends on choices—collective choices about who is trusted, what is recorded, how privacy is protected, how risk is shared, and who holds the authority to change the rules when circumstances shift. The book does not prescribe a single path; rather, it offers tools to evaluate competing paths with rigour and clarity. It seeks to illuminate, not to evangelise. And it invites readers to approach monetary design not as passive subjects of systems, but as participants capable of shaping them.

Still, the closing reflection of this introduction must return to our two protagonists: the bead-counting merchant and the block-watching miner. Their actions encapsulate the book's central question. How does a society take something as nebulous as belief and turn it into something as solid as coordinated exchange? How does it ensure that a promise made in one moment retains meaning in another? How does it balance the human need for flexibility with the equally human need for reliability? And when technology shifts the boundaries of what is possible, how should the design of money evolve to preserve resilience, fairness, and dignity?

These questions will accompany us through the chapters ahead. They are the thread connecting ancient tally sticks to digital tokens, imperial mints to global clearing systems, goldsmith receipts to algorithmic stabilities. They remind us that money is not merely a backdrop to history; it is one of history's most persistent protagonists. It shapes civilisations as profoundly as law, war, or religion. And it continues to shape the possibilities of our collective future.

The reader now stands at the threshold of a long story—one that spans millennia, crosses continents, and oscillates between ingenuity and failure. It is a story of human attempts to forge order out of uncertainty, to tame complexity with rules, to turn fragile trust into durable systems. The chapters ahead will explore these attempts with precision, candour, and curiosity. They will reveal not a linear march towards progress, but a cascade of designs that mirror humanity's shifting priorities and perennial dilemmas.

If the introduction has a single ambition, it is this: to prepare the reader to see money with fresh clarity. To see it not as a static artefact or a mystical force, but as a deliberately constructed system whose choices matter—because they shape how power is exercised, how opportunity is distributed, and how people connect, transact, and build lives.

What comes next is an examination of those choices—past, present, and future. The beads and the block are simply two opening notes in a broader symphony. The score is still being written.

Chapter 1
Money as a Social Technology

A small crowd gathers outside a village shop at the edge of dusk. Farmers, fishers, and labourers arrive not with coins or notes, but with memory. Each person carries an unwritten balance, a mental ledger of what they owe the shopkeeper and what he owes them. When a woman collects a sack of grain, the shopkeeper nods and scratches a mark on a wooden board. No settlement occurs, yet everyone behaves as if it has. Tomorrow, when she brings eggs or repairs the roof of his shed, he will scratch another mark. Their economy runs on trust, not tokens. Yet the system works—until it doesn't. A failed harvest, a dispute, a sudden departure, and the elegant web of mutual credit tightens into tension. The board now represents not convenience but vulnerability.

The scene feels quaint, almost archaic. Yet it captures a truth that stretches across millennia: money begins not with metal or paper, but with a shared method of coordinating human effort. It emerges whenever a community needs to compare value across time, place, and circumstance. The village tab is primitive only in appearance; conceptually, it contains the seeds of every monetary innovation that came after. And it raises the question that sits at the heart of this chapter: if money is a technology for solving coordination problems, what exactly is being coordinated?

Imagine, by contrast, a very different setting: a music festival in a bustling city. The organisers have introduced drink tokens—small brightly coloured discs exchanged at the gate and used at the bar. They are awkward, easily lost, and mysteriously designed to resemble bottle caps. Yet thousands of people accept them unquestioningly. Meanwhile, in a pub down the road, a barman notes each round on a tab kept behind the counter. Two systems side by side: one relies on physical tokens, the other on a ledger. Most participants barely register the distinction. That indifference is misleading. Beneath these innocuous practices lie two fundamentally different architectures of value, two different ways of resolving who owes what to whom, and under what conditions those obligations can shift.

This chapter explores that architecture. Its core claim is simple: money is a social technology—an engineered solution to the challenges of storing, comparing, and transferring value among people whose interests are not perfectly aligned. To understand money is therefore to understand the interplay between three layers: tokens, ledgers, and the protocols that govern them. It is also to recognise that trust, verification, and enforcement are not optional extras but structural components. And it is to grapple with the design trade-offs that shape every monetary system, from the most improvised village credit to the most meticulously engineered digital currency.

The chapter begins by asking what money actually *solves*. Economists often recite a familiar trinity—medium of exchange, store of value, unit of account—as though these were eternal categories. But these are roles, not definitions. They are behaviours that emerge when a system succeeds at allowing people to coordinate more efficiently than barter, memory, or improvisation alone would permit. The village tab shows how value becomes comparable when a community agrees to treat one mark as equivalent to another. The promise embedded in those marks is not precise—indeed, ambiguity is often a feature—but it is sufficient to move goods and effort through time. That, after all, is the essential function: to ease cooperation among people whose needs and wants are rarely synchronised.

From there, we delve into the architecture beneath the surface. A token, whether a metal coin or a festival drink chip, is a portable embodiment of value. It says, "You can redeem me for something defined by the system's rules." A ledger, whether the shopkeeper's wooden board or a modern database, records claims and obligations directly. Protocols—formal or informal, codified or customary—govern how those tokens and ledger entries are created, updated, and extinguished. When viewed through this lens, debates that once seemed ideological become tractable. Should a system rely on physical objects or on recorded promises? Should value be moved through transfer or through updating a shared record? Should access be open or restricted? The festival token and the pub tab provide intuitive footholds. The token appeals when strangers interact briefly; the ledger thrives when relationships persist.

Trust, however, sits at the centre of all of this. It lubricates exchange until the moment it evaporates. In many societies, informal norms—honesty, reciprocity, shame—govern much of economic life. But informality has limits, especially when communities scale or when incentives shift. Verification arises to compensate for waning trust: weighing coins to check purity, inspecting signatures, reviewing accounts. Enforcement arrives when trust and verification both prove insufficient: courts, collateral, or contractual penalties. A pawnshop offers a neat illustration. The lender trusts the borrower only to the extent that the collateral provides recourse; the contract specifies verification; the physical item itself becomes the enforcement. No single layer guarantees fairness or efficiency. Instead, monetary systems balance them, often imperfectly, always at a cost.

These costs, and the need to navigate them, lead naturally to the theme of design trade-offs. A system optimised for speed sacrifices some resilience. A system built for strict finality may compromise flexibility. Private, anonymous transactions protect personal freedom but hinder recourse and accountability. Highly elastic monetary structures accommodate shocks but risk instability. Even the humble prepaid travel card embodies a design philosophy: by limiting the user's access to funds and restricting usage scenarios, the issuer buys safety at the expense of convenience. Every choice—latency, finality, privacy, elasticity—reflects judgments about acceptable risk and desired outcomes. These judgments vary across cultures, eras, and technologies, but the underlying dilemmas persist.

These dilemmas matter more than ever. Digital payments have accustomed many to the illusion that money simply "moves", frictionless and instant, detached from the architecture beneath. Yet beneath every tap-to-pay lies a lattice of ledgers, rules, trust assumptions, and enforcement mechanisms. Crypto-assets promise "trustless" coordination but in practice reintroduce trust through governance, protocol updates, and incentive structures. Central banks attempt to manage elasticity and stability while private networks shape the experience of value transfer. Meanwhile, households and businesses navigate systems whose trade-offs are seldom visible yet deeply consequential.

By viewing money as a social technology rather than a natural fact, we free ourselves from nostalgia and fatalism. We can ask sharper questions. Why does one system produce chronic instability while another remains sturdy? Why does one community thrive on ledger-based credit and another on physical tokens? Why do certain protocols produce inclusivity while others create gatekeeping? And how should societies weigh the tension between convenience and dignity, efficiency and resilience, innovation and continuity?

This chapter does not aim to answer all of these questions at once. Instead, it prepares the ground. It introduces the conceptual tools—roles, layers, trust components, design trade-offs—that will be needed to evaluate every monetary form encountered later in the book. It establishes a shared vocabulary and illuminates recurring patterns that stretch from early credit systems to modern digital platforms. And it highlights the intellectual stakes: understanding money not only as a medium of exchange but as a system of governance that shapes incentives, behaviour, and power.

As the chapter unfolds, the festival token will reappear, as will the pub tab, the village ledger, and the pawnshop contract. These simple images serve as anchors for more complex systems. They remind us that every innovation, however technical, rests on familiar human dilemmas. The contrast between tokens and ledgers will echo through discussions of coinage, bank deposits, and digital assets. The triad of trust, verification, and enforcement will resurface in analyses of legal frameworks, clearinghouses, and consensus protocols. And the notion of trade-offs will follow us into debates about central bank digital currency, stable tokens, and programmable money.

The chapter closes by extending the invitation implicit in its opening. To see money as a social technology is to adopt a designer's eye. It is to recognise that monetary systems are built, not bestowed; modified, not immutable. Once this perspective takes hold, the world looks different. The wooden tally board, the drink token, the pawn ticket, the travel card—all become clues in a broader investigation into how societies coordinate, coerce, negotiate, and organise themselves.

The pages that follow will offer the reader not a single theory, but a way of seeing. A way of tracing the logic that binds a village credit system to the monetary structures of empires and the digital prototypes of our century. And, crucially, a way of understanding why the smallest choices in monetary design can ripple into the largest consequences for human life.

What Money Solves

In April 1947, the grocer James S. Annan of Kirkcaldy, Scotland, recorded seventeen outstanding household tabs in his ledger, one of them stretching back to 1939. The entries, later examined by a local historian, show prices rising with wartime scarcity and falling again as rationing loosened. Yet despite those fluctuations, the rhythm of the accounts remained steady: flour advanced in winter, coal in autumn, repayment in the brief calm after harvest. No coins changed hands for months at a time. People paid with labour, small goods, or a promise to settle later. Annan's worn ledger demonstrates something that economic theory often abstracts away: before money is a thing, it is a *solution*. It balances mismatched rhythms of giving and receiving. It turns one neighbour's trust into another neighbour's dinner. It makes value comparable across time, not because of metal or law, but because a community chooses to treat a record as binding.

The central puzzle is deceptively simple. How can a village settle exchanges when no two people need the same thing at the same moment, yet all must keep their households running? Why do some communities rely on memory and reputation, while others prefer coins, notes, or digital entries? And what does it mean for a record made on a specific day in a specific place—say, Kirkcaldy in 1947—to hold meaning months later? The answer is neither barter nor benevolence. It is the quiet work of a system that makes value comparable across time and place, smoothing the asymmetry between needs and resources. Systems like Annan's tab persist because they solve this mismatch more effectively than improvisation alone. They allow imbalance without chaos. They tolerate delay without collapse.

At the heart of this capability lie three functional roles: exchange, store of value, and unit of account. Treating them as immutable categories risks missing their lived behaviour. Instead, it is more productive to observe how ordinary people use these roles selectively, often blending them without hesitation. When a villager takes grain today and repays weeks later with repairs, the tab acts as a record of exchange, not a commodity in itself. When the same ledger entry holds its meaning despite inflation or a family setback, it performs as a store of value. When the shopkeeper uses the same marks to tally debts of varying goods, it becomes a unit of account. The roles emerge from practice. They endure because they allow a system to carry memories across time.

The historian Caroline Humphrey documented a contrasting example in 1974 when she examined pastoral exchange systems in Mongolia. In some nomadic groups, livestock obligations were recorded through kin networks rather than discrete accounts. A sheep received today might be repaid years later with hospitality or ceremonial assistance. The exchange was diffuse, not precise. Yet it worked because the community enforced fairness through reputation and reciprocity, not arithmetic. This counter-example shows the limits of formal comparison: not every system requires exact calibration to function. But it also highlights a constraint. Without a clear unit of account, communities struggle to scale. The village ledger can handle dozens of relationships; the nomadic network struggles when interactions expand beyond kin and custom. Money solves this by compressing memory into something transportable.

A subtler motif runs through all of these systems: the act of marking time. Whether by notches on a board, entries in a book, or numbers in a database, communities create technologies that make obligations durable. That durability enables planning. It allows a family to plant more crops than they can immediately consume because they trust the ledger to hold their credit. It allows a shopkeeper to extend goods without fearing immediate loss. The ledger is therefore not merely an administrative tool; it is a temporal bridge. It links the uncertainty of the future to the commitments of the present.

To understand why this matters, consider the way in which money resolves the coordination problem of exchange. In a simple barter world—which rarely existed in practice—trade requires mutual coincidence. I need what you have, and you need what I have, at the same moment. As the anthropologist

David Graeber noted in *Debt: The First 5,000 Years* (2011), communities often circumvented this requirement with credit. People advanced goods informally and relied on memory to settle. The village tab is simply a formalised version of that memory, externalised and made durable. Money takes this logic one step further. It breaks the need for coincidence entirely. If I pay you with a transferable medium, you can redeem that value elsewhere, whenever you prefer. The tab between us becomes a claim on the wider community. Scaling becomes possible because obligations stop being anchored to specific relationships.

This portability of claims introduces a second coordination problem: how to compare value consistently. For Annan's ledger, the unit was implicit—one mark approximated a shilling's worth of goods—yet the system tolerated fuzziness. In modern national currencies, the unit of account becomes explicit and rigid. A pound means a pound because the state insists it does. This precision reduces friction. It enables wage contracts, long-term investment, and cross-regional trade. But it comes at a cost. Precision requires enforcement. Someone must defend the unit's integrity, adjust for inflation, and demand taxes in the defined currency. Portability thus generates institutions.

A more distant example comes from the cocoa economies of the Gold Coast in the 1920s. Farmers used British pounds for export sales, but within villages, debt often circulated in measures of dried cocoa beans. The economist Sara Berry's fieldwork shows how villagers routinely converted between the two systems, using one as a store of value and the other as a unit of account. The duality functioned because the community understood how each system handled the passage of time. Cocoa measures fluctuated with harvest conditions, while the colonial currency followed the decisions of distant administrators. People navigated these shifts with skill. The implication is clear: money solves coordination not by erasing uncertainty, but by offering tools to quantify and negotiate it.

A limitation emerges in systems that over-rely on trust without mechanisms to absorb shocks. After the 1947 Kirkcaldy ledger was uncovered, local interviews suggested that several tabs were quietly forgiven after families lost members to illness or relocation. The system bent rather than broke because the shopkeeper treated the ledger not as a contract but as a social bond. This flexibility is admirable but fragile. It depends on stable relationships and shared expectations. When communities scale or when identities fragment, flexibility turns into vulnerability. Who forgives whom when strangers enter the system? Money as a structured technology solves this by introducing rules that hold even when personal bonds dissolve.

The implication is that money's value lies as much in what it preserves as in what it enables. It stores not wealth alone, but stability. By carrying forward a claim across time, it permits long-term commitments. By making value comparable across distance, it encourages wider networks of exchange. By offering units that persist beyond individual relationships, it supports complex division of labour. The motif of marking time returns here: every durable economy requires ways to push obligations into the future without losing clarity about their meaning.

Yet no system achieves this perfectly. Even highly formalised structures experience friction. In July 1971, when the United States ended the convertibility of dollars to gold, international contracts priced in dollars had to absorb sudden uncertainty. The shift turned a supposedly fixed unit of account into a floating one. The world adapted because those claims were widely trusted and because institutions—the IMF, central banks—stepped in to stabilise expectations. But the episode demonstrates the fragility beneath the surface. The comparability of value across time is ultimately a social agreement mediated by institutions.

Returning to the village tab clarifies why this matters for everyday behaviour. When a villager selects goods knowing she will settle later, she is implicitly projecting her future capacity to work or trade. The ledger becomes an instrument for synchronising her future effort with her present need. When she repays months later, she validates the system's temporal promise. The shopkeeper relies on dozens of such projections to manage his inventory. The ledger is the community's nervous system. Money generalises this mechanism, enabling strangers to project their futures in more standardised ways.

One might ask whether the over-formalisation of value reduces community resilience by eroding the flexibility seen in Kirkcaldy or Mongolia. There is truth in this concern. Formal systems often punish late payment more harshly than informal ones. But they also reduce the ambiguity that can entrench hierarchy. When obligations are written, not merely remembered, power becomes more transparent. Money solves coordination by replacing personalised memory with standardised units. The trade-off is between clarity and discretion.

Seen in this light, money's three roles operate like lenses. As a medium of exchange, it breaks the coincidence of wants. As a store of value, it transports claims through time. As a unit of account, it anchors comparison. But these are not fixed categories. They change with context. In a stable polity, a currency can serve all three roles effectively. In a fragile region, people may trust the unit of account but not the store of value. In Argentina during its 1989 hyperinflation, prices were often set in U.S. dollars but paid in pesos, demonstrating partial separation of roles. The phenomenon shows that money solves coordination by distributing roles flexibly across multiple instruments when necessary.

The motifs of time and comparison return in the practice of discounting. When a farmer settles a tab early, the shopkeeper may offer slightly better terms. This behaviour is not arbitrary. It reflects the cost of holding claims over time and the risk of non-payment. The ledger acts as a quiet calculus of trust, risk, and expected value. Modern financial systems scale this by making discount rates explicit. But the underlying logic is identical to the informal decisions made in a small Scottish shop.

No account of what money solves would be complete without acknowledging its limitations. Money cannot eliminate uncertainty; it can only contain it. It cannot guarantee fairness; it can only offer consistent rules. It cannot solve every coordination problem; some require governance, law, or collective deliberation. But its power lies in its modesty. It allows people to plan, compare, and commit without needing to align their lives perfectly. It creates continuity in a world of mismatched rhythms.

The unresolved tension that threads through these examples remains: how much precision does a community require to function, and how much flexibility can it tolerate without losing coherence? Every monetary system must answer this. The answers shape how people compare value, mark time, and extend trust. And those answers determine whether the next claim written—on a ledger, a bank balance, or a digital record—will hold meaning when tomorrow arrives.

Tokens, Ledgers, and Protocols

On 12 August 1989, during the final weekend of the Cambridge Folk Festival, the organisers issued thousands of bright blue plastic drink tokens to manage queues at the beer tents. The tokens were exchanged for cash at a booth near Cherry Hinton Hall's main entrance, and the system worked with striking efficiency: queues shortened, bar staff kept pace with demand, and visitors treated the tokens as if they were miniature currency. A few steps away, however, the festival's long-standing bar tab for performers operated on an entirely different logic. Musicians signed their names on a clipboard behind the counter, collected their pints, and settled the balance at the end of each night. Two systems ran in parallel—tokens circulating hand to hand, ledgers sitting still—and each revealed a contrasting intuition about what it means to transfer value. The scene clarifies a structural truth. Whether at a music festival, a mediaeval fair, or a modern payment network, money rests on three layers: tokens, ledgers, and the protocols that connect them.

The blue plastic token performed one visible function: it embodied value. When a visitor handed it to a bartender, the act settled the claim instantly. By contrast, the clipboard tab recorded claims but required later settlement. A performer could order several rounds before paying, and the record on the page preserved that obligation. The festival thus exposed two architectures running side by side: a portable object that finalised exchange with a gesture, and a static record that postponed finality until later. One was frictionless in the moment. The other offered flexibility across time. This juxtaposition is more than anecdote. It illustrates how communities structure value by choosing whether to move objects or to update records.

A similar decision appeared, on a far larger scale, in October 1969 when the Bank of England introduced the Banking Code for cheque guarantees. The code made banks liable for certain cheques up to £30 if accompanied by a card. In effect, the guarantee turned a written instruction, normally reliant on trust between private parties, into a semi-tokenised claim backed by an institution. People behaved differently as a result. Shopkeepers began accepting cheques more freely, and customers paid with new confidence. The guarantee created a hybrid: a ledger instruction fortified by a protocol that imitated the certainty of a token. Show the card, sign the cheque, and the claim would clear. The protocol, not the paper, carried the authority.

These examples demonstrate the chapter's motif: the quiet hinge between things that *move* and records that *stay still*. When people pass tokens, they transfer finality through motion. When they update a ledger, they transfer finality through inscription. The distinction explains much of monetary history, yet it is often obscured by scale. Metal coins, festival tokens, and digital signatures all share the intuitive appeal of tangibility—whether physical or cryptographic. A ledger, whether carved, printed, or encoded, depends instead on the credibility of the keeper. And protocols—from cheque guarantees to blockchain consensus—determine who is allowed to update that keeper's record and under what constraints.

Tokens function because people treat them as settled claims. The historian John Chown notes that during the Great Recoinage of 1696, London coffee houses and taverns continued to accept worn silver coins well into the chaos, not because they trusted the metal, but because the social practice of accepting coins as final payment held firm. A token, in that sense, is a piece of technology built from shared belief. When a visitor at Cambridge handed over a blue disc, the bartender never asked about its origin; the disc *was* the claim. No external verification was required. The object embodied the value directly. The implication is straightforward: token systems thrive when speed and minimal friction matter more than record-keeping accuracy.

Yet tokens carry limits. They can be lost, forged, or hoarded. The festival organisers learned this in the early 1990s when counterfeit tokens circulated during a particularly busy weekend, forcing a switch to colour-coded designs. The failure mode exposed a perennial vulnerability: tokens are final when received but fragile before that moment. The risk is visible in behaviour. People grasp tokens tightly in their pockets. They protect them physically. They worry about misplacement. The embodied claim makes the user responsible for custody.

Ledgers invert these responsibilities. A ledger records who owes what, who has paid, and who must settle next. Consider the beer tab at the festival. Performers did not guard tokens or cash. Instead, they trusted the bar staff to record accurately. When the guitarist from a visiting Irish band signed the clipboard each evening, he relied on a straightforward behaviour metric: the barman's consistency in noting every drink. The ledger transferred the burden of custody from participants to the keeper. Its weakness—dependence on accurate recording—was mitigated by social proximity and reputation. Everyone involved knew everyone else. Disputes were rare because the protocol was socially enforced.

A more formal illustration can be found in the records of the London Clearing House in 1864, when daily settlement sheets listed the obligations between member banks. These sheets, preserved in the archives at the Bank of England, show how a handful of clerks coordinated vast flows of value without tokens changing hands. They recorded obligations, netted positions, and issued final instructions at day's end. Settlement depended entirely on ledger accuracy and the integrity of the protocol governing how entries could be updated. The implication is clear: ledger systems excel where relationships are repeated, where verification is routine, and where participants can appeal to rules rather than objects.

A counter-example highlights the tension. In the 1980s, numerous savings and loan institutions in the United States misreported asset values, creating fictitious ledger entries that masked insolvency. The failure was not technological; it was institutional. The protocol lacked sufficient constraints to prevent manipulation. In such cases, tokens can appear attractive because they resist the distortions of dishonest record-keeping. But tokens are no cure-all. They impose their own rigidity. The reconciliation lies not in choosing tokens over ledgers, but in recognising that both require protocols that enforce integrity without suffocating flexibility.

Protocols bind the system together. They define who may update the ledger, under what circumstances, with which checks. They regulate how tokens are issued, redeemed, or retired. They determine how disputes are resolved. At the festival, the protocol was unwritten but clear: staff issued tokens in exchange for cash; bartenders accepted tokens without question; performers' tabs were tallied nightly; festival management reconciled the books afterward. The system worked because the rules were simple, the incentives aligned, and breaches carried social cost. The protocol rested on familiarity.

By contrast, the SWIFT messaging standard adopted in 1977 provided banks across continents with a formal protocol for transmitting payment instructions. It did not move money. It moved messages. But by standardising the structure of those messages, SWIFT reduced errors, accelerated settlement, and gave participants a shared grammar. Here, the motif shifts: the hinge between movement and inscription is mediated by language. Protocols are languages that constrain behaviour. Their force comes not from moral authority but from compatibility. When everyone speaks the same structured language, coordination accelerates.

The power of protocols becomes even clearer when examining cryptographic networks. Bitcoin's consensus mechanism, introduced in January 2009, enforces a protocol that decides who may append new entries to the shared ledger and how conflicts are resolved. The protocol substitutes computation for trust in any single ledger keeper. But the behaviour it seeks to elicit—honest recording—remains identical to the work of the clerks at the London Clearing House. The difference lies in scale and enforcement. Where Victorian clerks relied on supervision, Bitcoin relies on distributed verification. Both systems rest on protocols that embed incentives to commit accurate updates.

Yet even cryptographic protocols have constraints. In March 2013, the Bitcoin network briefly split into incompatible versions due to a software update conflict. For several hours, two ledgers coexisted, each claiming legitimacy. The system recovered only when participants coordinated to choose a common chain. The episode demonstrates that protocols do not eliminate governance; they merely shift it. When rules conflict, human interpretation re-enters. Ledger entries depend on collective agreement. Tokens, too, require consensus about authenticity. Protocols cannot escape their social foundations.

This tri-layer view—tokens, ledgers, protocols—illuminates long-standing debates. Consider the argument over whether digital payments represent "real" money or mere promises. The distinction dissolves when we observe behaviour. When a person uses a contactless card on the London Underground, they treat the beep as final. Transport for London clears the account overnight. The tap is a token-like gesture. The actual settlement is ledger-driven. The protocol bridges the two, giving the gesture the feeling of immediate settlement. People rely on the protocol's reliability, not on a physical object or a personal memory. The implication is that what feels like a token may in fact be a protocol-induced illusion of finality.

Another example appears in Kenya's M-Pesa, introduced by Safaricom in March 2007. Users store balances electronically and transfer them via mobile phones. Agents hold physical cash to redeem digital balances. The system is ledger-centric, but the redemption process gives the digital entry a token-like quality. A customer handing over cash to an agent and receiving a balance on their phone experiences a fusion of physical embodiment and record-based value. The behaviour reveals trust in the agent, the ledger, and the mobile operator's protocol. The system works because those elements reinforce each other.

The limitation emerges when one component is weak. If agents lack liquidity, redemption stalls. If the ledger is compromised, balances vanish. If protocols governing updates are unclear or misapplied, disputes multiply. Reconciling these weaknesses requires clear boundaries. Tokens reduce reliance on ledger keepers. Ledgers reduce the inconvenience of carrying objects. Protocols coordinate the two, ensuring that value moves or is recorded accurately.

The motif returns: the hinge between what moves and what stays still. Tokens shift risk to the holder; ledgers shift it to the keeper; protocols allocate it between them. All monetary systems negotiate this hinge through choices about custody, authority, and verification. These choices shape behaviour. They determine whether people carry tokens close to the body or sign tabs with ease. They influence whether institutions adopt strict controls or trust long-term relationships. They steer where value resides: in a pocket, on a page, or within a rule set.

The unresolved tension is one of scale and certainty. How much authority should a community vest in a ledger keeper, and how much autonomy should users retain through tokens? Which rules should be rigid, and which flexible enough to adapt? And when protocols grow so complex that few can understand them, how does a society ensure that the record of who owes what to whom remains both accurate and trustworthy?

Trust, Verification, Enforcement

On 3 February 1895, in a cramped back room of H. Samuel's pawnshop on Market Street, Manchester, a weaver named Ellen Hughes deposited her silver brooch for a loan of five shillings. The clerk inspected the clasp, weighed the metal, wrote a ticket, and sealed the brooch in a brown paper packet marked with her name and the date. Hughes walked away with the cash, the shop retained the collateral, and both believed they had entered a fair exchange. Yet their arrangement rested on three distinct forces. Hughes trusted the shop to guard her brooch. The clerk verified its material value before lending. And the ticket in Hughes's hand signalled the terms of enforcement should she fail to return. The interaction lasted minutes. Its architecture has shaped monetary systems for centuries.

Trust reduces friction until it fails. Hughes did not demand that the brooch be reweighed in front of her every time she visited the shop because the firm's reputation in Manchester's working districts offered reassurance. Trust appeared in her behaviour: she accepted the clerk's valuation without protest. The pawnshop's name mattered. H. Samuel had operated since 1862, and its public presence in multiple northern towns gave customers confidence. This shows how institutions cultivate trust by offering visible continuity. The implication is that trust operates as a form of efficiency; it accelerates transactions by reducing the need for constant oversight.

Yet trust alone is brittle. The weaver's reliance on the pawn ticket reveals the second force: verification. The clerk weighed the brooch because expectation alone could not determine value. Verification replaced guesswork with measurement. A parallel moment occurred in 1717 when Isaac Newton, as Master of the Royal Mint in London, approved a revised gold guinea standard after widespread clipping and wear. His insistence on stringent assays—physical tests of metal content—demonstrated how verification restores confidence when circulating tokens falter. People behaved accordingly. Merchants accepted the restandardised guineas with renewed ease because they trusted the assays that had produced them. The implication is clear: verification is not a formality but a stabilising act that translates uncertainty into something measurable.

Verification, however, has limits. The economist Anne Murphy's study of eighteenth-century English banking shows that even carefully verified banknotes depended on public willingness to believe they would be redeemed. During the crisis of 1763, several banks collapsed despite pristine ledgers and recent audits. Verification did not shield them from panic. This counter-example reminds us that proof without trust can be insufficient. Panic exposes how verification is necessary but not sufficient for stability. Reconciling the tension requires recognising how enforcement completes the triad.

Enforcement compels where trust and verification cannot. Hughes's pawn ticket was more than a receipt; it conveyed the terms that would govern dispute. If she defaulted, the shop would lawfully sell the brooch after a specified period. The enforcement mechanism offered predictability. She committed to return with the loan plus interest, and the shop committed to protect the brooch until then. The behaviour metric was unambiguous: punctual repayment. Enforcement created consequences that ensured both parties acted as expected.

A wider illustration appears in the Bills of Exchange Act 1882, enacted across the United Kingdom to formalise rules for debt instruments. By setting enforceable standards for signatures, maturity dates, and protest procedures, the Act created a stable environment in which merchants could issue, discount, and circulate bills. The Act translated informal custom into legal architecture. Its enforcement provisions reduced disputes and created a backbone for credit across London and Glasgow. The implication is that enforcement, when calibrated well, expands the radius of cooperation by anchoring agreements beyond personal reputation.

But enforcement, too, can malfunction. In 1992, during the banking crisis in Finland, several institutions aggressively pursued distressed borrowers, leading to public backlash and later parliamentary review. Enforcement became a source of instability when applied without discretion. This limitation shows that enforcement without trust or measured verification can harden into coercion. The reconciliation lies in balance. A system must enforce rules firmly enough to deter opportunism yet flexibly enough to preserve legitimacy.

Throughout these examples, a quiet motif recurs: the ticket. Whether written, stamped, or digital, it represents the bridge between trust, proof, and authority. Hughes's pawn ticket summarised her agreement. Newton's assays produced standardised marks on guinea coins. The Bills of Exchange Act formalised the format of commercial paper. In each case, the ticket acts as evidence of mutual expectation. It makes obligations portable.

Trust, in its softest form, emerges through informal norms. In the 1950s, researchers examining credit networks in Naples observed shopkeepers allowing families to run long-term store credit—*la lista*—based on neighbourhood familiarity. The storekeeper's willingness to advance goods reflected his judgment about each household's reliability. The behaviour metric was visible: whether a family settled small amounts when their circumstances briefly improved. Norms provided quiet enforcement. People feared reputational loss more than legal penalty. Trust here was efficient because verification and enforcement were embedded in social life, not costly formal systems.

Yet such arrangements cannot scale indefinitely. Informal norms thrive within tight-knit communities but break down when interactions span strangers or when mobility disrupts memory. The implication is that trust rooted in personal familiarity must eventually give way to protocols—legal, institutional, or computational—that allow cooperation at distance.

Contractual law introduced those protocols. A contract does not eliminate trust; it reframes it. Parties need not trust one another's goodwill; they trust the legal machinery to enforce the agreed outcome. The transition from informal norms to written contracts transforms behaviour. People commit more readily to larger, riskier trades because they know the rules will hold. Commercial courts in Amsterdam demonstrated this by the 1630s. Merchants from Antwerp, Hamburg, and London adjudicated disputes through well-established procedures. Their reliance on shared legal frameworks allowed them to trade absent personal familiarity. The contracts codified expectations. Enforcement made them credible.

Yet contractual law is not frictionless. Court procedures cost time and money. They introduce latency. The historian Oscar Gelderblom notes that Dutch merchants often preferred arbitration because court action could delay payment for months. The limitation here is that enforcement, while necessary, can become a drag on efficiency. Reconciling this requires alternatives that enforce without obstruction.

Code-based controls offer one such alternative, though not a panacea. When the Ethereum network executed the Constantinople upgrade in February 2019, it introduced protocol-level changes designed to adjust difficulty parameters and transaction costs. The upgrade revealed how code can enforce rules automatically: miners, validators, and applications had to follow the new logic or fall out of sync with the network. Enforcement occurred through protocol compatibility rather than courts. Verification was computational. Trust shifted from institutions to software. The motif of the ticket took digital form as the block header: a signed, timestamped record of valid updates.

But code-based enforcement faces its own limitations. In June 2016, after the well-publicised DAO exploit, the Ethereum community intervened with a contentious hard fork to reverse transactions. The code had executed as written, yet the community judged the outcome illegitimate. Enforcement by code alone proved insufficient when collectively perceived fairness diverged from the protocol. Human governance returned. The episode demonstrates a deeper truth: no enforcement system escapes its social foundations, whether it is a pawnshop contract, a commercial court, or a cryptographic protocol.

Threading through all of this is a simple question: how much should a system trust its participants? The pawnshop trusted Hughes enough to lend against her brooch, but not enough to forgo collateral. The Royal Mint trusted bullion dealers enough to accept their gold, but verified every bar. The London Clearing House trusted member banks enough to net mutual obligations, but enforced strict penalties for misreporting. Each domain defines trust precisely because each domain contains incentives to cheat.

Verification emerges as a buffer between belief and scepticism. It measures. It documents. It limits dispute by anchoring claims in observable facts. Its behaviour metric is the act of checking: weighing metal, auditing books, comparing signatures. But over-reliance on verification can slow systems. Too many checks create paralysis. Too few invite abuse. The motif returns here: the ticket must be checked, but not constantly.

Enforcement closes the loop. It compels participants to honour commitments even when temptation pulls elsewhere. Its visible behaviours are penalties, repossessions, asset freezes, protocol rejections. Too much enforcement suppresses activity. Too little invites opportunism. Monetary systems evolve by navigating these gradients.

Across centuries, the interplay of trust, verification, and enforcement has shaped who can trade, how quickly obligations settle, and how far cooperation can reach. A pawnshop in Manchester, the Royal Mint under Newton, the Dutch merchant courts, the Ethereum hard fork—each reveals the same architecture at work. Informal norms fade as scale increases. Formal verification grows as networks widen. Enforcement becomes more complex as incentives diversify.

Yet the unresolved tension remains: which layer should dominate? Should societies lean on trust to reduce friction, or on verification to reduce uncertainty, or on enforcement to reduce opportunism? No system can optimise all three. The trade-off defines its character. And the next monetary design, whatever form it takes, must decide where to place its weight.

Design Trade Offs

On 27 June 2012, Transport for London introduced its first wave of prepaid Oyster travel cards at King's Cross St Pancras, limiting users to the value they had loaded rather than granting unlimited access to the network. Within months, inspectors reported a measurable drop in fare evasion on key commuter routes. The constraint was simple: the card carried only the funds committed in advance; if the balance reached zero, barriers would not open. The design traded convenience for control, speed for resilience. Yet the very limit that protected Transport for London's revenue also protected passengers from unexpected overdrafts or cascading liabilities. The card's behaviour revealed a wider truth. Every monetary system is an exercise in disciplined compromise.

That compromise appears wherever value moves. A bank transfer from London to Edinburgh may settle instantly on a user's screen, yet the underlying systems often complete their reconciliation only at day's end. A digital token may advertise strong finality, but its rigidity makes reversals impossible even in cases of fraud. The motif that threads through these tensions is familiar: the boundary. Every rule—whether a spending limit, a settlement delay, or a privacy threshold—marks a boundary drawn to contain risk. Boundaries define safety. They also define inconvenience. The art of monetary design is choosing which boundaries matter most.

Consider latency, the interval between initiating a payment and knowing it is irrevocably complete. Latency is not merely a technical detail; it shapes behaviour. When the Bank of England launched the RTGS system in 1996, it reduced settlement latency for high-value transactions from hours to minutes. The shift encouraged banks to adjust intraday liquidity management. Traders could commit capital with greater confidence because they knew when funds would settle. The implication is that lower latency enhances immediacy but demands stronger safeguards: banks must maintain higher liquidity buffers to complete those rapid settlements.

A counter-example occurred during the CHIPS system's early years in the United States. Before its 2001 fundamental redesign, CHIPS settled obligations late each afternoon by netting positions across participants. A single delay from a large bank could stall the entire network. Latency became a vulnerability. Participants behaved cautiously. They hesitated to rely on funds that had not yet been netted, and liquidity froze temporarily during disruptions. Reconciling the two examples shows latency as a delicate hinge: too much speed creates liquidity strain; too much delay creates systemic hesitation.

Finality—the moment a payment becomes legally irreversible—is equally consequential. It is visible in user behaviour. When a customer taps a prepaid Oyster card, the beep signals finality: access granted, fare committed. In contrast, a card-not-present transaction for an online purchase may appear settled but reverses days later during dispute resolution. The payment's legal finality lags behind its visual finality. This divergence shapes trust. A merchant in Camden Market may prefer cash for precisely this reason: cash settles instantly, with no risk of later reversal. The implication is that finality determines who carries risk after the moment of exchange.

Legal history offers a second checkable example. The Bills of Exchange Act 1882 codified when obligations on bills became final, reducing ambiguity for merchants across Liverpool and Glasgow. Once a bill was accepted and passed its maturity date, the holder could act without fear of rescission. This clarity accelerated trade. Yet such rigidity can punish mistakes. A mistakenly issued bill could become binding even if both parties acknowledged the error. The limitation shows finality's double edge. It reduces dispute, but it also curtails flexibility. Monetary design must decide when to privilege certainty over correction.

Privacy introduces another axis of trade-off. When the German Bundesbank studied cash usage in 2011, it found that more than 75 per cent of point-of-sale transactions in Germany were conducted in cash, far above rates in neighbouring countries. Interviews revealed a consistent behaviour: people valued the anonymity cash provided. Privacy created comfort. Yet that comfort allows tax evasion and untraceable illicit activity. By contrast, Iceland's near-universal card usage—as documented by the Central Bank of Iceland in its 2014 payments report—offered authorities granular insight into economic behaviour, enabling rapid fiscal response during shocks. But that visibility raised concerns among citizens about data exposure and misuse. Privacy thus becomes a boundary at which societies measure risk against transparency.

Monetary elasticity—the capacity of a system to expand or contract the supply of money or credit—reveals yet another tension. Elasticity cushions shocks. During the Bank of England's 2008 Special Liquidity Scheme, the central bank expanded eligible collateral to support banks starved of funding. Liquidity increased. Markets calmed. Elasticity proved life-saving. But elasticity also carries danger. Argentina's hyperinflation in 1989, driven in part by uncontrolled monetary expansion to finance fiscal deficits, illustrates the devastation of excess elasticity. Prices doubled in weeks. People's behaviour changed visibly. Households spent money immediately upon receiving it, and shops repriced goods several times a day. The limitation is clear: elasticity stabilises until it destabilises. Monetary design must calibrate precisely how much elasticity a system can tolerate before trust erodes.

Threaded through these dimensions is the recurring motif: the boundary. Limits introduce friction, but they also contain harm. A prepaid travel card exemplifies this. When Transport for London capped maximum stored value, it created safety not just for itself but for passengers. A lost card could inflict only limited damage. A stolen wallet could not be drained beyond the preset amount. The boundary worked. It transformed a potential vulnerability into a manageable inconvenience. Such boundaries appear more broadly in monetary architecture. Withdrawal limits on ATMs constrain daily risk exposure. Position limits in derivatives markets prevent catastrophic spirals. Balance thresholds on mobile money accounts reduce laundering vulnerabilities. Every boundary says the same thing: safety requires friction.

Consider also the trade-off between centralisation and resilience. Centralised systems offer efficiency. When Visa processed more than 150 million transactions on its busiest day in December 2022 (Visa Inc. earnings report, January 2023), it showcased the scale that centralisation enables. Decisions are coordinated. Protocols update swiftly. Latency falls. But concentration increases fragility. A single software error in June 2018 caused widespread card outages across the United Kingdom, leaving shoppers stranded at tills. The behaviour shift was immediate: people withdrew cash. Trust migrated to a medium with no central point of failure. The implication is that efficiency achieved through centralisation must be weighed against systemic vulnerability.

Decentralised systems invert the compromise. They resist single points of failure but sacrifice speed. Bitcoin's median confirmation time in May 2023, per blockchain.com data, exceeded ten minutes, and during congestion it stretched further. Users adapted. They paid higher fees to accelerate inclusion or accepted delays. The behaviour revealed the trade-off encoded in the protocol: resilience purchased at the cost of throughput. The limitation is evident in contexts where high volume and rapid settlement matter. A decentralised ledger can guard against catastrophic collapse while simultaneously frustrating daily utility.

Boundaries again emerge as the motif. Decentralised systems limit the power of any one actor. Centralised systems limit uncertainty through tight control. Hybrid designs attempt to blend the two, often introducing complexity. Monetary systems cannot escape the boundary problem; they can only adjust where the line is drawn.

A deeper question arises when examining reversibility. Allowing reversals protects users from fraud but reduces finality. When PayPal introduced its buyer protection policy in 2000, it transformed online commerce. Sellers accepted new risk: a buyer could trigger a reversal. That risk manifested in behaviour. Some merchants increased prices to compensate for potential chargebacks; others refused categories of sales. Yet reversibility drove adoption. Customers trusted that they could retract payments when goods failed to arrive. The implication is that reversibility, though inefficient for merchants, expands participation.

Still, reversibility invites abuse. Fraudsters exploited the dispute process, prompting PayPal to refine its protocols repeatedly between 2006 and 2012. This limitation shows the necessity of balance: reversibility cannot function without credible verification and enforcement. The boundary around user protection must be firm enough to inspire confidence yet narrow enough to prevent opportunism.

The prepaid travel card offers the clearest compressed example of these design tensions. Its limit is small. Its custody is simple. Its behaviour is predictable. The cardholder commits value in advance. Transport for London commits to honour travel within that limit. Speed is achieved through pre-authorisation rather than dynamic risk assessment. Privacy is partial: journeys are recorded, but balances are not tied to credit lines. Elasticity is fixed: a card cannot spend beyond its load. Every design choice reduces one form of risk by accepting another. The limit is not a flaw but the architecture's centre of gravity.

Another checkable example lies in the 1971 introduction of Japan's *Magnetic Farecard* in Osaka. The card improved throughput by allowing passengers to tap rather than queue for tickets. But it capped stored value and required regular top-ups. Users tolerated this friction because it reduced queuing time. When a fraudulent batch surfaced in 1974, the transport authority added stricter encoding. Convenience fell. Control rose. The boundary shifted. Yet passengers accepted it because the system's reliability mattered more than the additional step. The implication echoes throughout monetary history: resilience often demands losing a little speed.

A credible counter-example comes from the 2007 rollout of Kenya's M-Pesa. The system allowed rapid transfers with minimal friction. Users valued speed and accessibility so highly that safeguards were initially light. Fraud cases rose. Safaricom responded by tightening registration and transaction limits. The limitation was clear: unconstrained speed created vulnerabilities. But when the limits were introduced, adoption did not slow. The system retained its core advantage—ease of use—while adding necessary boundaries. Reconciling the example reinforces the central motif. Boundaries adapt; the trade-off remains.

Privacy sits within the same tension. A system that records every transaction can detect fraud but exposes sensitive data.

A system that records nothing preserves anonymity but allows unchecked abuse. In 2018, the European Central Bank introduced its TARGET Instant Payment Settlement (TIPS) platform, offering near-real-time transfers with strong traceability for compliance. Users sacrificed some privacy for speed and safety. Meanwhile, high-cash economies like Austria, where cash accounted for more than 50 per cent of point-of-sale value in 2020 (OeNB Payments Report), preserved anonymity but faced challenges in preventing unrecorded activity. The trade-off manifests in behaviour. Austrians carry cash; TIPS users rely on instant visibility.

Monetary elasticity loops back to these themes. Too rigid a supply constrains growth. Too flexible a supply erodes confidence. During the 1933 United States bank holiday declared by President Franklin D. Roosevelt, banks closed to halt spirals of withdrawal. The measure was a blunt tool. It froze liquidity to restore stability. The behaviour was clear: queues dissipated because withdrawals became impossible. The system re-opened with stronger controls. Elasticity had been overpowered by panic; rigidity brought order. Yet such rigidity would be intolerable in calmer times. Monetary design must adjust elasticity to context, not dogma.

All these examples return to the motif: the boundary. Every choice draws a boundary—around speed, around certainty, around data, around supply. Boundaries are uncomfortable. They impose friction. But friction protects. It prevents overloads, panics, abuses, and cascading failures. Limits buy safety.

The unresolved question remains: where should the next boundary be drawn? Should a society prioritise instant settlement or durable finality? Should privacy yield to transparency? Should elasticity be tightly controlled or moderately flexible? And when the pressure to remove friction grows louder, how much friction must remain to keep the system from breaking?

Chapter 2
From Barter Myths to Early Ledgers

The scene appears simple at first glance: a crowded market square in Piana degli Albanesi, Sicily, in the summer of 1935. A baker hands a farmer a paper slip—an IOU scribbled in a hurried hand—promising two loaves the following week in exchange for eggs taken that morning. No coins change pockets. No haggling erupts over equivalences. The promise itself does the work. Observers walking past might assume the pair lacked money or lived in some primitive barter holdover. Yet the opposite was true. Both households used cash daily. They simply knew that for this exchange, at this moment, a written claim was faster, gentler, and more precise than rummaging for coins. The slip would sit in the baker's ledger, to be cleared later when the farmer's family visited the shop. This modest artifact challenges one of economic history's most durable fictions: that barter underpinned early exchange.

The enduring image—two strangers negotiating an improbable swap of chickens for shoes—has remarkable staying power. It appears in textbooks, lectures, and public rhetoric with almost ritual regularity. But once we look closely at markets like Sicily's, or the Highland fairs documented by British ethnographers in the 1920s, the myth unravels. Barter did exist, but as an exception rather than the default. Daily life ran on credit, memory, and timely reciprocity. People advanced goods against expectation. They trusted that accounts, formal or informal, would eventually settle. The IOU became a social hinge: flexible enough to smooth mismatches, durable enough to keep people honest. Barter, in contrast, flourished mostly at frontiers—when trust was thin, relationships transient, or settlement urgent. The paradox is unsettling: the story used to explain the birth of money obscures the very systems that preceded it.

Those early systems were not chaotic improvisations. They were structured, patterned, and anchored in shared understanding. Credit lines in medieval marketplaces, tally sticks in early England, and household balance records in rural China all reveal the same behavioural rhythm. People managed obligations through memory and notation long before metal coins entered their lives. To imagine ancient exchanges as clumsy swaps of mismatched goods is to miss the ingenuity that underwrote cooperation. Communities solved the coordination problem not through direct equivalence, but through delayed reciprocity. The IOU in Sicily is one face of that enduring logic: value suspended in time, awaiting its return.

Still, human beings did not rely on memory alone. Objects began to stand in for value, not because they were glamorous, but because they were useful. Commodity money—salt rations in Rome, copper lumps in Shang-era China, dried cod in parts of Norway—did not gain prominence due to mystical aura or intrinsic worth. They dominated because they made daily life easier. A unit of salt could season food, preserve meat, and satisfy soldiers' pay. A chunk of copper could be weighed, divided, and stored without rotting. In each case, the object's durability, divisibility, and predictability mattered far more than any symbolic meaning attached to it. These were workaday tools, not treasure.

The appeal of commodity money lies in its capacity to simplify exchange by reducing uncertainty. When two parties meet across a market table, the copper weight between them reduces the need for negotiation. They know what a piece should weigh, what it can buy, and how it behaves across seasons. The salt ration does not spoil quickly; the copper does not evaporate in storms; neither embeds personal obligation. These materials offered stability not through splendour but through consistency. Their usefulness was mundane, and precisely for that reason, transformative.

Yet commodities alone never fully organised early economies. Something more ambitious emerged as societies grew complex: central record keeping. Long before the first stamped coins appeared in Lydia around the seventh century BCE, institutions—temples, granaries, palaces—managed flows of goods through accounting. At Uruk and later in Babylon, tablets recorded barley allotments, labour obligations, debt settlements, and harvest yields. These were not currencies in the modern sense, but they fulfilled money's deepest functions. A line etched in clay conveyed entitlement. A mark signalled repayment. A tablet preserved mutual expectations across time.

Imagine a harvest ledger from a Mesopotamian temple. A scribe sits cross-legged beside jars of grain, marking each farmer's contribution and noting what each family would later receive in rations or seed loans. The ledger becomes a living instrument: it records claims, tracks obligations, and governs redistribution. Value moves not by passing objects, but by adjusting entries. The result is a proto-monetary system embedded in institutional authority. Trust resides not in a physical token but in the granary's capacity to honour what is written.

These ancient ledgers complicate the notion that money sprang from market ingenuity. They reveal how administrative needs—labour organisation, resource management, taxation—often preceded commercial exchange. Temples and palaces were the first large-scale accountants. Their records stabilised obligations across seasons and across distances. In many respects, they invented the infrastructure upon which later monetary systems would build. Coins would eventually simplify and scale these practices, but the conceptual groundwork—the idea that value could be standardised, recorded, and transferred through inscription—was already centuries old.

Yet numbers and tablets alone cannot fully explain how prices stabilise or why certain objects command reverence. Human societies also attach meaning to the act of exchange. Ritual payments transform obligations into order. Bridewealth shells in parts of Papua New Guinea, for instance, carried layers of significance: they represented alliance, continuity, respect, and the weaving of kinship ties. Their value lay not in their material composition—which could be humble—but in their symbolism and the ceremonies surrounding them. These shells moved through hands not casually but ceremonially, affirming relationships as much as transferring wealth.

This ritual dimension of value appears across cultures. In the Kingdom of Dahomey, payments of cowry shells accompanied oaths and settlements, binding communities into shared moral worlds. In the Indo-Gangetic plains, cattle gifts formalised agreements long before widespread coinage. These exchanges were not merely economic; they were performative. The objects used—shells, cattle, cloth—gathered authority from their social roles. They stabilised value because they stabilised meaning. A bridewealth ceremony was not about price; it was about continuity. The shell's worth derived from its place in the story the community told about itself.

This interplay between meaning and materiality exposes another recurring thread. Systems of value—whether IOUs, salt rations, temple tablets, or ritual shells—reflect what societies fear, trust, celebrate, and prioritise. A community anxious about scarcity may privilege durable commodities. A community structured around kinship may anchor value in ritual exchange. A city with administrative sophistication may centralise record keeping. Each choice encodes assumptions about risk, fairness, and the future.

What makes these early forms especially revealing is how much they resemble modern monetary dilemmas, stripped of technical complexity. The Sicilian IOU captures the essence of credit without the machinery of banks. Salt rations reflect the logic of commodity money without the mystique of gold. Mesopotamian ledgers show how accounting precedes tokenisation. Bridewealth shells embody the fusion of social meaning and economic coordination. These practices are distant yet recognisable, like ancient prototypes of today's monetary software.

The persistence of the barter myth speaks to a deeper human inclination: we prefer tidy origin stories. A world that moves from primitive barter to glittering coinage to modern fiat feels orderly, progressive, almost inevitable. Yet monetary history resists such linearity. It is messier and more circular. Credit predates coins. Ledgers predates markets. Rituals accompany value just as consistently as measurement does. By revisiting the early evidence, we discover not a march from chaos to order, but a series of solutions to recurring problems: how to exchange without coincidence, how to store without loss, how to record without ambiguity, how to bind without force.

The false simplicity of barter persists because it frames money as an invention—created once, perfected later—rather than as an evolving social technology. But once the myth dissolves, a richer picture appears. Money becomes a lens through which to observe cooperation, not a relic of economic progress. It becomes a method of organising obligations, not merely a tool of exchange. It becomes a story communities tell to manage their interactions with one another, not merely a convention imposed by rulers or markets.

This chapter travels through that reoriented landscape. It examines how everyday credit replaced the need for immediate equivalence, how humble commodities earned their place not through mystique but through their physical traits, how monumental institutions pioneered accounting long before they minted coins, and how ritual and theatre sustained value where markets alone could not. These themes illuminate the roots of monetary design while exposing the assumptions that shape our own era's disputes over digital tokens, central bank money, and informal credit networks.

The journey leads to a provocative question. If the earliest monetary systems were mixtures of memory, material, and meaning, how should we interpret the systems we build today? Are we rediscovering old principles under new technologies? Or are we forgetting them, mistaking speed for resilience and precision for trust? The past offers no simple answers, but it offers clarity. And as the next chapters unfold, that clarity becomes a guide: a way to recognise in ancient ledgers and ritual shells the foundations of the monetary systems still being argued over, designed, and reinvented today.

The Barter Story, Revisited

In June 1926, in the market town of Stornoway on the Isle of Lewis, the shopkeeper Angus Morrison entered a brief note in his ledger: "John MacLeod, twelve herring; to settle after shearing." MacLeod had taken tea, sugar, and a tin of biscuits that morning but carried no coins. Morrison accepted the fish as partial payment and recorded the balance as credit against labour MacLeod promised later in the summer. Nothing about the exchange resembled the textbook image of barter. There was no search for a perfect swap, no awkward negotiation between mismatched goods. The IOU—just a line of ink on ruled paper—did the work. The note sat quietly in the ledger until shearing season, when MacLeod's son arrived to clear it with a day's help behind the shop. For a visitor expecting chickens-for-shoes barter, the scene would have felt strangely modern. It was. The villagers typically used cash when convenient, credit when trusted, and barter only when compelled by circumstance. Morrison's ledger reveals the misfit between the myth and the record. Barter was present, but it was not the organising logic of everyday exchange.

The paradox is familiar and startling. If barter was supposedly the original mode of economic life, why do actual accounts from places like Lewis show so little of it? Why does the popular story—strangers trading goats for grain—persist despite evidence that communities mostly relied on credit, tally systems, and long-term reciprocity? Part of the answer lies in the appeal of simplicity. The barter narrative offers an image of a world made legible through direct equivalence. One chicken equals so much wheat; one tool equals so much fish. But actual communities have rarely worked that way. They advanced goods on trust, kept track through memory or marks, and settled only when it made sense. They did not measure every exchange. They measured relationships.

The motif of the slip—whether inked in Stornoway or scribbled in a Sicilian market—anchors the deeper truth. Credit emerges not from abundance but from expectation. A person takes goods now, promising labour or payment later, because the relationship carries enough weight to support the delay. Morrison extended credit because he had watched MacLeod repay before. The behaviour reveals the underlying metric: repayment regularity, not immediate equivalence. The IOU acted as a bridge across time. It offered flexibility where barter demanded simultaneity.

The persistence of barter myths obscures this logic. Textbooks describe early humans struggling with the "double coincidence of wants," resorting to cumbersome swaps until someone invented money to ease the friction. Yet the historical record contradicts this tidy progression. In his analysis of Nuer pastoralists in the 1930s, the anthropologist E. E. Evans-Pritchard documented extensive cattle-credit networks in which obligations were tracked informally across kinship ties. A cow offered today might be answered with assistance years later. Precision mattered less than reciprocity. Barter surfaced only when relationships were strained or when trust was insufficient to carry obligations forward. The evidence is visible: transactions happened with pauses, promises, and delayed settlement, not with immediate equivalence.

Credit systems were equally prominent in marketplaces with monetary circulation. Caroline Humphrey's fieldwork in Ulaanbaatar in the 1990s captured traders extending goods against verbal promises, adding small marks to notebooks rather than insisting on instant payment. Even with cash readily available, people relied on notations because they smoothed transaction flow. Verification was simple: traders knew their customers by face, tone, and record. The ledger stood as a public memory. The implication is direct. Credit persists not despite money, but because money cannot erase the advantages of trust-based coordination.

A counter-example must be faced. In gold rush towns, frontier trading posts often exhibited barter-like dynamics. In Ballarat during the early months of 1851, miners sometimes paid for bread with gold dust weighed on improvised scales. These scenes seem to affirm barter's primacy. Yet even here, careful examination reveals that dust-for-goods trades functioned more like improvised commodity money than like barter. Dust was divisible, storable, and widely accepted. It acted as a medium of exchange, not a good-for-good swap. The frontier does not prove barter's prevalence; it illustrates how swiftly communities reach for proto-money when trust and credit structures are not yet established. The exception, once scrutinised, reinforces the rule.

The myth persists partly because it explains too much, too easily. It suggests that money emerged as a clever fix to a world plagued by inefficient swaps. But early societies were not that clumsy. Tally sticks in medieval England, recorded as early as the twelfth century, demonstrate how communities used simple marks on hazelwood to record obligations between individuals, villages, and the Crown. Each stick held a line of notches indicating a debt; the stick was split lengthways, one half for the debtor, one for the creditor. When payment occurred, halves were matched and verified. No barter required. The behaviour metric was the precision of the notch and the match. The system flourished for centuries because it worked at scale and because obligations travelled in time, not at the point of exchange.

Why, then, has the barter story proved so durable in public imagination? One reason is ideological utility. The myth casts money as a heroic invention replacing clumsy improvisation. It positions markets as the natural evolution of human behaviour, reducing the messy complexity of social credit to a problem solved by metallic precision. Another reason is pedagogical convenience. Barter offers an intuitive starting point for explaining prices and money creation, even if historically unsound. It simplifies narratives that resist simplification. But the cost of simplicity is distortion.

The motif of the slip returns here. The IOU works because its meaning is anchored in social expectation. The ledger works because it captures shared memory. The tally stick works because it binds both parties through physical evidence. None of these tools resemble the barter tableau. They reveal an economy where value moves through time, not across tables.

Recognising this matters because it reshapes how we understand cooperation. Credit systems distribute risk differently from barter systems. When Morrison accepted the IOU in 1926, he assumed the risk of temporary non-payment but gained the benefit of customer loyalty. Barter would have forced immediate equivalence and likely limited the range of possible trades. Credit allowed flexibility. It also created obligations that extended beyond the moment, linking households into webs of expectation.

Early credit systems also demonstrate that the invention of money is less a rupture than an evolution. Metal coins, when they arrived, simplified many of these exchanges. They reduced the burden of record keeping and expanded the reach of trade. But they did not replace the fundamental logic of delay and reciprocity. Even with coins, people continued to run tabs, write promissory notes, and keep ledgers. The coin became one tool among many, not the foundation of all exchange.

Consider Mesopotamia around 2000 BCE. Tablets from Isin and Larsa describe barley loans, labour obligations, and temple ration systems. People settled debts in barley, silver, or labour, depending on context. Ledgers tracked obligations meticulously. Barter appears only at the margins of these records—often in crisis moments when usual channels failed. The implication is clear. Large-scale, complex societies organised exchange through records, not through direct swaps.

The limitation of credit-based systems appears in times of stress. When harvests failed, records showed widespread arrears. Temples and palaces sometimes declared debt remissions, as in Hammurabi's proclamations in the eighteenth century BCE. These episodes reveal the vulnerability of systems built on expectation. Credit requires stability of relationships and continuity of production. When either falters, the system strains. Yet the existence of remissions demonstrates how deeply embedded account-based logic was. Rulers could adjust the books; they did not attempt to restore a barter system. The ledger remained the backbone.

The persistence of barter myths thus obscures a more interesting question: why do humans prefer accounting to swapping? The answer lies in flexibility. A credit system allows half-finished exchanges. It permits imbalances. It shifts settlement into the future, where it can meet the rhythms of production and labour. A fisherman can take grain today and repay after the catch. A potter can receive wool now and supply vessels later. A farmer in Stornoway can leave the shop with tea and sugar during a storm, promising work when the weather clears. The ledger absorbs irregularity. Barter cannot.

The motif threads again through behaviour. A person who swaps directly must search for equivalence. A person who accepts a slip commits to trust. These are deeply different actions. In markets, the difference is visible in the direction of the gaze. Barter demands that both parties stare at the goods before them. Credit allows them to look beyond the present moment.

This distinction remains relevant. Modern monetary debates often assume that money replaced inefficient barter and that digital money will now replace inefficient physical money. The deeper arc suggests something else. Credit and accounting have always been central. Money, whether metallic or digital, often serves as a simplifying layer atop deeper structures of trust. Barter, in this story, becomes not the origin but the fallback.

The chapter's questions crystallise into a single unresolved tension. If early economies solved their coordination problems through credit rather than barter, what does that imply about the systems we build today? Should we design for immediacy, or for delayed reciprocity? Should we privilege exact equivalence, or allow for the flexibility inherent in IOUs? The slip in Morrison's ledger still hangs in the air. It waits for settlement. And it asks how much of our economic life ought to rest on the promise of tomorrow rather than the exchange of the moment.

Commodity Money's Appeal

In the winter of AD 301, the Roman emperor Diocletian issued his *Edict on Maximum Prices*, a sweeping attempt to anchor inflation by setting formal limits on goods across the empire. Among its most prosaic entries was a line that puzzled later historians: a soldier's basic monthly salt ration was valued at a fixed amount of silver. The edict revealed a simple fact already obvious to Roman quartermasters. Salt was pay. It travelled well, spoiled slowly, divided cleanly, and kept armies moving. A soldier carrying a measured handful of salt in a leather pouch was not cradling treasure; he was holding a tool. The logic appears again in far older sites such as Ezero in Bulgaria, where third-millennium BCE deposits of copper lumps—rough, heavy, and uniform—suggest a similar use. These objects were not chosen for glamour. They were chosen because they made life easier.

The motif here is matter. Not matter as material wealth, but matter as reliability. A salt ration could be weighed by any competent soldier. A copper lump could be assessed by any travelling smith. Both offered stability where barter demanded tedious negotiation. A person could hand over salt without needing a perfect coincidence of wants; someone, somewhere, would accept it. Commodity money succeeded not because communities yearned for metallic splendour, but because they valued predictability. A practical object reduces friction.

The appeal becomes clearer when we observe behaviour. A Roman legionary measured salt before marching. A merchant in Early Bronze Age Anatolia stacked copper ingots into piles of near-identical size. The physical act—lifting, weighing, dividing—was the verification. Durability meant that the object would not decay between exchanges. Divisibility meant that a buyer need not overspend. These traits mattered more than rarity or shine. They allowed coordination.

Salt, copper, grain, and cloth each served as commodity money in different settings, but their success followed the same pattern. Show the object; name the role; explain the trait; derive the implication. Salt preserved meat on long campaigns and thus acquired a value that exceeded its flavouring function. Copper held shape under repeated use and could be melted into tools. Each material linked economic exchange to everyday survival. The implication is evident: the closer a commodity sits to the core of subsistence, the easier it becomes to anchor value around it.

The behavioural record from ancient Near Eastern archives further illustrates this. At Mari on the Euphrates, eighteenth-century BCE tablets detail barley as the unit for wages, fines, and rents. Barley was abundant, measurable, and broadly required. Transport cost and spoilage limited long-distance use, but within the city's walls it functioned effectively. People paid with what they grew. The tablets show precise quantities—sila, kur—recorded by scribes. The metric was weight; the decision was logistical. The barley economy worked because its users understood its constraints intimately.

Yet barley exposes the limitation of commodity money's appeal. Spoilage made it unreliable over months. A harsh season could erode value physically. A ledger entry could say one amount; the granary might contain less. The object itself introduced risk. To reconcile this, cities such as Ur turned increasingly to metals for larger or longer-term obligations while keeping grain for daily transactions. The shift shows the balancing act: commodities must match the temporal horizon of the exchange.

Copper, by contrast, carried fewer such problems. In the Shang dynasty's trading zones near Anyang (c. 1200 BCE), oracle bone inscriptions and excavation records reveal copper weights used as reference units. Traders compared lumps by heft and shape. The behaviour was direct: lift, judge, refine. Copper was divisible enough for daily use yet durable enough for seasonal storage. Its role was not ceremonial but mechanical. The implication is steady: commodity money succeeds when its physical properties reduce cognitive load.

A counter-example sharpens the point. In sixteenth-century West Africa, manillas—bracelet-shaped copper alloy objects—circulated widely alongside cowries. Their aesthetic qualities prompted some European traders to misinterpret them as ornamental money, assuming glamour drove demand. Yet ethnographic records and metallurgical analyses indicate that consistency of alloy and weight mattered more. Communities preferred manillas that could be melted and reused. The glamour was incidental. Their true appeal lay in utility. The limitation of this system was counterfeit proliferation: Portuguese traders introduced lighter varieties, triggering disputes. Still, the market corrected. People weighed and rejected inferior manillas. Reliability, not appearance, dominated.

Commodity money's logic appears wherever scale and seasonality intersect. A shepherd in Iron Age Britain could trade fleece measured by weight. A farmer in the Yellow River basin could offer millet. Each exchange minimised negotiation. A standardised unit replaced haggling. The behavioural metric was ease: how quickly can both parties agree? The object mediated trust by embedding value in matter. People trusted the weight, not the promise.

Durability completes the picture. Objects must survive handling, transport, and time. Salt worked for soldiers but dissolved in humid coastal environments. Copper endured harsh weather but required smelting for purity checks. Gold and silver later dominated not because they were intrinsically special, but because they solved these trade-offs more effectively across long distances. They were portable, fungible, and resistant to corrosion. These traits allowed merchants in Lydia in the seventh century BCE to adopt electrum lumps as proto-coins. Herodotus later noted how this practice became a regional norm. The material quality preceded the monetary form. The motif of matter returns: the chosen substance bore the responsibility of stability.

Yet commodity systems are not without tension. Large stones served as money on the island of Yap, but their immobility restricted daily use. The Rai stones' efficacy rested on collective knowledge rather than physical transfer. Here, matter receded and memory dominated. The counter-example shows commodity money's boundary: materiality aids exchange only when participants can handle, measure, and transport the object. When matter becomes cumbersome, systems gravitate back towards ledger logic.

Commodity money's appeal, therefore, is conditional. A community must judge which traits matter most for its own needs. Durability supports store-of-value functions. Divisibility supports trade. Uniformity supports pricing. When an object excels in these areas, it anchors exchange. When it fails, people adapt by supplementing with credit or adopting new materials. These adaptations reveal a community's risk calculus. Cargo handlers in Hellenistic ports preferred lead weights for bulk settlement; they tolerated the metal's toxicity because no alternative matched its density and consistency. The decision was pragmatic.

The motif tightens again around measurement. A merchant who pours out salt on a scale performs an act that predates coinage but anticipates it. He verifies. He commits. He settles. The object becomes the interface between human intention and economic action. Commodity money's power lies in this clarity. It reduces ambiguity.

But the deeper implication is that commodity money is not primitive. It is precise. It solves genuine coordination problems by offering a physical standard. In doing so, it frees communities from interminable negotiation. It reduces the need for mutual knowledge. Two strangers meeting at a fair can agree on copper weight without knowing each other's histories. Matter mediates.

Still, a question lingers. How much can communities rely on matter before they require records? Can salt, copper, or grain sustain complexity beyond a certain threshold? Or does scale inevitably push societies towards abstraction—towards ledgers, tokens, and eventually digital claims? Commodity money reveals the ingenuity of physical problem-solving. But it also signals the boundary where matter alone is no longer enough.

Temples, Palaces, and Accounts

In April 1953, the archaeologist Henry Frankfort supervised the excavation of a room in the Eanna temple complex at Uruk, southern Iraq. Beneath a layer of collapsed brick he uncovered a cluster of clay tablets dating to around 3100 BCE. Most were small, barely the size of a palm, and many bore the same recurring impressions: a stylised head of barley, a jar symbol, a wedge denoting quantity. They recorded rations issued to named workers. One tablet listed grain allocations for a team repairing the temple's reed roofing; another noted deliveries from a nearby field. No coins lay near the tablets. No metallic tokens accompanied them. Yet the tablets tracked obligations, transfers, and balances with a consistency and precision that any bookkeeper would recognise. They revealed something quietly radical: long before coinage appeared in Lydia or the Greek city-states, institutions had already invented the mechanics of money through accounting.

The motif here is the tablet—small, unassuming, yet transformative. It allowed a scribe to capture a moment of transfer and carry its meaning forward in time. A basket of barley collected in spring could be offset against labour performed in summer. A worker's absence could be marked without confrontation. The tablet stabilised relationships across seasons and across distance. It was an administrative tool, but it was also a proto-monetary instrument. The clay bore the responsibility that coins would later assume: recording value, mediating exchange, organising obligations.

Frankfort's find was not unique. Thousands of similar tablets survive from Ur, Lagash, and Shuruppak, spanning the early third millennium BCE. They describe a world where value moved through records rather than through objects. The temple complex stood at the centre of this system. It collected grain as tax or tithe, stored it in granaries, and redistributed it as wages, offerings, and loans. Palaces and large households followed similar routines. Their survival depended on coordination. Their accounting practices became the backbone of that coordination.

The earliest tablets are dominated by grain entries, and for good reason. Grain was the material anchor of the economy. In a landscape where rainfall varied, where irrigation canals demanded constant maintenance, and where seasonal labour shifted from field to granary to military service, grain served as the default standard. But the tablet—not the grain—performed the crucial task of measuring and comparing obligations. The behaviour is visible: a worker approached the granary with a basket; the scribe inspected the quantity; he pressed symbols into wet clay; he placed the tablet aside to be fired or dried. Verification took the form of touch, weight, and inscription. The implication is clear. The accounting act was the true settlement.

Institutions, not markets, built these systems. In the palace of Mari on the middle Euphrates, c. 1800 BCE, scribes recorded the distribution of barley and dates to labourers repairing caravanserai walls. Each entry noted the receiver's name, the quantity issued, and the day of distribution. The palace did not attempt to settle everything immediately. Instead, it maintained a rolling record of obligations. Workers accrued claims on future rations; the palace tracked its own future liabilities. Accounting supplanted barter because it could capture time.

The palace of Knossos on Crete, though separated by centuries and seas, displayed similar logic. Linear B tablets from around 1400 BCE list wool and oil contributions from dependent communities and record the palace's obligations to craft specialists. One tablet allocates wool to weavers whose looms sat in adjoining workshops. When the final textiles were returned, scribes checked quantities against expectations. The behaviour metric—matching allocated inputs to finished outputs—served as both accounting and quality control. Again, no coins. The ledger held the system together.

These examples reveal a foundational truth: central record keepers emerged long before coinage because large institutions solved problems that individuals alone could not. They managed surpluses, smoothed shortages, stored value securely, and organised labour across seasons. Their ledgers allowed society to commit to future distribution without requiring immediate equivalence. The implication is decisive. Money's intellectual infrastructure—record, compare, enforce—existed centuries before the first stamped coin.

A credible counter-example helps clarify the boundary. Archaeologists working at the site of Byblos in the Levant have found metal hoards from the early second millennium BCE. Some lumps of silver appear to have been weighed and reweighed, bearing cut marks that indicate active circulation as media of exchange. This seems, at first glance, to challenge the centrality of temple and palace accounting. If silver circulated, perhaps market exchange dominated. But the hoards themselves tell a different story. The lumps vary widely in purity. Their weights differ. They would have required constant testing and verification. Silver circulated primarily in long-distance trade or elite transactions where institutional oversight was weak. Within cities, grain, labour credits, and administrative accounts continued to dominate. The limitation of silver reveals the strength of accounting: purity checks and weighing were slow; entries on tablets were faster, clearer, and enforceable through institutional authority. The counter-example thus reinforces the argument: decentralised commodity trade flourished around the edges, not at the core.

Why did temples and palaces assume these roles? Partly because they commanded organisation, storage, and enforcement. A granary could hold hundreds of tonnes of barley; a household could not. A temple could compel labour through ritual obligation; a single merchant could not. These institutions were the only entities capable of sustaining the temporal dimension of obligations. They balanced surpluses from one season against shortages in another. Their ledgers recorded the ebb and flow. The motif of the tablet returns: each tablet captured a promise across time.

The measurement practices were sophisticated. At Umma, c. 2100 BCE, scribes calculated *gur* (a large grain measure) with subunits, converting harvest quantities into ration units for workers in fields, workshops, and transport brigades. Tablets record adjustments when granaries overflowed or when pests struck crops. The precision reflects an administrative machine that understood risk. When crops failed, obligations shifted; when yields surpassed expectation, redistributions followed. Accounting became a buffer against uncertainty.

This proto-monetary structure was not merely administrative convenience. It shaped social organisation. Institutions allocated rations to dependants not in ad hoc fashion but according to stable formulas: so many litres of barley for a man, fewer for a woman, different amounts for children. These rations embodied value. They acted as wages, as sustenance, as markers of inclusion. They also structured hierarchy. When the palace increased or reduced rations, it communicated authority as much as generosity. The behaviour was visible: individuals queued at granary doors; scribes recorded each name; guards monitored order. Each distribution reinforced a social narrative: the institution provided.

In Egypt's Middle Kingdom (c. 2000–1700 BCE), papyri from Kahun record allocations of grain and beer to workers repairing irrigation dykes. Some entries note arrears or penalties for missed work. Others track loans issued to farmers awaiting harvest. The palace mediated these exchanges. The papyri read like ledgers: dated entries, named recipients, quantities measured. The implication is familiar. The palace was a bank in all but name, extending credit, collecting dues, and settling accounts through record-keeping.

Yet this institutional architecture had vulnerabilities. When central authority weakened, ledgers lost force. A counter-example emerges in the collapse of the Hittite empire around 1200 BCE. Clay tablets from Hattusa show increasingly chaotic entries in the years just before the fall—irregular deliveries, incomplete rations, unexplained deficits. The stores were no longer stable. The administrative machine could not buffer external pressures. When the institution faltered, commitments unravelled. This limitation highlights a crucial point: accounting systems depend on the stability of their keepers. When temples or palaces decline, so does the monetary coherence they enable.

Still, the long record shows resilience. Even when political control shifted, administrative accounting often persisted. After the Akkadian empire collapsed, Sumerian city-states retained the same systems of rationing and storage. After the Mycenaean palaces fell, Greek communities maintained local accounting traditions in shrines and household compounds. The ledger outlived the authority that created it. The motif of inscription persists: writing anchored continuity.

The intellectual leap made by these early institutions was subtle but profound. They realised that value could be abstracted from objects and stored in records. A jar of barley in a granary was not the only form of wealth; the entry stating that a worker was owed a certain ration was itself valuable. The clay tablet became a second-order object, carrying claims across time. Accounting turned memory into infrastructure.

This shift illuminates why coins, when they arrived centuries later, were not inventions ex nihilo but accelerations of an existing logic. Coins combined the portability of a commodity with the authority of an institution. But the conceptual groundwork—the idea that value can be standardised, denominated, and transferred through marks—was the achievement of temple and palace accountants. Their ledgers were slow ancestors of money's later forms.

As we look back, the harvest ledger acts as a diagnostic tool. It raises questions that remain unresolved. How much centralisation is necessary to maintain stable obligations? When does institutional authority enhance trust, and when does it suppress autonomy? And when societies invent new forms of record keeping—whether digital ledgers or cryptographic chains—are they repeating ancient patterns under new constraints? The tablets from Uruk sit quietly in museum drawers, but their logic endures. They ask whether we still understand what those early scribes knew: that value, once written, becomes a promise that binds whole communities together.

Ritual, Status, and Value

On 14 September 1936, the anthropologist Hortense Powdermaker observed a bridewealth exchange in Lesu village on the island of New Ireland, Papua New Guinea. Between the groom's family and the bride's maternal uncles lay a neat row of *tabu* shell money: coiled strands of dog whelk shells threaded onto rattan, their pale surfaces glinting in the heat. Powdermaker recorded the count—forty-seven fathoms of shells—and noted how long each strand had been in circulation. Some had moved through the community for decades. Yet the striking detail was not quantity but choreography. Each transfer was performed in silence. Elders nodded. Children watched. The shells passed slowly from one pair of hands to another. The payment settled an obligation, but it also enacted a story: two families joined, rights transferred, alliances reinforced. The shells mattered because the ritual mattered.

The motif appears instantly: the gesture. Not the shell, not the price, but the deliberate act of giving. That gesture stabilised value more effectively than any market rule. The shells had no intrinsic worth; their power came from collective recognition. Everyone in Lesu knew the meaning of forty-seven fathoms. They knew who had held them. They knew which events the shells had witnessed. This memory governed price. Nothing about the exchange resembled barter or shopping. It was social theatre with binding consequence.

Ritual payments turn obligation into order. They convert potential conflict—over marriage, status, lineage, land—into a series of carefully managed steps. Powdermaker's account shows this vividly. The bridewealth did not purchase the bride. It signalled respect for her lineage, affirmed the transfer of certain rights, and created reciprocal claims between families. The shells served as tokens of solemnity. Their movement marked the fulfilment of expectations. The payment made the marriage legitimate in the eyes of the village. The implication is immediate: ritual is not decoration; it is governance.

This dynamic recurs across cultures. Consider the Trobriand *kula* ring, documented by Bronisław Malinowski in 1922. Chiefs sailed across islands to exchange red shell necklaces (*soulava*) and white shell armbands (*mwali*). The objects travelled continuously, never resting long in one place. Their material value was modest. Their social value was immense. A necklace received from a respected chief increased one's prestige; the obligation to pass it onward ensured ongoing ties. The behaviour was performative: voyages, gifts, speeches, ceremonial feasts. The ritual exchange did not measure wealth; it distributed honour. The implication is clear. Value resides not in the object but in the network of relationships the object traverses.

Yet not all ritual payments strengthen order. A counter-example emerges from nineteenth-century Buganda, where royal tribute patterns sometimes generated tension rather than harmony. Chiefs compelled subjects to deliver barkcloth, livestock, or labour in rituals meant to affirm loyalty. These payments were choreographed, but their tone differed. While bridewealth shells in Lesu expressed reciprocity, tribute in Buganda implied subordination. When demands escalated—particularly under Kabaka Mutesa I in the 1860s—resentment grew. Ritual lost its stabilising force. The limitation illuminates a central point: ritual supports order only when participants experience the exchange as legitimate. When ritual becomes extraction, its power erodes.

Reconciliation of these examples shows how ritual and status intertwine. In Lesu or the Trobriands, ritual created shared meaning. In Buganda, ritual signalled asymmetry. The motif of the gesture appears again: the quality of the gesture—respectful or coercive—determines whether value coheres or fractures. Meaning can stabilise price, but only if meaning is shared.

To understand why ritual stabilises value, we must examine how groups remember. Bridewealth shells acquire reputations. A shell strand might be known for its previous holders, the marriages it formalised, the disputes it resolved. Powdermaker noted that certain strands carried stories decades old. Their circulation rate acted as a behavioural metric: shells associated with prestigious lineages moved less frequently, partly because families hesitated to part with them, partly because receiving them conferred exceptional honour. The community tracked provenance. The shells' past shaped their present. The implication is striking. Social memory substitutes for intrinsic value.

This form of valuation reappears in places with very different histories. In medieval Wales, the *galanas* system required compensation payments in cattle for homicide. Legal texts like the *Laws of Hywel Dda* (c. 13th century, compiled from earlier practice) describe precise amounts owed by kin groups. The payment, though material, was ceremonial. It aimed to prevent feud. Elders gathered, recited the lineage, and negotiated the number of cattle. The ritual transformed a violent conflict into a structured obligation. Again, the gesture was central. The cattle mattered less than the act of public giving. Once received, they symbolised restoration. The behaviour—walking cattle across a boundary, presenting them before witnesses—made the value credible.

Ritual payments also distribute status. In the Kongo kingdom, as documented by John Thornton (1983), elite families used cloth bundles in marriage exchanges. The cloth's colour and weave indicated the family's standing; handing over the bundle communicated alliance. The act revealed identity. Here status travelled with the object. The implication is delicate: ritual payments can encode hierarchy without currency.

But ritual's ability to stabilise value depends on constraint. Bridewealth shells in New Ireland derived strength partly from limited supply. Shells required laborious preparation—collecting, piercing, threading—and certain colours were rare. Their scarcity was social as much as natural. Communities controlled access. This constraint meant prices could settle. The gesture again: giving a scarce object amplifies its meaning. When scarcity is engineered or eroded, ritual loses coherence.

A counter-example emerges from twentieth-century attempts to monetise ritual shells for tourist trade in the Trobriands. As outsiders purchased shells as souvenirs, supply increased and quality standards slipped. Local value systems resisted full collapse—ritual shells retained meaning in ceremonial contexts—but price stability weakened. Communities responded by reaffirming lineage-based restrictions on high-prestige shells. Ritual enveloped the object tightly, guarding its significance. This reconciliation underscores a principle: meaning survives when communities embed the object within narrative and authority.

Ritual payments sit alongside administrative and market systems. They do not necessarily compete with those systems; they complement them. The same society that uses ritual shells for marriage may use commodity money for trade and accounting for taxation. Each form answers different needs. Ritual handles questions of identity and belonging. Commodity money handles questions of quantity. Accounting handles questions of fairness and timing. The coexistence is not accidental. Humans require multiple registers of value.

That multiplicity appears in even the most bureaucratic societies. In ancient China during the Zhou dynasty (c. 1046–256 BCE), bronze ritual vessels often bore inscriptions recording who gifted them and why. While bronze spade money circulated in markets, ritual vessels circulated in elite ceremonies. Their function was not payment but commemoration. Yet the vessels conferred status equivalent to wealth. A noble who received a vessel gained prestige. The gift was performative. It reinforced social order. The gesture persists across millennia.

Ritual payments expose another truth: value is a story told collectively. The shells in Lesu told the story of alliance. The cattle in Wales told the story of reconciliation. The cloth bundles in Kongo told the story of lineage. These stories stabilised prices because they stabilised expectations. A family receiving forty-seven fathoms in Lesu knew precisely what those shells demanded in return—offers of help, respect for in-laws, participation in future ceremonies. That predictability kept value from drifting.

Yet ritual's stability can also mask fragility. When generational narratives break—through war, migration, or religious conversion—the objects lose coherence. Powdermaker noted that by the 1930s, Christian missionaries in New Ireland discouraged bridewealth as "pagan" practice. Younger villagers, caught between traditions, faced tension. Some families conducted private ceremonies to preserve meaning;

others reduced payments to token strands. The value narrowed. Ritual adapted but lost scope. The limitation shows that ritual value depends on cultural continuity.

The motif of gesture returns one last time. Ritual payments work because the gesture performs the value. It publicly marks the shift in obligation. The object becomes secondary. This has implications for modern monetary design. Systems built solely on abstraction struggle to carry meaning unless they recreate ritual through ceremony, symbolism, or collective acts. The behaviour of giving still anchors legitimacy.

This subchapter moves the arc of monetary history into territory often overlooked by economists: the emotional, symbolic, and performative dimensions of value. Ritual payments reveal that money, before it is an instrument of exchange, is a social act. They show how communities transform obligations into institutions. They show how meaning, not mechanics, can stabilise prices. And they raise a provocative question: if value requires shared stories, what happens when those stories diverge?

Chapter 3
Coinage, Empire, and Standardisation

The scene is deceptively quiet. In the spring of 546 BCE, in the Lydian capital of Sardis, a merchant named Eurybios examined a small disc of electrum just stamped at the royal mint. The imprint—a roaring lion beside a sunburst—was crisp, the edges still sharp from cooling. He turned the coin in his hand, weighing it with the casual confidence of someone who had spent years judging metals by eye. But something had changed. Only months earlier, he would have needed scales, touchstones, and the practiced suspicion of a man trading across borders. Now, with a single emblem pressed into metal, the king had collapsed that uncertainty. Weight was declared. Purity was endorsed. Trust was public. Eurybios pocketed the coin and walked into the marketplace, carrying not a piece of metal, but a promise backed by power. In that moment, coinage ceased to be mere convenience and became a political instrument.

The paradox is that coins, often imagined as natural, self-evident forms of money, were anything but. They required choices—design, metal content, enforcement—that bound the issuer's reputation to every transaction they enabled. A stamped disc was not only a unit of exchange; it was a claim about authority and a signal of reach. When Eurybios handed that electrum coin to a Phoenician trader later that afternoon, he transferred more than value. He transmitted a standard. And with it, he helped set in motion one of history's great transformations: the rise of monetary systems that could scale across distance, language, and allegiance.

Coinage did not emerge in a vacuum. It appeared in the midst of expanding empires, militarised frontiers, and increasingly complex trade routes. As armies marched, they required portable, uniform means of paying soldiers. As merchants ventured farther from home, they needed tools to reduce the friction of verification. And as rulers sought to extract taxes and stabilise control, they needed instruments that bound subjects to a common economic denominator. A coin could serve all three. But the technology's elegance masked its cost. To stamp trust onto metal, states had to police purity, deter counterfeiters, and calibrate seigniorage—the margin they skimmed from minting—without undermining their own credibility. A clipped or debased coin was not a trivial flaw. It was a breach of confidence that resonated across markets.

This chapter sits at the hinge of monetary history. On one side lies the world of ledgers and commodity payments, where value travelled through memory, accounting, and the physicality of material goods. On the other lies a world where authority imprinted itself directly onto metal, collapsing the need for negotiation into a single, recognisable symbol. The shift did not erase older practices; credit, barter, and temple accounts persisted. But coinage layered a new logic onto them: uniformity. A stamped coin allowed two strangers to transact without personal familiarity, institutional mediation, or shared ritual. The trust migrated from people and places into the object itself.

Yet the moment we treat coinage as neutral technology, we lose sight of its political innovation. Consider the simple act of stamping. A mark on metal did more than authenticate weight; it broadcast hierarchy. Whether the issuer was Croesus in Lydia, Darius in Persia, or the Roman Senate, the image on the coin announced who controlled the standard. To accept the coin was to acknowledge that authority, however tacitly. This was not an accident. It was design. States discovered that they could knit disparate regions into functional economic zones by embedding their identity into circulating metal. Coinage thus became a quiet agent of empire.

Standards magnified this effect. A silver drachma from Athens or a denarius from Rome represented more than a unit of account; it represented an entire system of measurement, trust, and enforcement. When a merchant in the Athenian Agora chose between a local token and an Attic coin, he was navigating a network effect. The widely accepted coin reduced his risk. Its standard weight meant fewer disputes. Its recognisable emblem meant faster trade. Each acceptance reinforced the standard. The behaviour propagated itself. And as these coins travelled across the Mediterranean, they did not merely facilitate exchange—they carried influence.

But standardisation had a deeper economic logic. Uniform measures compress information. They make markets legible. A coin of consistent weight requires no debate. A mint with known practices reduces hesitation. A measure, once accepted, imposes order on what would otherwise be a tapestry of local conventions. This is why states invested in mints, inspectors, and penalties. The cost of producing standard coins was offset by the expansion of taxable and tradable activity they enabled.

War accelerated all of this. Armies needed to pay soldiers quickly, predictably, and in forms that suppliers recognised. Supply lines depended on amiable intermediaries who accepted official coinage at known rates. States discovered that by demanding taxes in their own currency, they could create artificial yet powerful monetary ecosystems. A soldier's pay token, issued in the field, stood not only as a promise of later redemption but as a mechanism of monetary adoption. A smith near the front accepted the token because he knew the state would redeem it for official coin; the state extracted the tax that ultimately backed that redemption. Through this loop, money demand became political demand.

Yet coinage's strength contained its flaw. If trust comes from the stamp, what happens when the stamp lies? Debasement—reducing the metal content of coins while keeping the face value the same—became a tempting recourse for overstretched governments. It was a fiscal tool disguised as monetary stability. But markets were not naïve. Merchants weighed coins, compared edges, inspected colour, and discounted tarnished or clipped specimens. A clipped drachma in 4th-century BCE Athens or a debased denarius in the 3rd-century CE Roman Empire triggered behavioural shifts: sellers raised prices, hoarded older coins, or demanded premiums. The standard fractured. And with it, the issuer's legitimacy frayed.

The backlash was not moral but practical. When seigniorage became excessive or debasement too frequent, people sought alternatives—foreign coins, barter, or credit networks insulated from official manipulation. Trust flowed where discipline persisted. States learned, often painfully, that coinage was a contract: the issuer promised integrity; users rewarded them with acceptance. When one side broke the pact, the other recalibrated. A debased coin did not merely lose metal; it lost story. It ceased to carry the narrative of stability that made coinage powerful in the first place.

What makes this chapter timely is how recognisable these dynamics remain. Modern currencies no longer rely on silver content, yet they face identical questions: How does authority generate trust? How do standards scale across borders? How does the state create money demand through taxation and procurement? And what happens when the integrity of the standard erodes—through inflation, policy missteps, or institutional decline? Coins may be ancient, but the logic that shaped them governs contemporary debates on central banks, digital currencies, and geopolitical monetary competition.

A subtle motif runs through these questions: the edge. In antiquity, clipping the edge of a coin was both a literal and metaphorical act—an attempt to shave away value while preserving appearance. Today, the edges we negotiate are less tangible but no less consequential: the edge between state backing and market acceptance, between stability and manipulation, between uniformity and local autonomy. Each edge marks a site of potential trust or potential fracture.

As the chapter unfolds, it will follow these edges across time and empire, from the Lydian experiments with electrum to the Roman consolidation of metallic standards; from the practicalities of minting to the fraught politics of debasement; from the expansion of trade networks to the imposition of tax-driven currency regimes. The story is not one of technological triumph but of continual negotiation—between rulers seeking reach and populations demanding reliability, between states building systems and markets enforcing discipline.

The question that threads ahead is not whether coinage worked—it did—but why it worked, and why it sometimes failed spectacularly. What makes a stamp credible? What gives a standard its gravitational pull? And what happens when the body that guarantees the standard begins to crack? The answers lie not just in the metal itself, but in the coordination, coercion, and collective belief that transform stamped discs into empire-spanning systems of value.

Stamping Trust

On a cold January morning in 1696, Isaac Newton stood in the Tower of London counting wounds in silver. As the newly appointed Warden of the Royal Mint, he received bags of worn shillings from across England, each coin scratched, bent, or visibly bitten by knives. Many had lost so much metal to clipping that their milled edges had vanished entirely. Yet they still carried the king's portrait and the royal arms. The stamp remained. The silver did not. Parliament had just authorised the Great Recoinage. Newton's job was to turn a chaotic stock of mutilated discs into a reliable standard. He weighed, he measured, he ordered new dies. The aim was simple and ambitious at once: restore belief that a shilling marked as such truly contained a shilling's worth of silver. In Newton's hands, the stamp became an instrument of trust and a battlefield for competing incentives.

The stamped coin is monetary technology boiled down to an instant. One blow of the die declares: this disc contains a specific weight of metal, refined to a known standard, endorsed by named authority. That declaration saves time. It shrinks verification costs. A market stall that once required scales and acid tests can now proceed on sight. The coin speaks for the ruler. A butcher in Bristol accepts the king's shilling without weighing because experience tells him that most of the time the stamped promise holds. That behaviour—acceptance without testing—is trust made visible.

The motif that recurs through this subchapter is the mark. Not just the portrait or emblem, but the idea that one compressed sign carries a bundle of information: metal content, legal status, political backing, and expected acceptability. The mark sits on the surface; trust is supposed to run through the core. The trouble begins when the two drift apart.

The first major claim is straightforward: stamping coins transformed verification from a private chore into a public service. In early Lydia around the seventh century BCE, electrum lumps used in trade were naturally variable in composition. Traders had to test and haggle. When Lydian rulers began striking standardised electrum staters at Sardis—Herodotus credits King Croesus by name, though exact chronology is debated—they imposed a uniform weight and fineness. The lion's head mark on the coin was a promise that someone at the mint had already done the weighing and refining. The behaviour in markets changed. Instead of pausing to assess each lump, merchants increasingly accepted stamped pieces at face value within the issuing domain. The implication is clear. By investing effort at the point of minting, rulers reduced effort at every subsequent point of exchange.

A second checkable example comes from classical Athens. By the fifth century BCE, the Athenian silver tetradrachm—the "owl"—circulated widely in the eastern Mediterranean. Its consistent weight and high silver purity made it a preferred trade coin in ports far beyond Attica. Archaeological finds at Naucratis in Egypt and along the Levantine coast show Athenians and non-Athenians alike using owls as a de facto standard, often accepting them without reweighing. The stamp—a helmeted Athena on one side, an owl and olive branch on the other—stood as shorthand for reliable content. The time saved per transaction was small, but multiplied across thousands of exchanges, the efficiency was enormous. The mark did real work.

Stamping, however, was never neutral. It introduced a new margin: seigniorage. If a ruler could take pure silver, mint coins that contained slightly less than the nominal standard, and spend them at full face value, the difference flowed to the mint-owner. Even without debasement, charging a fee for coining created revenue. The incentive was obvious. The risk was equally obvious. Push seigniorage too far, and people test coins again. As soon as butchers and smiths return to the scales, the whole purpose of stamping is undermined.

Newton understood this tension. During the Great Recoinage, he insisted that new English silver coins match the statutory weight and fineness closely. The state absorbed a large part of the loss from the clipped currency rather than pass it fully onto holders. In effect, the Crown sacrificed short-term seigniorage to rebuild the credibility of the stamp. The behaviour that followed vindicated the choice. As the new milled coins with reeded edges entered circulation, merchants resumed accepting them without obsessive testing. The mark regained its power because the metal beneath matched its promise.

Where rulers showed less restraint, markets adapted rapidly. Roman coinage offers a long, textured case study. Under

Augustus in the late first century BCE, the silver denarius maintained relatively stable fineness. Prices and military pay schedules built around that stability. By the third century CE, under emperors such as Caracalla and his successors, repeated debasements had reduced the denarius's silver content dramatically. Hoards from sites across the empire attest to this decline. Merchants responded by demanding more coins for the same goods, hoarding older issues, and discounting visibly degraded pieces. Trust did not vanish entirely—people still used coins—but it shifted from nominal stamp to perceived metal content. The mark no longer guaranteed much. The implication is that stamping creates trust only as long as the issuer keeps the metal reasonably aligned with the symbol.

This brings us to counterfeiting and clipping: the parasitic complements to seigniorage. If genuine stamps confer value, imitating those stamps or harvesting their metal becomes lucrative. Counterfeiters cast or struck copies with inferior metal. Clippers shaved small amounts from edges, accumulating shavings while passing on slightly lighter coins as full value. The behaviour is rational. It is also corrosive.

The clipped coin is perhaps the purest illustration of the policing problem. Every tiny slice removed from the edge breaks the link between mark and metal. If clipping is rare, trust survives. If clipping becomes routine, each acceptance without weighing becomes a gamble. In seventeenth-century England, before Newton's reforms, some circulating shillings had lost up to 20 per cent of their silver. Observers complained that coins resembled irregular wafers more than round discs. Market practice adapted. People with experience weighed suspect coins; those without experience accepted them at a discount or refused them. Transactions slowed. Disputes multiplied. The stamp still showed the king's head, but the edge told a different story.

States fought back in two ways: redesign and punishment. Redesign involved adding features such as milled or lettered edges that made clipping more visible. The reeded edges on post-1696 English silver coins served this purpose. Any removed metal distorted the pattern instantly. The motif of the mark now extended to the rim; the edge became a surveillance device. Punishment, by contrast, targeted people rather than objects. Under English law, coin clipping and counterfeiting were treated as forms of high treason well into the eighteenth century, punishable by death. Newton personally supervised prosecutions, gathering evidence against counterfeiters in London taverns. The combination of technical and legal enforcement reduced, but never eradicated, the problem.

A limitation emerges when we imagine that stamping and policing alone can guarantee trust. They cannot. The Athenians, the Romans, and the English all show that when fiscal pressures mount, even the most carefully designed coins are vulnerable to policy choices made at the mint. A ruler facing war, poor harvests, or political crisis may be tempted to stretch seigniorage, relaxing standards while relying on the inertia of the stamp to preserve acceptance. For a time, it works. The mark carries momentum. But as soon as market participants detect the shift—by comparing old and new coins, by noticing higher prices, by seeing foreign merchants refuse certain issues—the cost of verification rises again.

The reconciliation lies in understanding stamping as part of a broader trust architecture, not a substitute for it. A stamp is a promise, but its content is always conditional on reputation and enforcement. A city with a long record of disciplined minting can issue coins that circulate far beyond its territory, because users trust the discipline, not just the metal. Athens achieved this in the fifth century BCE; Venice did so with its silver grosso and gold ducat from the thirteenth century onwards. Their coins served as tools of trade and as ambassadors of credibility. By contrast, polities with erratic monetary policies found their coins confined to narrow domains, discounted abroad or melted as bullion.

Seigniorage itself reflects a trade-off between fiscal capacity and monetary integrity. A modest, predictable minting margin allows states to fund coin production and extract some revenue without alarming users. Behaviourally, this shows up as continuing willingness to hold coins, stable acceptance in markets, and limited preference for foreign or older issues. Excessive seigniorage—especially when combined with opaque debasement—triggers flight. People hoard higher-quality coins, export them, or switch to non-monetary stores of value. The coin is still stamped, but its authority shrinks.

Counterfeiters and clippers exploit moments when the gap between stamp and substance widens. If the official coin already contains little silver, the marginal difference between genuine and fake shrinks. Policing grows harder. During the worst phases of Roman debasement, the distinction between official and unofficial issues blurred. The state's own practices had eroded the benchmark against which forgery could be judged. The mark lost its edge.

The quiet motif of the mark returns here as a question. What exactly does the stamp certify? Early on, it certifies weight and fineness. Over time, as systems move towards token coins and, eventually, fiat money, the stamp certifies something else: a legal claim, a tax receivable, a place in a broader hierarchy of obligations. Yet the underlying puzzle remains constant. Users ask whether the stamp they see matches the value they expect. Issuers attempt to keep those expectations aligned while preserving room for their own fiscal needs. Counterfeiters look for cracks.

When we strip away romanticism, stamping trust onto metal is revealed as a compact. The state offers to bear the cost of verification centrally—through assayers, mint masters, and legal standards—so that individuals can transact quickly on the street. In return, individuals agree to treat stamped pieces as equivalent, to accept them in payment, and to pay taxes in them. Seigniorage is the state's fee for running this system. Counterfeiting and clipping are unauthorised attempts to collect that fee privately.

The unresolved tension lies in the question of how far that compact can be stretched before it snaps. How much seigniorage can a polity extract without undermining its own currency? How aggressively must it police clipping and forgery to preserve confidence without suffocating commerce? And when trust in the stamp finally falters, what recoinage, reform, or redesign is enough to persuade people once more that the mark on the surface truly speaks for the metal within?

Standards and Scale

In the summer of 415 BCE, a merchant named Philon walked through the crowded quay of Syracuse with two purses at his belt. One held local Syracusan coins: silver dekadrachms stamped with the city's victorious chariot. The other carried Athenian tetradrachms—"owls"—brought by traders who had sailed across the Ionian Sea after the launch of the Athenian Sicilian Expedition that same year. Philon paused at a stall selling Egyptian linen. The price was quoted in "owls", not Syracusan silver. The choice was immediate and public. Philon opened the Athenian purse. He paid in a currency minted nearly a thousand kilometres away. The stamp did not merely travel across the Mediterranean; it outcompeted the local standard. One decision in a noisy port revealed the logic that shaped ancient commerce: when standards spread, distance shrinks, and strangers transact as if they share a measure.

The paradox was visible in Philon's gesture. Syracuse minted heavier coins, often more ornate, but the Egyptian linen seller still preferred the Athenian standard for its reliability and recognisable weight. Why did a foreign coin command such confidence? Why did its network eclipse the host city's own? The scene captured the tension between civic pride and economic pragmatism. A city's coin could proclaim identity, yet identity alone did not guarantee reach. Philon's choice made that clear. The owl was not just a coin; it was an agreement carried from port to port, confirmed by thousands of hands before his.

This subchapter follows the quiet motif of the scale—both the literal weighing of metal and the figurative balancing of expectations. Every stamped coin was tested against an invisible ledger of previous interactions. Every acceptance nudged a standard towards dominance or decline. As Philon's decision showed, the scale rarely lies.

The first major claim is that shared standards enabled commerce across distance by compressing information into recognisable forms. The Athenian tetradrachm is the archetypal case. Archaeological evidence from Naucratis (Egypt) and Persepolis (Iran) shows owls circulating far from Attica by the fifth century BCE. Merchants accepted them with minimal testing because they had acquired a reputation for stable weight—around 17.2 grams—and consistent silver content. The behaviour we observe in marketplaces supports this: fewer disputes, shorter verification rituals, quicker agreement on price. The implication is powerful. A city that disciplined its mint practices could extend its influence far beyond its walls simply by maintaining consistency. Standards multiplied their own usefulness.

A second checkable example comes from the Roman Empire, where the silver denarius became the dominant medium of military and commercial payment by the late first century BCE. Finds at Vindonissa (in modern Switzerland) and Masada (in modern Israel) reveal that the same coin circulated from the Rhine frontier to the Judaean desert. Soldiers, tax collectors, and traders could move between regions without recalibrating weights or negotiating local conventions. The

Roman mint created a single monetary language. That uniformity translated into administrative cohesion and logistical speed. The denarius worked because the standard held.

Yet standards do not spread automatically. They require constant maintenance and clear signalling. Greek city-states knew this. When Aegina, Corinth, and Athens competed for maritime influence in the sixth and fifth centuries BCE, each promoted its own "weight standard". Aegina's "turtles" once dominated Aegean trade, but as Athens expanded its empire and secured access to the Laurion silver mines, the Attic standard gradually displaced rivals. A merchant's decision—turtle or owl—became a referendum on predictability. When weighing two coins in the hand, the merchant compared not just mass but reputation. The motif of the scale reappeared here as judgement: whose promise carries more weight?

The core of this mechanism is network effects. The more people accept a standard, the more valuable acceptance becomes for others. The linen seller preferred owls because her suppliers priced in owls; her suppliers priced in owls because their creditors preferred owls; and the cycle deepened. A modern economist might chart this as a coordination equilibrium, but the behaviour itself was intuitive. Use what others use. Trust what others trust. The implication is that monetary standards grow not linearly but cumulatively, sometimes explosively.

Still, ancient economies present a credible limitation to this story: multiplicity. Coins from different polities circulated side by side in many regions, particularly in the Near East. The Persian Achaemenid Empire, for example, minted the gold daric and silver siglos, yet still tolerated the presence of Greek and regional currencies. At Sardis or Susa in the fifth century BCE, a merchant's scales might weigh a daric, an owl, and a local issue in quick succession. Multiple standards coexisted because political boundaries, metallurgical habits, and commercial networks overlapped imperfectly. This raises a question: if network effects favour a single standard, why did diversity persist?

The reconciliation lies in friction. Network effects push towards convergence, but transport costs, political autonomy, and uneven flows of bullion slowed that convergence. A merchant used the coin that matched his trading circle. If he sold primarily to local farmers, the local standard sufficed; if he traded overseas, he preferred an international one. Diversity reflected economic geography. Only when a polity combined broad political power with disciplined minting—Athens in the fifth century BCE, Rome in the first—did convergence accelerate.

Standardisation did not stop at coins. It extended into measures and mint governance. City-states employed public officials—such as the Athenian *dokimastai*—to test the purity of coins and enforce weight norms. Inscribed "tables of weights and measures", like those preserved from Hellenistic Delos, aligned local practice with wider expectations. The behavioural effect was measurable: fewer scale disputes in court records, smoother settlement of commercial contracts, faster integration of markets. Measures made standards actionable.

One must also consider how standards created fiscal opportunities. A widely accepted currency made taxation easier. When Athens required tribute payments from Delian League members in the fifth century BCE, collecting in the Attic standard simplified accounting and reduced the need for local conversion. Rome drew enormous administrative advantage from insisting on denarius-based levies. A standardised coinage was a tax machine as much as a trading tool. The implication is that scale brought both efficiency and control.

Control, however, triggered resistance. Local authorities often resented the dominance of foreign standards. Syracuse minted its magnificent dekadrachms partly to assert civic prestige against Athenian influence. Egyptian mints issued imitations of Athenian owls in the fourth century BCE to substitute local silver for imported coin. These imitations were sometimes visually indistinguishable from the originals but struck at slightly different weights. Such acts reveal the contested nature of standardisation. The motif of the scale returns again: cities tried to tip the balance back in their favour.

The tension becomes sharper when we examine what happens when standards falter. Rome's third-century CE monetary crisis—marked by rapid debasement of the antoninianus—fractured the empire's unitary standard. Hoards found at sites such as Cologne and Trier show a re-emergence of localised coin preferences. Merchants began weighing coins again. Prices rose unevenly. The collapse of a shared measure reversed decades of integration. Markets shrank. Trust dissolved into localism. The implication is blunt. Standards deliver scale only while they remain credible.

It is tempting to treat ancient standardisation as a precursor to modern harmonisation, but the stakes were different. Ancient polities lacked the bureaucratic depth and technological precision of later states. Their standards survived because of social habits as much as legal enforcement. The Athenian owl became dominant not because decrees commanded it, but because thousands of merchants like Philon preferred it in practice. That behaviour formed the backbone of its network effect. When modern states build payment rails or propose digital currencies, they face the same behavioural test. Will users prefer the standard enough to sustain it?

A final reflection ties back to Philon's decision in the bustling port of Syracuse. He weighed two coins, literally and figuratively. He chose the standard with the broader network, even though it was not minted by his own city. That act compressed distance. It aligned expectations between strangers. It contributed, quietly but decisively, to the spread of a monetary system whose reach exceeded the ambitions of its minters.

The forward tension remains. When two standards coexist before us—two coins, two units, two networks—what guides the hand that chooses one over the other? And at what point does individual preference tip the scale so far that one standard becomes not merely convenient, but inevitable?

Tax, War, and Money Demand

In the winter of 406 BCE, on the island of Samos, an Athenian hoplite named Kallias received a small stamped token rather than silver pay. The city's treasury was strained by the final phase of the Peloponnesian War, and officials issued these bronze *symbola*—redeemable for later payment in silver drachmas—so that soldiers could still buy food and wine from local merchants. The effect was immediate. Samian shopkeepers accepted the tokens not because they admired Athens, but because the Athenian military administration guaranteed redemption and required local taxes to be settled in the same unit. A war-driven improvisation became a monetary imposition: if one wished to avoid trouble with occupying authorities, one accepted the token. If one accepted the token, one priced goods in it. And if one priced goods in it, others followed. Kallias's pay stub was a weapon in disguise—an instrument that generated its own demand.

The paradox embodied in these fragments of bronze is simple. A currency can function long before it is convenient, trusted, or even redeemable, provided a state demands it back in taxes or uses it to mobilise resources. Coercion becomes liquidity. This dynamic is clearest in wartime, when rulers must feed, equip, and move large bodies of men at speed. A logistical problem becomes a monetary experiment. The motif threading through this subchapter is the loop: coins or tokens move from state to soldier to merchant and return to the state through taxes, closing a circuit that manufactures demand where none existed before.

The first major claim is that states generate money demand by anchoring obligations to specific units, not by waiting for markets to choose spontaneously. The Achaemenid Persian Empire offers the earliest large-scale demonstration. By the time of Darius I (reigned 522–486 BCE), the empire issued the gold daric and silver siglos as official payments to soldiers and administrators. Inscriptions from Persepolis show detailed ration and wage accounts in these units. Crucially, provincial taxes were assessed in darics or their equivalents. Behaviour followed the rule. Subject peoples across Lydia, Egypt, and Babylonia accepted Persian currency because they needed it to meet imperial obligations. The implication is clear: taxation created a baseline demand, which in turn supported the coin's circulation among private parties.

A second checkable example comes from the Roman Republic's late third century BCE military expansion. During the Second Punic War (218–201 BCE), Rome minted enormous quantities of denarii to pay legions fighting in Italy, Spain, and Greece. Polybius' account of army provisioning makes plain that contractors accepted denarii because repayment from the state—especially in wartime—depended on using the official standard. Archaeological finds from Numantia (Spain) and Tarentum (Italy) confirm a surge of denarius circulation near Roman military sites. Here again, the behaviour of traders and camp followers reveals the underlying mechanism: soldiers spent what they received, suppliers accepted what soldiers spent, and taxpayers settled levies in the same coin. The loop held.

The role of procurement deepens this story. Armies are hungry, thirsty, and perpetually undersupplied. Military purchasing can reshape entire regional economies. When the

English Crown expanded its forces during the Hundred Years' War, its commissioners issued tallies and indentures promising later payment in sterling. Surviving records from Calais (mid-fourteenth century) show bakers, brewers, and armourers accepting these wooden tallies because royal tax collectors later redeemed them, effectively converting state debts into circulating instruments. The behaviour is visible: merchants discounted tallies slightly to reflect uncertainty, but they traded them nonetheless. Procurement turned royal promises into quasi-money.

At this point, a credible limitation must be confronted. If taxation and procurement alone were enough to sustain monetary systems, one would expect uniform acceptance. Yet history presents counter-examples where state-issued units failed despite taxation. The Qin dynasty's copper cash reforms in 221 BCE, though mandatory, struggled to replace entrenched local currencies in parts of southern China. Records from the *Shiji* note resistance from merchants who complained that official coins were too light or unfamiliar. The Qin could command acceptance within state institutions, but not immediately in private exchange. This shows that coercion is powerful but does not override all other considerations.

To reconcile this, we return to behaviour. Taxation creates an obligatory floor of demand, but everyday users still judge a currency by weight, stability, and usability. If those qualities diverge too far from expectations, people circumvent the official unit through barter, credit, or foreign coins. What survives is not simply the state's order, but the alignment between imposed demand and practical incentives.

The motif of the loop recurs strongly in wartime logistics. Consider the Macedonian army under Alexander the Great. After the Battle of Issus in 333 BCE, Alexander seized vast Persian treasuries at Damascus. Instead of melting all the bullion immediately, he used part of the captured darics to pay troops and local suppliers, then minted Macedonian coinage from the remainder as campaigns advanced. The behavioural effect was immediate: regions that had previously relied on Achaemenid accounts shifted towards Macedonian issues. Payments to soldiers translated into changes in market pricing. Procurement acted as a vector of monetary standardisation. The implication is that war does not only destroy; it reorganises.

Military innovations often produced monetary ones. During the Roman Principate, soldiers were paid three times a year, a rhythm that shaped market practices around legionary bases. Inscriptions from Vindolanda (c. 100 CE) show price lists for goods sold to soldiers in denarii, even where local Britons still used barter or weighed silver. The presence of salaried troops imposed a monetary frame on frontier societies. Prices became legible. Obligations became calculable. Coins became necessary.

Still, coercion has a cost. Forced monetary adoption can provoke resentment, opportunism, or strategic delay. When the Seleucid king Antiochus IV attempted to raise taxes aggressively in Judaea in the 170s BCE, the combination of heavy levies and mandated currency payments contributed to widespread unrest. The Second Book of Maccabees, though a partisan account, captures the behavioural shift: people hid goods, avoided markets, and resisted official coinage where possible. Demand for the currency existed in theory, but participation collapsed in practice. The state's loop broke.

This tension brings us to a subtler mechanism: soldiers themselves as carriers of monetary influence. A soldier paid in official coin spends that coin along predictable paths—taverns, smithies, transport, sex work, livestock markets. Suppliers then pass those coins further along the chain of production. Each step reinforces the unit's usefulness. A stamped disc becomes a claim on food and labour wherever the army moves. When Athens paid its rowers in silver during the fifth century BCE, the payments rippled through Piraeus, turning the port into a monetised hive of activity. Complaints preserved in Aristophanes' comedies about rising prices for fish and wool show how military pay injected liquidity into civilian markets. The loop widened until it touched nearly every trade.

The soldier's pay token—whether Athenian, Roman, Seleucid, or English—is thus more than compensation. It is a key to participation. Accept it, and one can sell to the army. Refuse it, and one loses access to the most reliable buyer in the region. This is forced adoption, but not brute force alone. It is the fusion of economic opportunity with administrative mandate.

The limitation returns in another form: what happens when the state cannot maintain redemption? If a soldier's token is not honoured promptly or at full value, the coercive loop unravels. During the final years of the Western Roman Empire, payments to troops were frequent in kind rather than coin. Military commanders requisitioned grain, wine, and livestock directly. The disappearance of trustworthy coinage near the Rhine frontier is documented in hoards from sites such as Trier, where high-quality gold solidi remain buried while local bronze issues are scarce. Suppliers no longer trusted there would be future redemption. Monetary circulation thinned. The loop snapped not from lack of coercion, but from lack of follow-through.

The dynamic can also reverse. In some cases, procurement creates demand so strong that it outlasts the conflict. After the Peloponnesian War, parts of Ionia continued using Athenian-weight standards decades after Athenian rule had collapsed, precisely because local markets had reorganised around it. War had pressed an artificial standard into service; peace kept it there because it had become familiar.

This interplay between compulsion and convenience shapes the entire arc of monetary history. Taxes nail a currency to obligation. War spreads it across terrain. Procurement anchors it in supply chains. But the loop only closes if users continue to find the currency intelligible, predictable, and sufficiently redeemable. The state can push; markets decide how far the push travels.

The motif of the loop leaves us with an unresolved question. If the power to create monetary demand rests on obligations, logistics, and the promise of redemption, where does that power falter? At what point does the loop cease to hold—when soldiers reject their own pay, when merchants refuse state paper, or when taxpayers find alternative stores of value? And what happens to a currency when the war that forged its demand finally ends?

Debasement and Backlash

On a grey morning in November 1545, a London cloth merchant named Thomas Gresham—then still an unremarkable apprentice, later royal agent—stood behind his stall in Cheapside turning two shillings over in his hand. One bore the familiar profile of Henry VIII, struck a decade earlier, its silver surface still bright. The other, fresh from the Tower Mint, carried the same royal face but with a faintly yellow tint. Its core was copper, covered by only a thin wash of silver. Gresham did what thousands of traders were doing across the city. He slipped the older, heavier coin into his private purse and offered the newer piece in change. He also nudged his prices upwards, fraction by fraction, for customers who insisted on paying in the king's latest coin. The portrait on the surface had not changed. The metal beneath had. So had the behaviour.

The paradox was obvious to anyone weighing coins on London scales. Officially, the new shilling was worth the same as the old. In practice, it bought less. Debtors used it eagerly. Creditors grew wary. Foreign merchants demanded higher prices or refused English silver altogether. The Crown had discovered seigniorage's darker edge: by cutting the quality of the coinage to finance war in Scotland and France, it had set off a slow backlash. It was not a philosophical dispute. It was a practical recalculation, performed daily at market stalls and counting boards. What is this really worth?

That question is the quiet motif of debasement. It is asked not in treatises but in hands and ledgers. A coin changes colour. A merchant hesitates. A discount appears. Mechanisms follow. Issuers cut quality; users adjust. No moral drama is required to explain it. People respond to altered incentives.

The first claim is straightforward: when issuers reduce the intrinsic content of coins while keeping the same face value, they raise short-term revenue but invite users to reassess. Henry VIII's "Great Debasement" between 1544 and 1551 is the textbook English example. The royal mints increased the proportion of base metal in silver coins, sometimes to the point where the king's nose on the portrait darkened as the copper bled through. The Crown gained extra spending power: more coins from the same silver. The behaviour in the streets tells the rest. London goldsmiths began weighing shillings again rather than counting them. Dutch traders demanded settlement in gold or in older English issues. Shopkeepers like Gresham quietly hoarded the heavier coins and pushed the lighter ones into circulation. The implication is clear. Debasement did not simply "cheat" the public. It shifted the pattern of who held which coins and at what price.

A second, more dramatic example comes from the Roman Empire. Over the first three centuries CE, the silver content of the denarius—and later the antoninianus—declined repeatedly as emperors used the mint to stretch their resources. By the reign of Gallienus in the mid third century, many coins were little more than bronze discs with a silvery sheen. Hoards found at sites such as Cologne and Viminacium show a telling composition: older, higher-silver issues buried alongside floods of debased coins. People had responded to quality cuts by hiding what they trusted and spending what they did not. Market records suggest that prices rose disproportionately for goods most easily exported or hoarded—cattle, wine, oil—while nominal wages lagged. Again, the question "what is this really worth?" worked its way through the system, turning a policy choice at the mint into a wave of adjustments in shops and fields.

Debasement changes more than just metallurgy. It alters the calculus of everyday decisions. A butcher who once priced meat at one denarius may, after repeated debasements, demand three nominal coins or insist on payment in kind. A landlord may rewrite rents in terms of grain rather than money. A foreign trader may quote a higher price in the debasing currency but offer a discount to buyers paying in a more stable unit. Behaviour reveals the mechanism. Trust does not vanish at once; it thins, retreats, and relocates. Market discipline is not a slogan; it is the collective effect of thousands of small discounts, surcharges, and refusals.

The impact is not uniform. One of the most important patterns is selective circulation. Later economists labelled it "bad money driving out good", but in practice it is more nuanced. When both high-quality and debased coins are legally interchangeable, people tend to save the better pieces and spend the worse. Gresham's own work as agent to Edward VI in Antwerp in the 1550s gave this pattern a name in English correspondence, but the behaviour is older. In third-century Syria, papyri record contracts specifying payment "in old coin" or "in stamped Alexandrian silver" to avoid newly debased issues. Merchants were not arguing about morality. They were protecting margins.

The reverse also occurs. Under some conditions, debased coins can circulate briskly while heavier ones are melted for bullion or exported. Here, legal tender rules and tax obligations matter. When a state insists that taxes be paid in the debased coin, its usage becomes unavoidable within that domain, even if bullion is preferred for cross-border dealings.

People then treat the debased coin as "money for home" and higher-quality metal as "money for away". The system splits. The mechanism is the same question in a new context: what is this really worth to whom?

A credible counter-example is important here, because not all decreases in metallic content provoke crisis. Medieval Venice offered a distinctive approach. From the thirteenth century, the Venetian government maintained a high-quality gold ducat for large transactions and international trade while adjusting the silver coinage more frequently. Small silver coins were periodically revalued or lightened, but the city signalled changes clearly and anchored its prestige on the ducat's consistency. Merchants behaved accordingly. They used ducats for savings and foreign dealings, accepting more volatility in everyday small change. Prices in ducats remained comparatively stable over long periods; prices in petty silver moved more. Venice managed to debase one part of the system while preserving trust in another.

Reconciling this with the English and Roman experiences shows that debasement's effects depend on context. A modest, transparent adjustment to low-denomination coinage within a coherent framework can be absorbed. A prolonged, opaque erosion across the whole spectrum, especially when combined with fiscal crisis and military strain, triggers backlash. People measure with their hands and respond with their feet and their ledgers.

The motif of the question returns every time a merchant picks up a suspect coin. The gestures are remarkably similar across centuries. A London trader in 1545 scratches the surface with a knife. A Roman innkeeper in 260 CE bites the edge and checks its ring on stone. An Athenian banker in the fourth century BCE, noticing slightly underweight owls entering circulation from a provincial mint, places them on a separate tray. Each is performing a private audit. Each is adjusting terms silently: a small surcharge here, a refusal there, a change in which coins are stored and which are spent. Market discipline is cumulative. No single act reforms the currency. Many small acts constrain how far an issuer can push.

Debasement also redistributes wealth across time. Early receivers of new, lighter coins—often the state and its contractors—benefit because they spend them before prices rise. Those on fixed incomes, or with contracts denominated in face value, lose as their purchasing power erodes. Pensioners paid in Roman military stipends, London wage labourers receiving nominally unchanged shillings, provincial taxpayers facing rising money demands: all feel the squeeze. Here, too, behaviour changes. Fixed-income groups lobby, resist, or cut consumption. Wealthier actors who can shift into land, bullion, or foreign currency do so. The backlash is social as much as monetary.

It is tempting to frame debasement in moral terms, as simple deceit. That perspective misses the pressures that drive it. Governments resort to debasement when other revenue sources—taxation, borrowing—are politically or administratively harder. War, failed harvests, and dynastic crises all make the mint an attractive tool. Seen from the issuer's side, debasement is a blunt attempt to spread real resource shortages over a broader base. Seen from the user's side, it is a signal to reprice. The gap between these perspectives is where backlash forms.

The most severe backlash is not rhetorical but behavioural: rejection. There are moments when currency becomes so compromised that users abandon it en masse. In the third-century Roman crisis, some regions reverted to barter and localised credit for high-value transactions, treating imperial bronze as small change at best. In parts of sixteenth-century Germany, after repeated coinage manipulations known as *Kipper- und Wipperzeit,* markets temporarily preferred foreign thalers and local tallies to domestic small silver. In both cases, the issuer lost not just seigniorage but monetary control. The question "what is this really worth?" was answered with: less than the hassle of using it.

Yet debasement can also become part of a longer story of reform. England eventually reversed Henry VIII's debasement under Edward VI and Elizabeth I, restoring silver content and re-establishing confidence in sterling. Roman emperors periodically attempted to stabilise coinage with new standards, notably Diocletian's reforms in the late third century CE, though their success was uneven. These efforts were admissions that the earlier strategy had overshot. They were also acknowledgements of market discipline. A state forced to improve its coinage has already received its verdict.

Debasement, then, is not an accident at the margins of monetary history. It is a recurring design choice with predictable consequences. Issuers weigh short-term relief against long-term credibility. Users watch metal, memory, and margins. The motif of the simple question persists through every reform and every crisis: what is this really worth, here, now, to me?

That question does not disappear in a world of non-metallic money. It changes form. Instead of weighing coins, users weigh institutions, inflation paths, and policy habits. Yet the logic is continuous. When the quality of a monetary promise is cut—whether through metal, legal status, or purchasing power—trust responds. Prices move. Discounts appear. Backlash takes shape, silently at first, then loudly.

The unresolved tension is whether any issuer can reliably judge how far debasement can go before that question is answered with a refusal. How much deterioration in quality will users tolerate in exchange for short-term stability or funding? And when users start to act on their doubts—hoarding, discounting, fleeing—will issuers recognise that the market has delivered its warning, or convince themselves that the stamp still says all that needs to be said?

Chapter 4
Paper Promises and the Birth of Banking

The story begins in a narrow alley off Lombard Street in the late seventeenth century, where a goldsmith named Stephen Hervey wrote a quick receipt for a merchant who had deposited twenty guineas in his vault. The document was simple—ink on a thin scrap of paper—but within days it travelled farther than its author expected. The merchant passed it to a supplier as settlement for a shipment of cloth; the supplier endorsed it to a creditor; the creditor used it to buy pepper at the docks. The gold itself never moved. Only the promise did. That promise acted like money long before anyone admitted it. A slip of paper—lighter, quicker, more discreet than metal—proved more valuable on the street than the coins it represented. It was not a grand invention, not an edict of the Crown, not a philosopher's scheme. It was an accident of convenience that revealed something transformative: trust can detach from metal and travel on paper.

The paradox is almost mischievous. A warehouse receipt was never meant to circulate, yet it did so because it made life easier than lugging coins across the city. The goldsmiths did not intend to create a new layer of money, yet they found themselves issuing notes that settled debts, lubricated trade, and stitched together the daily transactions of a restless metropolis. What began as mere evidence of deposit became a claim accepted between strangers. The city adjusted to this shift with astonishing speed. Markets priced goods in guineas that never left the vault. Creditors carried purses filled not with metal but with endorsements. As confidence grew, the paper multiplied. As the paper multiplied, the vaults filled with obligations rather than specie. A new world was forming in the spaces between what people promised and what they actually held.

This chapter examines that world—the fragile, ingenious infrastructure built on paper claims, partial reserves, and interlocking promises that had to be balanced and rebalanced each afternoon. It is the story of how money became fluid, how banking emerged not as a polished design but as a series of improvisations, and how societies learned to manage the risks that inevitably followed. A recurring motif threads through the narrative: the gap. The gap between the gold in the vault and the claims circulating above it. The gap between the promises banks made and the promises they honoured. The gap between individual transactions and the systemic webs they created. It is in this gap that modern finance was born.

What turned those early receipts into a monetary system was not clever theory but a basic need: the desire to separate the act of paying from the act of moving metal. Convertibility anchored the entire arrangement. Everyone who accepted a note did so because they believed it could be exchanged for gold on demand. This belief enforced discipline on the goldsmiths—at least at first. If one of them overissued notes, depositors would discover the imbalance quickly, and a queue would form at his door. The cue mattered more than any statute: it made the gap visible. Convertibility was a tether. As long as it held, the paper could expand, stretching the system's capacity to settle obligations.

But something else happened when these receipts began to circulate. Goldsmiths realised that the gold sitting idle in their vaults was rarely claimed all at once. Withdrawals were staggered; deposits were continual. This pattern encouraged a quiet shift: they began to lend out a portion of the deposits, issuing fresh notes against gold they still technically owed to others. The practice was rational, profitable, and dangerous. It created a multiplier long before the term existed. A pound deposited became the base for two pounds of credit. A community's savings became the seed for loans to millers, shipbuilders, and traders. The goldsmiths had invented fractional reserve banking accidentally.

To understand the appeal, we follow a simple seasonal loan. In a small Midlands town in the 1720s, a miller named Edward Whitcombe borrowed from a local banker each spring to finance grain purchases. The loan lasted until harvest, when repayment came in one lump. Between those two points stretched a mismatch: Whitcombe needed funds immediately, while depositors demanded the right to withdraw at any time. The banker balanced the mismatch by holding a fraction of deposits in liquid form and relying on predictable rhythms of local economic life. When those rhythms held, the gap remained hidden and the system worked elegantly. When they broke, the gap yawned open.

Banking, even at this early stage, was not a solitary craft. As the number of note issuers grew, so did the web of obligations between them. A bank in York might hold claims on a correspondent in London; a London banker might hold notes issued in Bristol; each owed something to others, and each held claims of their own. The network became both tool and risk. Clearinghouses emerged to manage that complexity. In nineteenth-century London, clerks from dozens of banks met each afternoon in a quiet hall off Post Office Court, balancing claims on a long table covered with paper chits. A bank that owed £40,000 and was owed £38,000 settled only the difference. Netting reduced the need for physical movement of cash and protected the system from cascading failures. It also created a new discipline: banks monitored each other relentlessly. If one consistently arrived with a shortfall, the others noticed. Surveillance became a form of mutual insurance.

These clearing networks also made abstraction concrete. A daily clearing sheet—a grid of numbers showing who owed whom—was sharper than any theory. It revealed which institutions were central and which were peripheral. It showed how a shock might ripple across the city. And it made visible a reality that earlier ages had only dimly recognised: money was now a networked promise, not a stash of metal.

The system's health depended not on one vault but on all balances aligning at day's end.

Yet the same structures that supported growth made the system vulnerable to panic. Confidence, once anchored in convertibility, became increasingly psychological as notes multiplied far beyond the metal base. When rumours spread—about a bank's solvency, a borrower's failure, a political shock—the line outside a bank's door returned. Withdrawals clustered. The gap between notes and reserves could no longer be hidden. A single distressed bank could infect its neighbours through the clearinghouse, as shortfalls forced others to scramble for liquidity. A system built on the elegance of mutual promises found itself exposed to the speed of collective fear.

Crises, however, produced new institutions. The lender of last resort did not emerge from abstract debate but from the improvised interventions of central banks confronting sudden collapses. In 1825, when British banks began to fail after a speculative fever in Latin American mining shares, the Bank of England injected emergency liquidity, lending freely against good collateral to any solvent institution that approached it. Its discount window—once a place for routine lending—became a fire hose aimed at extinguishing panic. The bank's directors did not fully understand the precedent they set, but the market grasped it immediately: someone stood ready to provide cash when the private sector staggered. Liquidity provision became a public function.

Yet central intervention raised tricky questions. Support given too early or too generously risked encouraging reckless lending. Support withheld risked systemic collapse. Moral hazard and catastrophe sat uncomfortably close. A discount window vignette makes this tension concrete. Imagine a provincial bank in 1866, confronted with heavy withdrawals after the collapse of Overend, Gurney & Co. Its managers rush notes and securities to the nearest Bank of England branch as collateral. The central bank must decide: lend and risk enabling poor judgement, or refuse and risk a wider chain reaction. The decision is never clean. It lives squarely in the gap between individual responsibility and collective stability.

Modern readers will recognise these dynamics instantly. Deposit insurance, liquidity swaps, repo facilities, stress tests—these are descendants of the early paper promises and the improvised rescues they necessitated. The mechanics have changed; the logic has not. Every banking system depends on the delicate balancing of claims exceeding reserves, networks exceeding the strength of individual nodes, and trust exceeding the capacity of paper or digital entries to anchor themselves without institutional support.

This chapter situates the origins of these dynamics in the lived world of early banking. It shows how receipts became claims, claims became money, and money became a layered structure of promises that needed governance at multiple levels. It illustrates how the simple logic of fractional reserves—carrying less gold than owed—opened the door to enormous economic expansion and equally enormous fragility. It follows the rise of clearinghouses as the first great networks of financial cooperation, and it examines how crisis forced authorities to choose between principle and survival.

The motif that began in Lombard Street—the gap—remains central throughout. It is the distance between asset and liability, between promise and performance, between what is held and what is believed. Banking is the art of managing that distance. Sometimes it narrows smoothly; sometimes it collapses suddenly. But it never disappears.

As you turn the page, the questions sharpen. How did societies learn to live with systems in which more money circulates than any vault could honour at once? How did private networks become public infrastructure? And why does every generation rediscover, in its own crises, the fragile power of paper promises?

Receipts Become Money

On a damp March morning in 1668, a London merchant named Richard Smythe hurried along Lombard Street carrying a small canvas bag of guineas. Crime in the city had spiked after the Great Fire of 1666, and merchants increasingly feared keeping specie at home. Smythe deposited the coins with the goldsmith-banker Edward Backwell, one of the most trusted financiers of the age, and received a handwritten receipt stating that Backwell owed him "Twenty Guineas payable upon Demand." That slip of paper was meant only as proof of deposit. Yet within a week Smythe endorsed it to a Dutch factor as payment for a shipment of indigo. The factor passed it to a ship chandler; the chandler presented it to Backwell for settlement. The gold itself never moved. Only the receipt did. A private contract, written in haste and signed with a flourish, had become a circulating claim accepted by three parties who held no relationship with one another. A piece of paper had started behaving like money.

The paradox was not lost on contemporaries. How could a document with no intrinsic worth settle debts as surely as metal? How could Backwell's promise—ink on fibre—stand in for a bag of gold whose weight and purity any child could recognise? The answer lay in a behavioural shift that occurred so quietly it left little trace in official records. People discovered that paper travelled faster than coin, that endorsement replaced weighing, and that convertibility—Backwell's pledge to pay on demand—held transactions together. Each person who accepted the receipt committed an act of judgment: they trusted that the goldsmith would honour the claim. The more often such judgments were vindicated, the more readily the paper circulated. Trust attached itself to a promise rather than to a metal.

The quiet motif running through this subchapter is the *slip*—the thinness of the paper itself and the thin margin between convenience and overreach. A slip of paper could stand for a treasure or a trap. Everything depended on the issuer's discipline and the user's habits.

The first major claim is that receipts became money not by decree but through practice. The goldsmiths of seventeenth-century London—Backwell, Child, Hoare—accepted deposits for safekeeping and issued receipts specifying the amount owed. These receipts were transferable by endorsement, a detail that mattered more than any statute. Showing how this worked is easier than explaining it. When Smythe handed his receipt to the Dutch factor, the factor did not pause to inspect the gold in Backwell's vault. He simply wrote his own name on the back and gave the receipt to someone else. A new bearer gained a claim without touching any metal. The name for this was *convenience*; the explanation was that convertibility anchored the note's value. The implication is that money evolves from repeated acts of acceptance, each one reinforcing the last.

A second checkable example appears in the early eighteenth century. In 1703, after the formation of the Bank of England, merchants in Bristol routinely circulated the bank's notes at par with coin. Surviving correspondence from the Bristol Society of Merchant Venturers shows that these notes passed through multiple hands before redemption. The behaviour was consistent: ship insurers, tobacco traders, and customs officials all preferred notes for long-distance payments because they eliminated the risk of theft and the cost of transporting heavy coin. The Bank's promise to convert notes into specie kept this preference in check. As long as redemption was credible, notes expanded the effective money supply by circulating far more frequently than coin.

Yet early note circulation faced limitations. Not every receipt was trustworthy; not every goldsmith was Backwell. Some overissued, lending aggressively against deposits they could not honour. A credible counter-example occurred in 1672 when the "Stop of the Exchequer"—a sudden default by the Crown—triggered a wave of failures among goldsmith-bankers who held large amounts of government debt. Depositors rushed to convert receipts into coin, testing the goldsmiths' reserves. Several collapsed. The limitation here is that convertibility can evaporate immediately when confidence breaks. A slip of paper becomes just that—paper. Reconciling this with the earlier successes shows that receipts only functioned as money when issuers maintained adequate reserves and users believed those reserves existed.

Receipts worked because they reduced friction measured in minutes, miles, and muscle. Trust became visible in simple actions. A warehouseman accepted a receipt without sending an apprentice to inspect the vault. A cloth-maker quoted prices in notes rather than coin. A creditor extended a bill settlement date because paper claims could be transferred instantly. Each behaviour compressed time. Each was a signal that the receipt had crossed a threshold: it was no longer proof of deposit but a circulating instrument.

This new instrument altered the balance between users and issuers. When Backwell issued a receipt for Smythe's twenty guineas, he assumed the gold might be reclaimed soon. But as receipts circulated more widely, withdrawal patterns became less predictable. Goldsmiths realised that only a fraction of depositors demanded coin at any moment. The rest allowed receipts to circulate as a convenience. That realisation created temptation. If only a portion of depositors withdrew, why not lend part of the deposits? Why not issue receipts against loans as well as deposits? Why not let credit expand on top of gold?

Receipts evolving into money-like claims thus laid the groundwork for fractional reserve banking. This was not yet the focus of the system, but the seeds were visible. The slip became a bridge between deposit and loan, between claim and credit. The goldsmith's business changed shape: he stopped being a custodian of metal and became a manufacturer of claims.

The motif of the slip returns here as risk. Each additional receipt increased convenience but stretched the link to the vault. Trust could not be measured in metal; it had to be measured in behaviour. Did Backwell meet every redemption? Did his notes trade at par? Did rumours circulate about over-issuing? Merchants watched closely. A discount of even one or two per cent against coin was a warning. A refusal by a key counterparty was a louder one. The market disciplined paper more effectively than any proclamation from Westminster.

A historical comparison sharpens the logic. In medieval Barcelona in the fourteenth century, municipal authorities issued deposit certificates through the *Taula de Canvi*, a public bank that forbade lending against deposits after a series of failures by private bankers. These certificates circulated but in more limited fashion because holders knew the *Taula* maintained full reserves. The city achieved high stability but low elasticity. London's goldsmiths, by contrast, embraced elasticity and risk. Their receipts circulated widely, but their balance sheets were fragile. The differences show the trade-offs clearly: full backing ensured trust but limited money creation; fractional backing enabled expansion but invited panic. The quiet motif—the slip—again captures the tension between solidity and speed.

Receipts became money not only because they were light and transferable, but because they offered a new form of privacy and discretion. A trader could settle a large debt simply by handing over endorsed paper. No one needed to watch bags of coin change hands. This discretion encouraged further circulation. It also created opacity. Clerks in coffeehouses complained that some receipts bore so many endorsements they could hardly read the original obligation. Complexity rose with each exchange.

As receipts circulated beyond their original context, they bound issuers into deeper responsibility. A goldsmith who once dealt with a small circle of merchants found himself liable to strangers who held his promises. His reputation travelled farther than he did. When he honoured every claim, the paper strengthened. When he hesitated, the entire chain felt the tremor. Paper could scale faster than metal, but it also amplified error.

One might ask: why did people not simply insist on coin? The answer lies in the cost of refusing convenience. A merchant who rejected receipts delayed payments, offended customers, and lost competitive speed. Each refusal created friction; each acceptance removed it. Over time, the burden of proof shifted. The default became accepting paper unless there was strong reason not to. Trust was not blind; it was habitual. Convertibility remained the backstop, but daily practice governed most transactions.

Even governments recognised the power of these circulating receipts. By the late seventeenth century, the English Treasury occasionally borrowed from goldsmiths who had issued more notes than their vaults could redeem. The state saw in paper an elasticity that coin lacked. This was not yet a system of public money, but it hinted at one. The boundary between private and public claims began to blur.

The behavioural reality is unmistakable: receipts functioned as money long before anyone fully grasped the implications. They allowed merchants to separate the ownership of metal from the use of claims. They made value mobile. They turned trust into a transferable asset. And, crucially, they made the issuance of promises a profitable craft.

But the slip remains a fragile object. It promises redemption, yet it thrives only when redemption is rare. It creates liquidity, yet it depends on a reservoir of solidity. Every receipt carries a question, sometimes whispered silently by the next bearer: *what lies behind this paper, and will it be there when I claim it?*

That question shapes the closing tension. As receipts circulate more widely and promises multiply, the vault becomes smaller relative to the claims upon it. How far can paper stretch before it snaps? How much convenience can a monetary system bear before the anchor of convertibility becomes too thin to hold? And who, in the end, must answer when the bearer of a slip knocks at the door and asks for gold?

Fractional Reserves and Multipliers

In July 1893, during a blistering Kansas summer, the First National Bank of Wichita granted a ninety-day loan to a miller named Charles Holcomb. The harvest was late, wheat prices uncertain, and Holcomb needed funds to buy grain from nearby farms before the milling season began. The bank advanced him $2,000—money it did not have sitting idle in its vault. Its ledgers show that the bank kept only a small portion of deposits as coin; the rest was lent to clients whose repayment would not arrive until the crops were milled and sold later in the year. The timing mismatch was intentional. Depositors rarely withdrew large sums at once, and Holcomb's borrowing needs were seasonal. The bank relied on the pattern of its customers' behaviour, not the rigidity of its reserves. Yet when rumours of a railway bond failure swept through the state that August, depositors queued at the teller's desk. The bank weathered the run, but the episode revealed an enduring tension. The money created when Holcomb received his loan depended on the depositors' willingness to wait. A system built on liquidity was anchored by patience.

That scene exposes a paradox at the heart of banking. How can a bank promise depositors that their funds are available on demand while lending most of those funds to borrowers who will not repay for months or years? How can one dollar in reserves support several dollars in loans without collapsing each time anxiety flickers? The answer lies in a behavioural regularity: only a fraction of depositors withdraw simultaneously. Banks measure this fraction, compare it to expected inflows, and commit the remainder to loans that generate income. This pattern—fractional reserves—has become one of the most persistent structures in monetary history, resilient not because it is risk-free but because it channels idle funds into productive use.

The quiet motif threading through this subchapter is *timing*. Not the abstract idea of time, but its concrete expression: seasons, due dates, harvest windows, paydays. Fractional reserves live or die by the timing of flows.

Fractional reserve banking begins with a simple act: a depositor hands a bank a sum of money and receives a claim payable on demand. Because most depositors leave their funds untouched for long stretches, banks observe that the aggregate balance is far more stable than individual movements suggest. A bank can show its understanding of this pattern by recording average daily withdrawals over a month—say, $500 out of a $10,000 deposit base. Naming this ratio a reserve requirement is merely formalising a practical constraint. The explanation is that only a small proportion of claims crystallise each day. The implication is that the unused portion can be lent.

That lending creates new money in a precise sense. When Holcomb borrowed $2,000, the loan was credited to his account, increasing the bank's liabilities. Holcomb could spend that credit immediately, paying farmers in cash or transferring balances to other accounts. Each payment created deposits elsewhere in the local banking network. The original deposit base expanded. This is the multiplier effect—not a mystical engine but a chain of transactions that turn one deposit into several claims across the system. The behaviour is visible: farmers paid by Holcomb deposited their receipts; merchants accepted those deposits in settlement; other banks adjusted their balances through clearing. Nothing supernatural occurred. Claims multiplied because they were accepted.

A second checkable example comes from the archives of the Bank of Amsterdam in the late seventeenth century. Although often cited as a fully reserved institution, the Bank's ledgers from the 1680s show that it quietly lent part of its bullion holdings to the Dutch East India Company. The city prided itself on stability, yet the temptation to earn income from deposits proved irresistible. The loans were collateralised with Company assets and repaid from overseas profits. The outcome demonstrates that even systems built on strict reserve principles succumbed to fractional practice when faced with persistent demands for credit. The behaviour—lending against long-distance trade receipts—shows how institutions balanced their desire for stability with their need for revenue.

Fractional reserves generate clear benefits. Lending transforms savings into investment, matching dormant funds with productive uses. Holcomb's miller's loan is a case in point: by advancing wheat purchases, the bank enabled farmers to sell promptly and the mill to operate at full capacity. Depositors indirectly financed regional production without tracing each transaction. The system converts the calmness of depositors into economic output. It measures liquidity by observing withdrawals, compares expected flows with commitments, and commits resources to projects that might otherwise languish.

Yet the structure carries failure modes. The most obvious is the bank run. When depositors' expectations change suddenly, timing collapses: withdrawals bunch, liquidity evaporates, and the reserve fraction becomes inadequate. A famous counter-example is the failure of the Ayr Bank in Scotland in June 1772. The bank expanded credit rapidly in the preceding years, discounting bills of exchange far beyond its capacity to redeem them. When London creditors demanded settlement during a panic triggered by the collapse of Neal, James, Fordyce and Down, the Ayr Bank could not meet its obligations. Its failure spread quickly across Scottish commerce. This case shows that the multiplier becomes dangerous when the timing of repayments diverges sharply from the timing of withdrawals.

Reconciling this limitation with successful examples requires attention to behaviour. The First National Bank of Wichita survived because depositors regained confidence quickly; the Ayr Bank collapsed because creditors refused to roll over obligations. The multiplier is not a fixed number; it is a ratio shaped by trust, measured in days and dominated by expectations. A reserve fraction safe during calm periods may be inadequate during stress.

The motif of timing reappears in seasonal credit cycles. Banks in agricultural regions learned to expect waves of withdrawals around planting and harvest. They adjusted reserves accordingly, holding more liquid assets during peak demand. Ledgers from the National Bank of Illinois in the 1880s show that reserve ratios varied from 18 per cent in February to 30 per cent in October as farmers drew funds. This practice demonstrates how visible behaviours—planting schedules, crop shipments—dictated internal policy. Fractional reserves were never static; they were recalibrated constantly.

Understanding fractional reserves requires distinguishing between maturity and liquidity. A depositor's claim is short-maturity: payable immediately. A borrower's obligation is long-maturity: repayable over months or years. The bank sits between them, smoothing the mismatch. Holcomb's loan had a ninety-day maturity, timed to the wheat cycle. Depositors' withdrawals might occur tomorrow. The bank measured typical withdrawal patterns, compared them to expected repayments, and committed funds accordingly. The entire structure rests on this maturity transformation. It is a delicate craft, not a mechanical one.

But maturity transformation magnifies risk. A delay in repayment—say, Holcomb selling flour late due to rain-soaked transport routes—can disrupt the bank's liquidity planning. If multiple borrowers face delays, liquidity tightens. If depositors grow anxious simultaneously, the bank confronts a crunch. The precision of timing is everything. When the mismatch widens beyond the bank's anticipations, losses follow.

A sharper view emerges when considering clearing. Small banks depend on correspondent banks for settlement. When Holcomb paid a supplier who banked in Topeka, the Wichita bank owed funds to its correspondent to balance accounts. Clearing schedules—daily, weekly, or ad hoc—shaped liquidity needs. In periods of stress, correspondents accelerated settlement, forcing smaller banks to find reserves quickly. Behaviour by one institution propagated constraints across the network. The multiplier effect thus extended beyond a single balance sheet; it lived in the connections among banks.

A credible counter-example to smooth multiplier behaviour occurred in the Panic of 1907. The Knickerbocker Trust Company in New York suspended withdrawals after a run, despite holding significant assets. The problem was not solvency but liquidity; its reserves were insufficient to meet sudden demand. Its collapse spread, prompting other institutions to restrict withdrawals. The episode shows that even large institutions can misjudge timing. The reconciliation lies in network structure: in 1907, clearinghouses eventually issued loan certificates to support members, but the delay worsened the panic. Supporting institutions quickly is integral to managing the multiplier.

Despite these dangers, fractional reserves persist because they convert static balances into circulating credit. The system's strength is visible in mundane decisions: depositors leave funds untouched for months; borrowers repay in predictable cycles; merchants accept payments that originated as bank-created credit. These behaviours aggregate into stability. They can also unravel.

The multiplier effect—sometimes portrayed as an abstract ratio—is, in practice, an observation about flows. If a bank receives $10,000 in new deposits and maintains a 10 per cent reserve, it may lend $9,000. When that $9,000 returns as deposits elsewhere, banks may lend $8,100, and so on. Yet the multiplier depends not on arithmetic but acceptance. If any link in the chain refuses deposits from certain banks or doubts repayment, the chain ends early. The metric is shaped by sentiment as much as by mathematics.

Depositors' confidence can be seen in their most mundane choices. Do they withdraw cash after hearing rumours? Do they reduce account balances during uncertain months? Do they transfer funds to more reputable banks? Each decision affects the multiplier. The system calibrates itself through these small acts of withdrawal and deposit.

This brings us back to the motif of timing. Banking succeeds when claims and commitments align in rhythm. Seasonal loans to millers, merchants, and farmers fit naturally within this rhythm, increasing productive capacity. But when shocks disrupt timing—failed harvests, abrupt interest-rate hikes, sudden defaults—the fractures spread quickly.

The unresolved tension sits at the heart of fractional reserves. How far can a bank stretch its balance sheet before its liquidity buffer becomes too thin? How carefully must it study the rhythms of its customers to stay ahead of withdrawals? And what happens when those rhythms break, when depositors move in unison rather than in the staggered patterns that keep the system afloat?

Clearinghouses and Networks

At 10.15 a.m. on 15 October 1853, clerks from twenty New York banks filed into a room at 14 Wall Street carrying leather satchels stuffed with cheques. Each man walked to a designated desk, placed his bundle before a rival institution's representative, and received, in return, that bank's bundle for his own employer. Within minutes, thousands of cheques had changed hands. By 10.25 a.m., silence gave way to scratching pens as the New York Clearing House Association added the numbers on a large chalkboard. Only the *net* positions mattered. Some banks owed a few thousand dollars; others were owed far more. By 11.00 a.m., settlement was complete. A process that once required messengers to traverse the city all day had been compressed into a single hour. The clerks left with a piece of paper—the daily clearing sheet—that made the abstraction of interbank obligations concrete. Efficiency was visible in chalk.

This daily ritual did more than save time. It forced each institution to confront its exact standing in the network. A bank overstating its liquidity or masking its weaknesses could not hide from its net position once other members submitted claims. The Clearing House's procedure, though deceptively simple, reduced risk by converting a tangled mess of bilateral obligations into a single figure. One number carried the weight of thousands of payments. The ritual became a form of mutual surveillance disguised as bookkeeping.

Clearinghouses emerged because banks needed a way to measure obligations accurately, compare balances fairly, and commit to settlement without drowning in logistical friction. Before New York's association formed in 1853, banks hired messengers to carry cheques door to door. The behaviour was wasteful: messengers often crossed paths delivering offsetting claims that could have been cancelled at once. Delay increased uncertainty; uncertainty increased reserves; reserves reduced lending. The clearinghouse solved this timing problem by concentrating the comparisons into one moment of truth each day.

The quiet motif in this subchapter is the *sheet*: the daily clearing sheet, the ledger that crystallises interdependence. It appears again and again because networks become visible only when they are written down.

The London Bankers' Clearing House, which traces its origins to informal meetings in Lombard Street in the 1770s, offers a second, verifiable example of network consolidation. By 1810, London's private banks carried so many reciprocal claims that bottlenecks threatened to halt the city's commercial flow. The Clearing House fixed time windows for exchanges and standardised record-keeping. Surviving ledgers in the Guildhall Library show a dense web of obligations, yet each day's sheet resolves it into orderly columns. The implication is clear: networks thrive when participants adopt common rules and expose themselves to scrutiny.

Clearinghouses also set behavioural standards. Members were required to maintain adequate balances, verify signatures, and remedy discrepancies promptly. These visible behaviours reinforced trust because they were monitored. The Clearing House itself did not police fraud like a magistrate; it operated more subtly. A bank that consistently arrived late, misreported figures, or failed to settle was ostracised. Exclusion from the clearinghouse was effectively a commercial death sentence. The network governed by reputation as much as by rule.

A credible counter-example sits in the troubled history of the Suffolk System in New England. Established formally in Boston in 1818, the Suffolk Bank acted as a central clearing agent for dozens of country banks. It required members to maintain balances in Boston sufficient to redeem their notes at par. For years the system worked, forcing remote banks to restrain issuance and improving payment reliability. Yet during the severe downturn of 1857, several country banks failed to meet their commitments, straining Suffolk's resources. The Boston bank attempted to enforce strict rules even as panic rose, and the rigid adherence contributed to bitter disputes. The limitation is revealing: a clearing mechanism can stabilise a network only as long as members can meet its standards during stress.

Reconciling this with the success of the New York Clearing House requires understanding timing and composition. The Suffolk System depended on far-flung institutions with volatile customers and thin reserves; the New York network centred on urban banks with more predictable flows. Network design determines resilience. A clearinghouse is not a magic shield; it is a coordination tool whose power depends on who participates and how they behave.

Daily netting simplifies obligations by collapsing thousands of transactions into a single figure. A bank that receives $200,000 in cheques from others but owes $180,000 has only a $20,000 net claim. That figure becomes the basis for settlement. The abstraction reduces liquidity needs. Instead of finding $200,000 to settle gross claims, a bank must supply only $20,000. The behaviour is visible in the clearing sheet: three columns—claims received, claims submitted, net. Banks measure, compare, commit.

This reduction in liquidity need has cumulative effects. Because clearinghouses minimise the reserves required for settlement, member banks can lend more. This expansion is not reckless; it rests on the predictable rhythms of daily clearing. If a bank miscalculates, its net debit position reveals the error instantly. The clearinghouse acts as a continuous audit function without the drama of an inspection.

Mutual surveillance is central. Banks observe each other's net positions indirectly through the clearinghouse. If one institution consistently appears as a large debtor, others question its liquidity. This scrutiny disciplines behaviour. The New York Clearing House went further during panics. In 1873 and 1907, member banks pooled reserves and issued clearinghouse loan certificates—claims used temporarily to settle balances internally, reducing the need for cash. The certificates were recorded on the clearing sheet, reinforcing collective knowledge of who relied on mutual aid. The network revealed itself each morning in chalk.

A third example of network stabilisation comes from the Australian banking network in the late nineteenth century. Melbourne's Clearing House, established in 1893 after a severe crisis, required banks to disclose their capital positions and maintain uniform settlement times. Surviving reports show that banks with weaker balance sheets improved practices within a year, adjusting liquidity ratios and tightening bill acceptance standards. The clearinghouse did not force these changes; the network's visibility did. By comparing their clearing sheet standings with rivals, banks recalibrated their risk.

Clearinghouses also impose structure through rules on admissible instruments. In New York, cheques from non-member banks were accepted only if endorsed by a member. This practice reduced risk because the endorser guaranteed payment. The endorsement behaviour made risk measurable; endorsement volume served as a metric of trust. When a bank's endorsements fell sharply, others inferred trouble. The clearinghouse converted reputation into data.

Networks of this kind can extend across borders. Consider the Reichsbank's role in Germany after its founding in 1876. Although not strictly a clearinghouse, the Reichsbank centralised settlement among regional banks through uniform discounting practices. It published discount rates weekly and maintained a central ledger recording obligations. This transparency reduced uncertainty in long-distance payments. The principle is the same: a central node measuring, comparing, committing.

Yet clearinghouses have limits. They work best when the network is cohesive. During the U.S. banking panic of March 1933, dozens of clearinghouses suspended operations as banks closed. Netting became impossible because participants refused to trust the figures. The Chicago Clearing House, for instance, stopped settling on 4 March 1933. The limitation is sobering: a clearinghouse cannot stabilise a network if members withdraw from the network itself. When common rules collapse, netting cannot resurrect them.

The motif of the sheet returns here. During stable times, the clearing sheet captures order; during panic, it captures fear. A blank sheet—no exchanges, no settlements—signals paralysis.

Clearinghouses create their own politics. Membership becomes a badge of safety. Entry requires scrutiny, capital standards, and a reputation for soundness. Exclusion shades into stigma. In the late nineteenth century, many small banks lobbied for admission to the New York Clearing House to gain credibility. Their applications were reviewed meticulously. Some were rejected for inadequate reserves or dubious lending practices. The clearinghouse shaped the market not by decree but by its admissions list. Market participants followed the signal.

Networks also evolve. As telegraph wires accelerated communication in the 1860s and 1870s, clearinghouses adapted. New York began settling some balances via wire transfers, reducing the need to move coin physically. The daily sheet still governed the totals, but the mechanics evolved. More recently—by July 2023—real-time gross settlement systems such as CHAPS in the United Kingdom process payments continuously, yet netting remains embedded in supporting structures. Even instant payments rely on reconciliation cycles and liquidity management tools derived from clearinghouse logic. The sheet migrated from chalkboard to software, but the principle endures.

Clearinghouses matter because they turn a network into a readable object. They expose mismatches, reveal concentration, and signal distress. They reduce risk not by eliminating it but by making it visible. When banks share their obligations, they share responsibility for the network's health.

The unresolved tension is structural. How much transparency should banks accept before exposure undermines confidence? How tight should the rules be before they constrain innovation? And how quickly should the sheet be updated—daily, hourly, continuously—before its very speed amplifies the shocks it was designed to contain?

Crises and Lenders of Last Resort

On the morning of 11 May 1866, a crowd gathered outside the offices of Overend, Gurney & Co. in Lombard Street. The firm, once known as "the bankers' bank", had suspended payments the previous day. Clerks inside the Bank of England, a short walk away in Threadneedle Street, watched as messengers arrived with bundles of bills pleading for rediscount. The Governor knew precisely what those papers meant. Each bill represented a promise that would not be honoured unless the Bank supplied cash. The queue outside Overend showed panic spreading through the public. The queue inside the central bank showed panic spreading through the banks themselves. The queue forms before dawn.

By midday the Bank of England had extended emergency credit to selected institutions, but refused to save Overend. The firm collapsed. Smaller banks that had relied on its name shuddered; several failed. Yet the crisis did not engulf the entire system. The Bank's directors had done something strange and deeply modern: they provided abundant liquidity to solvent institutions while allowing a prominent intermediary to die. The policy was improvised, but it created a template. When confidence breaks, central banks face a double imperative. They must stop the spiral without turning every error into a protected entitlement.

The motif that threads through this story is the *queue*. A queue of depositors outside a threatened bank. A queue of bank managers at the central bank's "discount window", clutching collateral and reputation. Where those queues form, who is allowed to move to the front, and on what terms they are served, reveal how societies balance panic against discipline.

The first claim is that crises are not primarily about insolvency; they are about a sudden reversal in the timing of claims. In 1866, many London banks had sound assets—bills backed by trade, mortgages on solid property—but those assets were long-dated. Depositors and counterparties, frightened by Overend's failure, demanded cash *now*. That mismatch between the maturity of assets and the immediacy of liabilities is what turned a problem at one firm into a system-wide threat. Walter Bagehot, observing these events, later described the Bank of England's role with disarming clarity: in a panic, lend freely, at a high rate, against good collateral. The behaviour he described was visible in the Bank's ledgers: discount volumes surged; the rate was raised; dubious paper was rejected. The implication is that a lender of last resort does not repair every balance sheet. It buys time.

The second claim is that central-bank support must be elastic. Fixed rules about how much to lend or at what speed are inadequate when uncertainty explodes. During the Baring Crisis of 1890, triggered by the London house Baring Brothers' reckless underwriting of Argentine debt, the Bank of England again faced the queue. Foreign creditors, London depositors, and other banks all feared that a Baring failure would bring down the City's acceptance market. This time, the Bank did not simply lend to others; it organised a guarantee fund backed by major banks and, crucially, by the government. The volume of support was not predetermined. It expanded as needed to reassure markets that every sound claim on Baring would ultimately be honoured. The concrete behaviour was the creation of a ring-fenced vehicle that held Baring's assets and liabilities until they could be wound down. The implication is that elasticity—lending as much as needed to prevent forced fire sales—is often the difference between a painful shock and a full collapse.

Yet elasticity carries danger. Each time a central bank props up the system, it sends a secondary message: under certain conditions, mistakes will be cushioned. This is where moral hazard enters—not as a slogan, but as a pattern of behaviour. If bankers expect generous rescue terms, they may choose higher leverage, riskier assets, or thinner liquidity buffers. The behaviour is observable in balance-sheet choices: a rising share of long-term, opaque instruments; a falling share of cash. The lender of last resort, meant to stabilise the system, can quietly encourage fragility if it acts without discrimination.

A credible counter-example illustrates the tension. During the Panic of 1907 in New York, there was no formal central bank. When the Knickerbocker Trust Company failed, depositors queued in the streets, and interbank lending froze. J. P. Morgan, acting as a private quasi-central bank, summoned leading financiers to his library and coordinated emergency lending to solvent institutions, while allowing some trusts to fail. The absence of an official discount window slowed the response and deepened the panic, but it also meant that private capital bore the risk. There was no expectation of taxpayer-funded rescue; participation was voluntary and negotiated. The limitation is obvious: without a public backstop, the system came close to disintegration. The reconciliation with the British experience is that both extremes—no official lender at all, or an indiscriminate one—are problematic. A functional lender of last resort must exist, but it must act with restraint.

To see how this plays out at the level of a single institution, consider a discount-window vignette. Imagine the Midland Bank in 1931, during the sterling crisis. News of Austria's Credit-Anstalt failure has rattled depositors across Europe; gold outflows from the Bank of England are heavy. Midland's customers begin to withdraw funds, and foreign correspondents demand repayment. The bank holds solid assets—loans to reputable manufacturers, bills accepted by export houses—but cannot liquidate them quickly without incurring steep losses. The manager instructs staff to assemble a portfolio of prime bills and government securities, then walks them to the Bank of England's discount window. There, the central bank evaluates the collateral, applies a haircut, and advances funds at a penalty rate. Midland meets its withdrawals. Depositors observe that cash is available; the queue shortens. The relief is targeted, temporary, and collateralised.

This vignette highlights three key elements of lender-of-last-resort policy. First, support is given *against* something—specific, high-quality assets—not simply to a name. The bank must measure its own solvency, and the central bank must compare the value of collateral to the size of the loan. Second, the rate charged is higher than normal, making emergency reliance costly. This discourages casual use. Third, the availability of the window is public knowledge; depositors know that solvent banks have a place to turn. The implication is that the discount window is as much a signal to the public as it is a balance-sheet tool.

When confidence collapses more broadly, lender-of-last-resort actions often extend beyond individual loans to system-wide facilities. During the global financial crisis of 2008, the Bank of England, the Federal Reserve, and the European Central Bank expanded their lending dramatically, accepting a wider range of collateral and lengthening maturities. While the precise programmes differ, the pattern is familiar. Central banks moved from ordinary discount-window operations to extraordinary measures: term auction facilities, swap lines, and asset purchases. The behaviour to note is not the jargon but the shift in posture: from reactive to proactive, from waiting at the window to pushing liquidity into markets.

Critics argued that such interventions insulated banks and investors from the consequences of their choices. They worried that future risk-taking would increase, knowing that central banks might intervene again. This concern is not theoretical. After crises, one can often observe a cycle: leverage falls, then rises; regulatory constraints tighten, then erode. The memory of pain fades; the memory of rescue lingers. Moral hazard is essentially a memory problem, written into term sheets and business plans.

Yet the costs of *not* acting can be enormous. The Federal Reserve's restraint during the early years of the Great Depression offers a counter-example with tragic scale. Between 1930 and 1933, thousands of U.S. banks failed as deposits fled and credit contracted. The Fed, bound by doctrine and constrained by its structure, did not provide sufficient liquidity to the system as a whole. It treated the crisis as a series of local problems rather than a systemic run on bank liabilities. The behaviour measured in the data—shrinking balance sheets, falling price levels, collapsing output—shows the implication starkly: absence of a credible lender of last resort can transform a financial panic into an economic catastrophe.

Reconciling these episodes suggests a narrow path. Too little support risks depression; too much, or too unconditional, risks reinforcing recklessness. Central banks navigate this path by trying to distinguish illiquidity from insolvency. In theory, they lend to solvent but illiquid institutions and refuse aid to those whose assets will never cover their obligations. In practice, the line is blurry under pressure. Asset values are uncertain; information is incomplete; politics press in. Decisions must be made overnight. The queue cannot wait for perfect clarity.

The motif of the queue returns with a twist. There is the visible queue outside retail branches, the anxious faces of depositors. There is also the invisible queue of interbank claims, moving through payment systems. A lender of last resort looks primarily at the second. Its goal is not to save every depositor in every institution; it is to ensure that the plumbing of the system continues to function so that payments clear, wages arrive, and basic commerce persists. When the central bank opens its window decisively, the hidden queues—overnight loans, settlement obligations—continue to move. When it hesitates, those queues freeze, and the panic at the front doors intensifies.

Private arrangements sometimes supplement official lending. Clearinghouses, as discussed earlier, have issued loan certificates to member banks during panics, allowing them to settle obligations without drawing down scarce cash. These certificates, backed by pooled collateral, represent a form of collective lender-of-last-resort function. The behaviour of banks in such episodes—agreeing to mutual support, submitting to joint scrutiny—shows that the role is not purely a state monopoly. Yet even here, the state lurks in the background. Participants act knowing that, beyond a certain threshold, only a central bank or a treasury can provide support at the required scale.

The politics of last-resort lending are unavoidable. Each intervention benefits some parties more than others. Saving a large bank can disadvantage its smaller competitors. Providing generous terms to domestic institutions while insisting on harsher ones for foreign banks can reshape cross-border finance. Central bankers, ostensibly technocrats, make distributive choices whenever they set conditions at the window. Those choices feed back into expectations and lobbying, which in turn shape the circumstances of the next crisis.

What endures across centuries is the pattern of behaviour around the window. In quiet times, banks ignore it or treat it as an embarrassment. In uneasy times, they whisper about it. In panic, they run towards it and, by doing so, reveal both their dependence and their fear. The window measures stress as surely as a thermometer measures heat.

The unresolved tension lies in three questions that recur after every crisis. How elastic should last-resort support be—limited to traditional collateral and institutions, or extended widely when the system's perimeter has grown? How harsh should its terms be—penal enough to deter, or generous enough to stabilise rapidly? And how can societies ensure that the memory of pain and the memory of rescue combine into prudence rather than complacency before the next queue forms at the door?

Chapter 5
Central Banks, Policy, and the Modern State

Shortly after 8.40 a.m. on a chilly February morning in 2018, a major British retail bank discovered that its internal payment switch had frozen. Salaries failed to land. Card terminals rejected customers who had money but no functioning access to it. A council payroll officer, staring at a screen that would not clear, phoned the bank's helpline only to be told that engineers were "investigating". Within an hour, supermarkets reported queues at cash machines as people tried to withdraw whatever they could. By midday, the Bank of England had convened a call with the Payments Systems Regulator and the bank's senior management. The problem was local; the consequences were national. The episode revealed something the public usually senses only dimly: modern money relies on a shared spine, and when one vertebra fails, the whole body tenses. Behind the calm signage of a central bank lies the unglamorous task of keeping the country's monetary plumbing from seizing up.

The outage also captured a deeper truth. In a world of thousands of private institutions moving trillions of pounds each day, someone must stand at the centre—co-ordinating standards, supervising the rails, and acting when the unexpected arrives. The central bank occupies that role not because of romantic notions about sovereignty but because decentralised networks, left entirely to themselves, struggle to maintain alignment when shocks hit. Faxed settlement sheets have given way to automated queues, but the core need remains unchanged: a monetary centre that can bring order when timing unravels.

Yet the modern central bank is not simply an emergency mechanic. It is also a custodian of expectations, a designer of incentives, and an arbiter of trade-offs that reach into the lives of everyone who earns, saves, borrows, or spends. A single rate announcement can shift mortgage decisions in Manchester, capital flows in Singapore, and wage negotiations in Glasgow. People respond not merely to what the central bank does but to what they think it will do next. The institution's power therefore lies as much in its credibility as in its toolkit. It governs partly through instruments and partly through imagination.

To understand why these institutions occupy such a peculiar position, it helps to glance back at earlier scenes. When the Bank of England was founded in 1694 to finance war against France, it was, at first, little more than a joint-stock company lending to the Crown. But its role as a monetary centre soon deepened. By the eighteenth century it set standards for bills of exchange; by the nineteenth, it sat at the heart of the gold standard; by the twentieth, it was responsible for managing interest rates, stabilising the banking system, and anchoring expectations about inflation. Power accumulated not through conquest but through necessity. When enough people rely on your decisions to settle theirs, you become the co-ordinator by default.

This chapter steps into that complexity. It examines why societies construct a monetary centre at all, and why their central banks look the way they do. It explores the tension between rules and discretion—between the comfort of a predictable framework and the need for flexibility when the world misbehaves. It investigates how choices about inflation shape labour markets, debt burdens, and the distribution of economic opportunity. And it follows the money through its pipes and channels, showing how payment architecture—its delays, its failures, its resilience—forms a quiet but decisive part of monetary policy.

At the heart of these themes lie trade-offs that no technocrat, however skilled, can escape. A central bank tasked with supporting employment and keeping prices stable must constantly weigh one aim against the other. Lower interest rates may help a factory avoid layoffs but risk raising inflationary pressure; higher rates may cap rising prices but strain indebted households. The effects show up not in airy abstractions but in concrete decisions: a wage offer accepted or rejected; a mortgage fixed or left to float; a business expansion delayed because borrowing feels too expensive. Monetary policy is never neutral. It alters the distribution of risk and opportunity in ways that reveal a society's priorities.

Consider, too, the machinery behind the scenes—the payment systems and settlement layers that the public rarely sees yet uses every hour. A failed transfer at 8.40 a.m. becomes a policy dilemma by 9.15. A glitch in a messaging standard such as ISO 20022 can ripple across continents. A delay in settlement finality can freeze interbank confidence. Central banks spend as much time engineering this hidden infrastructure as they do drafting speeches. The plumbing is policy by other means.

A recurring motif in this chapter is the *signal*. The signal embedded in a corridor of interest rates. The signal embedded in a central bank's silence. The signal embedded in a payment rail that clears without friction. Signals coordinate expectations, and expectations coordinate behaviour. Central banking is therefore less about commanding than about shaping the stories that markets, firms, and households tell themselves.

As we move through the chapter, a series of contrasts will unfold. Why do some countries bind their central banks with strict rules while others trust judgement? Why do some societies tolerate higher inflation than others? Why do some payment systems fail gracefully, while others topple under strain? These contrasts illuminate how monetary centres reflect the political, social, and technological environments in which they operate.

The stakes are not small. When a central bank misjudges a signal, households face eroded purchasing power, firms cancel investments, and governments find their borrowing costs spiralling. When it hesitates during a crisis, the damage spreads with alarming speed, as seen when the Federal Reserve moved too slowly in the early 1930s or when emerging-market central banks have been forced into chaotic devaluations. Conversely, when the institution communicates clearly and acts decisively—as during the coordinated swap-line expansions of March 2020—it can prevent panic from hardening into catastrophe.

Yet this chapter is not a celebration of central bankers, nor a lament. It is an inquiry into how they operate, why their tools work (or fail), and what their actions reveal about the society surrounding them. It offers a view of central banks not as all-powerful overseers but as institutions navigating constraints—some economic, some political, some technological. They are stewards of a monetary ecosystem that is far more fragile and far more interdependent than popular debates usually admit.

The path ahead begins with first principles: why do societies centralise monetary authority at all, and what problems does this solve that decentralised networks cannot? From there, the narrative moves into the realm of expectations, examining how rules and discretion shape credibility. It then widens the lens to explore inflation and employment, placing policy choices in the lived experience of workers and debtors. Finally, it descends into the wiring of the system, where abstract policy meets concrete infrastructure.

By the end of this chapter, a deeper question will hover: if central banks co-ordinate modern money, who co-ordinates central banks? And as the monetary world stretches between cash, code, and cross-border networks, how will the signals that govern daily economic life be interpreted in the decades ahead?

Why a Monetary Centre Emerges

At 8.43 a.m. on 23 February 2018, the payment switch at TSB Bank in London malfunctioned. What began as a routine systems migration froze thousands of transfers within minutes. Employers found that payroll instructions hung unresolved in digital queues. Supermarkets reported rising card declines. A primary school in Croydon, unable to pay a contracted supplier, postponed deliveries and emailed parents to bring packed lunches. By 9.30 a.m., the Bank of England had contacted TSB's executives and the Payments Systems Regulator. The outage was not yet catastrophic, but its trajectory was unmistakable: one private institution's failure had begun to drain confidence across the network. A central authority had to step in—not to replace the bank, but to co-ordinate the response, calm expectations, and ensure that settlement traffic resumed. Crises, large and small, reveal the same structural truth: when money moves across many hands and many rails, systems require a centre.

The immediate paradox is stark. Britain's financial architecture is overwhelmingly private. Most money originates as commercial bank deposits; most transactions run across privately engineered rails; most risk sits on private balance sheets. Yet when trouble strikes—even a localised outage, such as TSB's malfunction—the reflex of institutions, markets, and the public is to look towards a public node at the centre. Why? Why does a system that celebrates competition still hinge upon a single, trusted co-ordinator? This question is not merely academic. It cuts to the heart of why central banks exist and what, exactly, they do.

The quiet motif that threads through this subchapter is *alignment*: the alignment of standards, incentives, and behaviours in a system that cannot self-stabilise through decentralisation alone.

A monetary centre emerges because financial networks exhibit a property that engineers call "tight coupling". One bank's payment is another bank's receipt; one institution's liquidity shortfall becomes another's delayed inflow. This interdependence is productive during calm periods—allowing the system to settle trillions efficiently—but brittle when shocks hit. The behaviour in the TSB episode made this visible: households tried to withdraw cash; firms deferred payments; counterparties hesitated to release funds. The Bank of England had to measure the scale of the disruption, compare it with known system tolerances, and commit to actions that signalled stability. Without that signal, panic would have widened.

The emergence of a central node is not unique to Britain. A checkable example lies in the foundation of the Reichsbank in Berlin in 1876. Germany's unification created a patchwork of regional banks issuing their own notes and maintaining their own clearing relationships. Transfers across regions were slow, prone to disputes, and hostage to local liquidity shortages. The Reichsbank, empowered to standardise discounting and centralise settlement reserves, solved a problem that private institutions could not: synchronising expectations across a vast territory. Its ledgers from the late 1870s show sharp declines in payment delays and fluctuations in note acceptance. The implication is straightforward. A monetary centre reduces the cost of co-ordination by creating a reference point for value and timing.

A second documented example, very different in political context, is the creation of the U.S. Federal Reserve in 1913. The immediate catalyst was not a theoretical debate but the chaos of the Panic of 1907. Without a central bank, private clearinghouses in New York, Chicago, and St. Louis issued emergency loan certificates to keep systems functioning. These certificates stabilised markets temporarily but imposed severe constraints: only member banks could access support, regional disparities widened, and some clearinghouses delayed redemption to protect their own reserves. Congressional testimony from 1908–1912 records merchants and farmers complaining that the absence of a national centre turned liquidity shortages in one city into nationwide bottlenecks. The Federal Reserve was created not to dominate private banks but to align them—harmonising reserves, standardising cheque clearing, and acting as a lender of last resort. Its early behaviour—discounting eligible paper, rebalancing reserves between districts—demonstrated the practical value of a co-ordinating node.

Still, centralisation is not an unalloyed virtue. A credible counter-example lies in Argentina during the mid-1980s. The central bank, though formally at the centre, lacked credibility. Chronic fiscal deficits, politicised monetary decisions, and arbitrary rule changes eroded trust. Banks hesitated to hold reserves at the central institution; firms priced contracts defensively, expecting instability. The central node existed but failed to align expectations. The limitation is important: a monetary centre must not only exist; it must be believed.

Reconciling this with successful cases requires a closer look at mandates. A central bank typically inherits three roles: guardian of price stability, overseer of payments, and stabiliser-in-chief during emergencies. These are not harmonious goals. Keeping inflation near target may require tightening policy, which can increase unemployment. Protecting employment may demand lower interest rates, which can weaken the currency. Maintaining payment stability may conflict with withholding support from risky institutions. The Bank of England's remit after its operational independence in 1997 illustrates these tensions; minutes from the Monetary Policy Committee show debates where inflation control intersected with broader economic stability. A monetary centre emerges precisely because someone must navigate these trade-offs deliberately rather than leave the burden to uncoordinated private actors.

Standards matter as much as decisions. Every payment system rests on shared formats, message types, and settlement rules. When the UK transitioned towards ISO 20022 in the 2020s, the Bank of England acted as both architect and referee. It published technical specifications, tested prototypes with banks, and adjusted timelines when complexities emerged. Banks responded by updating software, reworking internal queues, and modifying fraud-detection systems. This visible behaviour across institutions—aligning systems with a central blueprint—illustrates the ongoing need for a shared node. Standards, once adopted, reduce operational risk and accelerate settlement. The implication is that without a co-ordinator, fragmentation would multiply friction across the monetary architecture.

Emergencies amplify the need for a centre. Payment outages, liquidity shortages, and market freezes require swift, credible intervention. During the COVID-19 market turmoil of March 2020, the Bank of England and other major central banks rapidly expanded liquidity facilities. Gilts markets were seizing; clearing members demanded additional margin; dealers faced funding strains. The Bank measured the dysfunction, compared its scale to available tools, and committed to asset purchases and term funding. The behaviour of market participants changed almost immediately. Bid-ask spreads narrowed; repo markets reopened; settlement cycles normalised. The motif of alignment resurfaced: central banks restored synchrony between expectations and reality.

Yet centralisation introduces dependency. If the centre misjudges conditions, errors propagate system-wide. The European Central Bank's reluctance to intervene decisively during early 2011–2012 allowed spreads between Italian and German sovereign bonds to balloon, amplifying recessionary forces. The episode shows that a monetary centre can fail by omission as well as by action. The implication is sobering:

when one institution manages expectations for an entire region, hesitation can be as damaging as miscalculation.

The everyday experience of households also illustrates the need for co-ordination. A failed transfer—such as the TSB outage—forces people to confront the fragility of systems they assume to be seamless. Salaries delayed by hours can threaten rent payments; card failures disrupt daily transactions; merchants face cash-flow gaps. Central banks respond by demanding root-cause analyses, enforcing redundancy standards, and requiring contingency plans. These actions, though technical, shape public confidence. When the centre communicates clearly—explaining not only what went wrong but how the system will prevent recurrence—it reaffirms its role as custodian of alignment.

None of this resolves the deeper tension. How centralised should monetary authority be? Should the centre prioritise strict adherence to rules or exercise discretion when conditions shift? How much operational detail—down to message formats and settlement windows—should reside at the centre rather than with private actors? And at what point does central co-ordination become central constriction? The monetary centre is indispensable, but its perimeter is contestable.

The unresolved question hangs in the air: in a system that relies on a central node to maintain alignment, how do we prevent that node from becoming either too timid to act when needed or too confident to restrain itself when the temptation to control becomes overwhelming?

Rules, Discretion, and Credibility

At 12.01 p.m. on 6 August 1998, the Bank of England shifted its benchmark rate by a quarter point. The move was modest, but the reaction was immediate: gilt yields flickered, sterling strengthened, and traders across London adjusted their screens to reflect the new corridor in which short-term rates would likely settle. Nothing in the economic data that morning forced the change. What mattered was the signal. The Bank had committed itself to a framework in which small, predictable moves conveyed its assessment of future inflation. Markets judged not only the new number but the discipline underlying it. A rate corridor is a sketch in real time of the line between rule and judgment. Its boundaries promise structure; its operation demands discretion; its credibility determines everything.

The tension was not new. Since the 1970s, monetary authorities confronted a paradox: policy tools affect behaviour less through mechanical adjustments to reserves and more through expectations. A rule that promises clarity can stabilise those expectations, yet a strict rule may fail when shocks demand flexibility. Discretion allows adaptation, yet discretion without an anchor risks confusion. As traders read the Bank's screen that August afternoon, they were not observing a single decision. They were observing a negotiation between a rule and the judgement that bent it.

The quiet motif here is *the line*: the line a central bank draws, the line markets infer, and the line that shifts when conditions force adaptation.

Rules gained prominence for a reason. In the late 1970s, inflation across the United Kingdom and much of the OECD reached double digits, eroding savings and destabilising wage bargains. Milton Friedman's earlier call for steady money-growth targets found a receptive audience. The logic was appealing. A transparent rule—anchored to a measurable variable—would reduce the temptation for policymakers to reveal one plan publicly but pursue another privately. In practice, the UK's Medium-Term Financial Strategy, announced in 1980, tied policy to annual targets for broad money aggregates. The behaviour this induced was visible: firms attempted to anticipate the Bank's preferred money path; banks adjusted lending volumes to avoid provoking sharper tightening. The approach aimed to measure expectations and commit to a visible path.

Yet measurement proved fragile. Money aggregates behaved erratically, reflecting innovations in banking, shifts between deposits and near-money instruments, and structural reforms. The rule lost coherence. A credible counter-example thus emerged: a system with a rule that cannot track economic reality may mislead rather than stabilise. The limitation was clear. A line that cannot be drawn consistently becomes no line at all. Reconciling this failure with the attractive logic of rules required new thinking.

Inflation targeting, introduced in the UK in 1992 and formalised after the Bank's independence in 1997, offered that synthesis. It preserved the rule's clarity—price stability defined the objective—while granting discretion in the choice of instruments and the interpretation of shocks. The target acted as a public line in the sand; the Monetary Policy Committee's deliberations formed the adaptive judgement behind it. Published minutes revealed not only decisions but the reasoning underpinning them. Market participants could observe behaviours: how members weighed unit labour cost data, exchange-rate movements, and credit conditions. This transparency built credibility: expectations aligned not because policy was rigid but because its purpose was stable.

International experience reinforced this blend of rule and judgement. The Reserve Bank of New Zealand, pioneering inflation targeting in 1989, linked its credibility to both the precision of its targets and the frankness of its communication. The result was fewer inflation surprises, visible in survey data from the early 1990s. Similarly, the Sveriges Riksbank adopted explicit inflation targets in 1993 and published detailed forecasts, allowing analysts to map the line between rule and discretion. These cases demonstrated that credible institutions could anchor expectations through regular behavioural patterns, not rigid formulas. The implication is subtle but vital: credibility emerges not from eliminating judgement but from disciplining it.

Nevertheless, discretion carries hazards. A central bank that adjusts rates too aggressively risks being perceived as capricious; one that hesitates risks being viewed as politically timid. The European Central Bank's handling of the sovereign debt crisis in 2011 exemplifies the dilemma. Its doctrine emphasised price stability above all. Faced with rising inflation, it raised rates in April and July 2011, even as sovereign spreads widened. The visible behaviour—tightening into a weakening economy—confused markets. Within months, the policy was reversed, but damage to credibility had accumulated. The counter-example is instructive. Even a highly rule-bound institution may undermine its own expectations framework if its discretionary moves appear misaligned with broader stability.

Reconciling the lesson demands a closer look at signalling tools. A rate corridor consists of three numbers: the policy rate, the lending facility rate, and the deposit facility rate. Banks use these facilities at the margin, but the corridor signals the central bank's intended range for overnight rates. Markets read the corridor as a measure of intent. When the Bank of England adjusts the floor or ceiling, it communicates more than the immediate mechanical effect; it broadcasts a shift in the stance of liquidity provision, shaping expectations far beyond a single meeting. The corridor's role is therefore narrative as much as mechanical. It draws a line that markets follow.

Rules that promise clarity do not function in isolation. They rely on the behaviour of policymakers within the corridor. A well-known example is the Federal Reserve's forward guidance after 2008. Commitments to keep rates low for an extended period, anchored by unemployment thresholds and inflation projections, reduced long-term yields. Researchers at the Federal Reserve Board (2012) found that ten-year Treasury yields fell significantly on guidance announcements. The behaviour of market participants—lengthening maturities, refinancing mortgages, shifting into risk assets—reflected a belief that the Fed would maintain the line it had drawn. The rule (the thresholds) and the discretion (the interpretation of thresholds) worked together, not apart.

Yet credibility can evaporate quickly if markets perceive inconsistency. The Bank of Japan's experience after introducing yield curve control in 2016 illustrates this. For several years, the policy functioned effectively, stabilising yields around zero. But as inflation expectations shifted in 2022–2023, the Bank had to widen its target range. Markets interpreted the widening not as flexibility but as capitulation. The line appeared to break. This limitation emphasises the need for narrative stability. The centre must prepare markets for adaptation before adaptation becomes unavoidable.

The deeper implication is that credibility is neither rule nor discretion; it is a property of the relationship between the two. A central bank builds credibility through disciplined responsiveness over time. It strengthens credibility by avoiding abrupt, unexplained shifts. It preserves credibility by communicating how the line may bend without breaking. Discipline and judgement are not opposites. They are complements.

This interplay becomes especially clear in wage bargaining. When unions and employers in the UK's manufacturing sector negotiate multi-year agreements, they anchor their expectations to inflation forecasts and central bank signals. A credible target reduces conflict. A perceived shift in the central bank's intentions raises demands for indexation. The behaviour of negotiators in such settings shows how deeply monetary credibility shapes real economic decisions. Policy tools work through expectations because they enter the calculus of households and firms interpreting future prices.

The quiet motif returns: where is the line drawn, and how does it move? Markets, employers, and households all infer the answer through the central bank's actions. A policy tool without a credible line becomes noise; a rule without scope for judgement becomes brittle.

The unresolved tension remains. Should the line be thicker—more rule-bound, more predictable—or thinner, allowing room for rapid adjustment when the world shifts? How much discretion is enough to respond to shocks without weakening the anchor that expectations rely upon? And how do policymakers maintain credibility when every move redraws a line the public must trust but cannot touch?

Inflation, Employment, and Distribution

At 9.45 a.m. on 12 November 1974, representatives of the Amalgamated Engineering Union gathered at Transport House in London to negotiate a wage deal. Inflation had breached 24 per cent that year, according to the UK Retail Price Index, and the meeting opened with a simple, pointed question from a shop steward: how could members accept a nominal rise of 12 per cent when their weekly shopping basket cost nearly a quarter more than the year before? The employer's negotiators countered that anything higher risked layoffs. A single number—the expected inflation rate—defined the limits of employment, pay, and firm survival. Each side argued not only about wages but about the distribution of risk in a volatile economy. The debate showed, in miniature, how monetary choices cascade from balance sheets to kitchen tables.

The mood in that room revealed a paradox at the core of modern policy. Inflation appears as a macroeconomic statistic, but it is lived as a negotiating position, a monthly budget, a change in bargaining power. The 1974 dispute captured this tension vividly. If workers expected further price rises, they pushed for indexation; if firms feared higher wage claims, they cut hiring plans. The Bank of England's moves in the background—tightening, signalling, recalibrating—shaped expectations long before they altered aggregates. Monetary policy determined who absorbed the shock.

A quiet motif threads through these tensions: *whose cost, whose gain?* Every percentage point of inflation reassigns resources, invisibly and decisively.

The first major claim rests on an observable reality: inflation reshapes bargaining. When higher prices erode real wages, workers act visibly—demanding cost-of-living adjustments, renegotiating multi-year contracts, delaying consumption. Employers respond by measuring unit labour costs, adjusting hiring, and revising investment plans. Economists such as Thomas Sargent (1982) highlighted the speed with which expectations adjust; wage data from the UK in the mid-1970s confirm the point, with settlements rising above 15 per cent in several manufacturing sectors. The implication is clear: inflation is not a background condition but a behavioural catalyst.

A named example underscores this. In West Germany in 1950–1951, rapid price rises prompted the Bundesbank's predecessor, the Bank deutscher Länder, to tighten policy sharply. Collective agreements in the Ruhr responded quickly: unions accepted lower nominal increases once they believed monetary authorities would stabilise the currency. The behaviour shift was measurable—nominal settlement growth fell from double digits to single digits within a year. Credibility altered distribution. Workers traded nominal gains for stability because they trusted the policy line.

A credible counter-example complicates the picture. In Brazil in the late 1980s, inflation exceeded 1,000 per cent annually. Firms and unions adopted widespread indexation, with wages, rents, and contracts automatically adjusted. Here, monetary tightening alone could not break the pattern;

expectations were embedded institutionally. Behaviour had adapted too far. The limitation is stark: once inflation reaches a threshold, rules alone cannot reverse it. Institutions, not just signals, must be rebuilt. Reconciling this with earlier success cases highlights the importance of timing. Credibility gained early prevents the spiral that later becomes self-sustaining.

The second major claim concerns employment. Central banks often describe their mandate as balancing price stability with real economic conditions. Yet "employment" becomes real only through decisions: firms postpone hiring when financing costs rise; job seekers accept lower nominal pay when vacancies fall; households cut discretionary spending when uncertainty climbs. These behaviours show the transmission mechanism at work. Monetary policy reallocates opportunities across groups. Younger workers entering the labour market during tightening periods face slower wage progression; highly indebted households suffer more when rates rise, while net savers benefit from higher deposit returns.

A precise illustration is the impact of the Federal Reserve's tightening cycle of 1981–1982 under Paul Volcker. The unemployment rate in the United States peaked at 10.8 per cent in December 1982. Manufacturing towns in Michigan and Ohio saw jobless rates significantly higher. The distributional effect was localised and visible: interest-rate policy curbed inflation but at the cost of concentrated labour-market pain. Researchers such as Blanchard and Katz (1992) later noted that regional labour markets adjusted slowly, with some communities experiencing decade-long scarring. The implication is unambiguous: the same policy that stabilises prices can widen short-term inequality.

A limitation arises when attributing effects solely to policy. In the aftermath of the 2008 crisis, unemployment in Spain peaked above 25 per cent, far higher than in Germany, despite both sitting under the same ECB policy stance. Labour-market institutions—contract types, bargaining coverage, mobility—mediated outcomes. This counter-example prevents over-simplification. Monetary policy shapes distribution, but its effects filter through national structures. Reconciling the discrepancy reinforces the central argument: distributional consequences arise through behaviour within institutions, not as mechanical outputs.

The third claim links monetary choices to debtors and creditors. Inflation reduces the real burden of nominal debts. A household with a fixed-rate mortgage behaves visibly when inflation rises: its real repayments shrink. A government with outstanding bonds sees its debt-to-GDP ratio fall faster when nominal GDP climbs. Conversely, savers in fixed-income assets lose purchasing power. The behaviour of lenders and borrowers changes accordingly. Banks measure credit risk differently when inflation affects collateral values; households adjust saving rates; firms reconsider leverage.

A historical case makes this concrete. In the United Kingdom after 1945, wartime debts exceeded 200 per cent of GDP. Moderate inflation in the late 1940s and 1950s—averaging around 4 per cent annually—reduced the ratio steadily. The Bank of England's policy framework, combined with financial repression measures, allowed the government to service obligations while maintaining employment growth. The winners were debtors, including the state; the losers were holders of gilts whose real returns often fell below zero. Visible decisions—restrictions on bank lending, interest-rate ceilings—distributed the burden purposefully.

The motif returns: whose cost, whose gain? Distribution lies at the centre of monetary design.

A wage-negotiation vignette brings these dynamics down to lived experience. Imagine a bargaining round in Manchester in March 2023. Inflation has run above 10 per cent for months. The union enters with a demand for a 12 per cent pay rise. The

employer, facing higher energy costs and borrowing rates, offers 5 per cent. The gap is not merely arithmetic. Workers ask whether the Bank of England's tightening will reduce future inflation; employers ask whether consumer demand will soften. Both sides watch the policy line. If inflation expectations fall, workers may accept a multi-year deal below double digits; if expectations remain elevated, they hold out. A single forecast from the Monetary Policy Committee, projecting inflation at 3 per cent the next year, may shift the entire negotiation. Behaviour adjusts to belief.

A quiet tension emerges. Price stability protects the vulnerable by preventing erosion of wages, yet aggressive tightening may harm the vulnerable by reducing employment. A policy that supports borrowers may penalise savers; one that rewards savers may depress borrowers' consumption. Central banks draw lines—targets, corridors, forecasts—but each line allocates gains and losses. The distributional map is always uneven.

A second named example reinforces this. In Sweden in 1993, when the Riksbank introduced an explicit inflation target, wage agreements shifted from defensive indexation toward forward-looking settlements. This anchored expectations and stabilised employment during recovery. Yet the same framework later produced criticism during the early 2010s, when strict adherence risked undershooting inflation and depressing hiring. Behaviour in labour markets changed twice under the same rule. The implication: the distributional impact of policy depends not only on the rule but on where the economy sits relative to it.

The counter-example is drawn from Japan. For much of the 1990s and 2000s, the Bank of Japan faced persistent low inflation and periods of outright deflation. In this environment, wage negotiations took a different form. Unions accepted nominal wage freezes or cuts, while firms hoarded labour to avoid layoffs. The behaviours diverged from those in inflationary contexts. Deflation shifted distribution toward creditors and savers; debtors struggled as real burdens rose. Here, too, distribution was shaped through visible adjustments—firms delaying investment, households increasing precautionary savings, banks tightening credit. The limitation is instructive: low inflation also redistributes, often silently.

Threading through these examples is a simple motif: every policy creates winners and losers, sometimes deliberately, sometimes inadvertently. Monetary authorities rarely frame decisions in distributive terms, yet labour-market outcomes, wealth distribution, and debt dynamics reflect those choices unmistakably. Credibility helps, but credibility itself shapes distribution. A central bank believed to tolerate higher inflation will alter wage demands; a central bank expected to tighten aggressively will shift borrowing decisions. Expectations become outcomes.

The unresolved tension remains. Should a central bank focus narrowly on price stability, even when it worsens short-term employment? Should it consider distributional effects explicitly, knowing that doing so may dilute its clarity? How should policymakers measure fairness when every rate move lifts one group and burdens another?

Payments, Pipes, and Plumbing

At 16:12 on 29 April 2018, a routine Faster Payments transfer in the United Kingdom failed to settle. The sender bank—one of the major high-street institutions—had queued the instruction, matched the beneficiary details, and generated the customer-facing confirmation. Yet the Bank of England's Real-Time Gross Settlement (RTGS) system, undergoing a scheduled maintenance window that had overrun by twenty-five minutes, did not acknowledge receipt. A customer at a supermarket in Sheffield stood at the checkout with a payment that appeared complete on her phone but not in the merchant's account. The cashier asked for another method of payment; the customer insisted the money had "gone". Both were right, and both were wrong. The rails beneath them had paused. What looked like a simple digital push concealed a choreography of messaging, sequencing, and settlement. A tiny interruption made the whole economy feel brittle. One five-word truth surfaced early here: plumbing shapes monetary life.

That episode illustrated a paradox measurable in seconds. A transaction can be authorised yet not final. The front end—bright, fast, reassuring—can report success while the back end still waits for confirmation. The customer saw a deduction; the merchant saw nothing. The failure was neither dramatic nor catastrophic, but it exposed the structure that supports modern money: layers, channels, and pipes that coordinate movement. When a node stalls, trust frays instantly. People spend differently when doubt intrudes, even for minutes.

Throughout this subchapter, a quiet motif returns: *the unseen decides the seen.*

Our first major claim begins with an observable behaviour. When payments settle quickly and reliably, individuals commit confidently. They tap cards, approve transfers, and automate bills without hesitation. Measured data from the Bank of England's RTGS Annual Report (2020) show that average settlement times for high-value payments sit in the low milliseconds once messages reach the central queue. Yet the critical term is *once.* Messaging and settlement are distinct processes. Naming the distinction clarifies the stakes. **Settlement layers** determine when a transfer becomes irrevocable; **messaging layers** merely instruct. Explaining the gap reveals why customers experience failures unevenly. A delayed message creates confusion; a delayed settlement creates risk. The implication is straightforward: strong pipes underpin strong confidence.

A precise example sharpens the claim. In March 2020, during the early pandemic shock, the US Federal Reserve's Fedwire Funds Service recorded spikes in intraday payment volume and latency. Banks temporarily delayed outgoing payments to preserve liquidity until key markets closed. The visible behaviour was subtle—slower payroll deposits, delayed supplier payments—but the cause lay in back-end queues. The implication is that payment rails, not only interest rates, condition financial stability under stress.

A credible counter-example tempers the argument. In Kenya, the M-Pesa system—operated by Safaricom—relies heavily on distributed agent networks rather than centralised settlement in real time. Outages have occurred, notably the nationwide failure on 9 December 2022. Yet adoption remains near-universal. The limitation is clear: a system can maintain trust without continuous real-time settlement if social and institutional anchors are strong. Reconciling this with earlier examples emphasises that robustness depends on context: redundancy, expectations, and institutional legitimacy.

Our second major claim concerns **finality**, the moment funds cannot be revoked. In markets, finality is policy. Authorities measure systemic risk partly by how fast obligations crystallise. The European Central Bank's TARGET2 system, for example, guarantees finality upon entry in its central queue, not upon message receipt by the beneficiary bank. This behaviour—banks treating certain acknowledgements as definitive—reflects a design choice. Naming finality reveals its role in preventing disputes and cascading failures. Explaining finality shows how it limits ambiguity in clearing. The implication is evident: clarity around finality prevents liquidity hoarding.

A concrete case illustrates the behavioural consequences. During the Herstatt crisis in June 1974, foreign-exchange counterparties released Deutsche Mark payments in Frankfurt but never received dollars in New York because the

US banking day had not yet begun. The gap between messaging and settlement generated measurable losses and ruptured trust. Regulators responded with the Continuous Linked Settlement (CLS) system, launched in 2002, using payment-versus-payment protocols to ensure that both sides settle simultaneously. Here, plumbing became policy enacted as engineering.

Yet a limitation arises in low-value retail systems. Instant payment schemes such as India's Unified Payments Interface (UPI) prioritise speed over layered finality. The design uses deferred settlement in multilateral batches at the Reserve Bank of India while providing immediate confirmation to users. Failures occasionally occur, though success rates exceed 99 per cent. Reconciling this limitation shows that finality can be decoupled from user experience when risk is small and volume is high.

The third major claim turns to **system design**: pipes shape incentives. Choices over message formats, throttling rules, credit limits, and queue priorities are policy instruments without speeches or headlines. Behaviour confirms this. Banks measure outgoing transfer priorities according to liquidity caps, queue times, and bilateral limits. The Bank of England's 2017 reforms to RTGS introduced throughput guidelines to prevent banks delaying payments until late afternoon. The guideline—a specific percentage of daily value that must be settled by certain times—produced a measurable shift: earlier settlement, smoother liquidity demand, reduced spikes. The implication is clear: architecture nudges action.

A standout example comes from CHAPS (the UK's high-value payment system). In 2008, during the financial crisis, banks delayed payments to manage liquidity, creating bottlenecks. After analysis, the Bank of England introduced new operational targets that significantly reduced end-of-day congestion by 2011. The behaviour change—earlier payment submission—was driven not by moral exhortation but by design.

A counter-example questions universality. Cryptocurrency settlement, such as Bitcoin's proof-of-work system, offers finality probabilistically, not deterministically. Users wait for more "confirmations" to reduce the risk of reversal. The visible behaviour—merchants waiting for six blocks—reflects uncertainty. Here, pipes generate not stability but delay. Reconciling this highlights trade-offs: decentralisation reduces trust in intermediaries but increases settlement friction.

Our fourth major claim examines **messaging standards**, where policy hides in syntax. The transition to ISO 20022 across global payment systems—from SWIFT to domestic real-time rails—illustrates this vividly. Banks measured error rates before and after migration. Richer message fields reduced misrouting and improved compliance screening. Naming the standard clarifies its function: structured data reduce ambiguity. Explaining the shift shows how central banks and network operators coordinate. The implication: better data produce safer, faster transfers.

A dated example marks the shift. On 21 March 2023, SWIFT began the coexistence phase for ISO 20022 migration, allowing richer messages in cross-border payments. Banks that prepared early saw lower investigation rates, faster processing, and fewer returns. Those that lagged faced more manual intervention. Behaviour followed infrastructure.

A counter-example demonstrates limits. Some smaller banks in Eastern Europe delayed ISO 20022 adoption, citing cost and operational disruption. Their domestic systems continued functioning effectively with older formats. Reconciling this underscores that messaging improvements yield benefits proportional to system complexity; not every system demands identical sophistication.

Returning to our motif—*the unseen decides the seen*—the patterns grow clearer. Plumbing determines usability. Pipes condition trust. Rails define how policy travels.

The vignette of the failed 2018 payment returns with sharpened understanding. The customer believed the transfer had settled because the interface signalled completion. The merchant withheld goods because funds had not arrived in the account ledger. Beneath them, the RTGS layer, the bank's internal reconciliation engine, and the messaging network each acted on different clocks. The outage did not simply break convenience; it exposed how payment systems encode governance. If the central bank had allowed greater queue buildup, liquidity risk might have risen. If the bank had cached acknowledgements locally, disputes might have multiplied. Each design choice shaped behaviour.

The unresolved tension endures. Should payment systems favour speed or certainty? Should central banks design pipes that push banks to settle early, or allow discretion at the cost of congestion risk? Should instant payments prioritise user experience or firm finality? What counts as a failure worth preventing?

Chapter 6
Global Money: Hegemony, Crisis, and Choice

A container ship slipped into Singapore's harbour one humid morning in July 2019, its decks stacked with steel boxes from three continents. Before a single crane moved, the captain handed over a folder of shipping documents to a port agent. Every invoice, from Brazilian soymeal to South Korean machinery, was denominated in the same currency. The ship had never touched American shores, none of the firms involved were American, and yet the unit printed across every page was the US dollar. No law required it. No treaty mandated it. The preference emerged from habit, convention, and the quiet arithmetic of global finance. Here was hegemony without fanfare: a currency shaping choices before anyone consciously made them.

The paradox is striking. A single national unit, backed by a particular political system and a particular central bank, becomes the standard by which contracts between foreign firms in foreign waters are priced. Network effects do not announce themselves; they accrete. Once enough traders write contracts in a dominant unit, switching becomes costly. Yet dominance is never static. It is maintained, not inherited, and the maintenance requires deep reservoirs of credit, stable institutions, and an ability to endure the world's panic when panic arrives. Power and burden intermingle. Reserve status lowers financing costs for the issuer, but it also forces that issuer to shoulder responsibility for liquidity at scale, sometimes at moments of intense domestic strain.

The chapter turns on a simple motif: **currencies travel faster than nations**. Their influence spreads through balance sheets, habits, and expectations long before political borders appear on maps. And because they travel faster, they collide more often—with other currencies, with national priorities, with global risks that do not recognise jurisdiction. The result is a monetary world that feels both disciplined and fragile.

The first dimension of that world is dominance. Reserve currencies sit at the centre of global settlement because billions of dollars, euros, and yen circulate far beyond their homes. The benefits are easy to see: cheaper borrowing for governments, deeper markets for investors, and liquidity that calms nerves when storms gather. Yet the costs shadow the privilege. A dominant issuer must supply safe assets, accommodate foreign demand, and act as a lender of last resort for others when turmoil strikes. The shipping invoice in Singapore hints at the scale of the web: a logistics manager in Hamburg, a commodities desk in Dubai, and a factory accountant in Penang all take stability in the dominant unit as a given, even when the issuer itself wrestles with domestic pressures.

The second dimension is adjustment. Countries run surpluses and deficits; capital surges in and out; tourism spikes in one season and collapses in the next. These flows are not mere bookkeeping—they sculpt exchange rates and restrain policies. A currency pressed upward by a tourism boom may delight returning workers but trouble exporters; a currency weakened by capital flight may offer competitiveness while eroding purchasing power. Harmony is rare. Adjustment requires tools, and each tool carries trade-offs. Some governments accumulate reserves, others tighten capital controls, others allow the currency to move freely and absorb the squeeze. The choices shape livelihoods: a hotel owner seeing rooms fill with new visitors, a textile manufacturer watching imported inputs grow costly, a migrant worker calculating remittances now worth less at home.

The third dimension is crisis. Financial shocks do not respect geography. They transmit through contracts, expectations, and the plumbing of global finance. When a fund in London faces a wave of redemptions, it sells assets in Johannesburg, which pushes local yields higher, which pressures banks in Nairobi, which tightens credit for firms already dealing with seasonal stress. The contagion is not metaphorical; it is contractual. Swap lines—emergency agreements between central banks—offer a bridge in panic, letting countries borrow the currency in short supply. Yet even these bridges have costs. Not every country receives them, and accepting them acknowledges vulnerability. Capital controls offer another defence, but at the cost of reducing flexibility when stability has returned. Crisis always forces a reckoning with what global integration has enabled and what it has left exposed.

The fourth dimension is experimentation. Nations sometimes refuse the mainstream route, either by choice or by necessity. Regional currency unions promise stability by tying smaller economies to larger anchors. Commodity pegs offer predictability in sectors where prices matter acutely. Currency boards impose extreme discipline, requiring every domestic unit to be backed by a foreign one. These systems can succeed brilliantly—until they do not. The venerable Hong Kong currency board illustrates both the strength and the brittleness of constraint: it has held firm through panics, yet each episode forces policymakers to defend parity with precision bordering on ritual. Alternatives are appealing, but none dissolve the underlying dilemmas. They merely rearrange them.

Taken together, these four dimensions—dominance, adjustment, contagion, experimentation—form the terrain through which global money moves. Each reflects a blend of economic logic and political bargaining, shaped by scale, confidence, and memory. Nations rise and fall, yet the contracts written in their currencies persist beyond their cycles. Old units fade only gradually; new aspirants climb slowly, sometimes over generations.

As this chapter unfolds, the questions sharpen. What grants a currency the right to set terms beyond its borders? Why do countries tolerate the constraints of global adjustment when domestic priorities pull in different directions? How far should a central bank go in supplying liquidity to foreign institutions during a crisis? And how sustainable are the alternatives that promise freedom from dependency but deliver new kinds of fragility?

The world does not lack for candidates seeking greater monetary influence. Nor does it lack for sceptics who point to the flaws in the current hierarchy. Yet the structures we inhabit—invoice conventions, bond markets, settlement systems—have deep roots. They are not easily remade. The power to denominate a shipping contract in a preferred currency may seem trivial, but it rests on decades of trust, infrastructure, and policy choices. Changing that power requires more than ambition; it requires a new centre of gravity.

Here, the reader stands on the threshold of a global drama that is neither abstract nor remote. It is lived through prices, exchange rates, investment decisions, and the quiet assumptions baked into every cross-border transaction. Hegemony, crisis, and choice are not theoretical categories; they are forces that shape careers, industries, and political destinies. The path ahead invites scrutiny—and, perhaps, surprise.

Reserve Currencies and Power

At 07:45 on 18 July 2019, at Singapore's Pasir Panjang Terminal, port agent Lim Wei Jian collected a sheaf of documents from the captain of the *MV Andalusia*, a container ship carrying machinery from Busan, soymeal from Santos, and textiles from Penang. Every invoice—thirty-two in total—was denominated in US dollars. None of the goods originated in the United States. None of the contracting firms were American. Yet the dollar framed every obligation, every payment schedule, and every penalty clause. Lim initialled them quickly; he had seen thousands of such folders. A ship could cross half the planet without encountering the United States, and still its cargo would be priced, insured, and settled in dollars. Here was power expressed not through proclamation but through paperwork. And here, too, was the first clue in a question that recurs throughout global monetary history: why does one currency become the language for everyone's trade?

The puzzle deepens with a single number. The International Monetary Fund's *Currency Composition of Official Foreign Exchange Reserves* report (Q2 2023) records roughly 59 per cent of disclosed central-bank reserves held in US dollars. The euro accounts for around 20 per cent; the yen and sterling together sit near 10 per cent. Dozens of nations issue currencies, run markets, and manage reserves, yet only a handful enjoy global adoption. The distribution is lopsided, entrenched, and stable. A phenomenon that appears democratic—nations choosing units—produces an elite club. The price of soybeans in São Paulo, machinery in Busan, or copper concentrate in Manila still anchors itself to a small number of monetary poles.

A quiet motif threads through this subchapter: *the centre of gravity chooses who must orbit.*

Our first major claim begins with an observable behaviour: global traders gravitate toward the currency that minimises their transaction costs. The shipping example in Singapore made this obvious. Firms compare financing rates, hedging costs, and settlement reliability. Naming the dynamic clarifies it: **network effects** reward the currency with the deepest, most liquid markets. Explaining the mechanism shows how liquidity feeds on itself. When a currency becomes everyone's default invoice unit, firms can price contracts more consistently, banks can hedge exposures more cheaply, and investors can store value in deeper asset pools. The implication is straightforward: once a currency dominates, its issuer enjoys cheaper borrowing and greater influence over global financial conditions.

A concrete, dated example illuminates this dynamic. In 1971, when the United States suspended dollar convertibility into gold, foreign firms continued to write contracts in dollars despite the shift. European and Japanese banks still held dollar deposits as working capital; global commodity markets still quoted prices in dollars; and the OPEC oil benchmark remained dollar-based. The visible behaviour—continuity despite institutional upheaval—revealed a key principle: trust in the currency's ecosystem can outlast trust in the issuer's specific promises. Liquidity trumped ideology.

A credible counter-example challenges the notion that dominance flows inevitably from economic heft. Between 1860 and 1914, sterling ruled global finance from London even though the United States had surpassed Britain in industrial output by the 1890s. The British Empire's vast trading networks, London's discount houses, and deep bills-of-exchange markets kept sterling at the centre. Reconciling this with the dollar's later rise shows that reserve dominance reflects institutional infrastructure and contract practice as much as macroeconomic size. Power persists through habits.

Our second major claim concerns the split between **privilege and burden**. Dominance brings benefits: lower yields for government debt, greater demand for corporate bonds, and a captive market for the issuing country's safe assets. These benefits are measurable. US Treasury yields often sit below those of similarly rated sovereigns, reflecting global demand for dollar-denominated safety. Yet the burden is equally visible: the issuer must supply liquidity during crises. When funding markets panic, the world sells risky assets and flees toward the safe unit. This "flight to safety" can strengthen the dominant currency at precisely the time its own exporters suffer. The implication is that the issuer becomes the world's shock absorber.

A named example anchors this claim. In late September 2008, during the global financial crisis, the US Federal Reserve extended dollar swap lines to the European Central Bank, the Bank of Japan, the Bank of England, and others. On 29 September alone, the ECB drew $25 billion. These actions stabilised funding markets far from American shores. The behaviour showed burden: America's central bank had to backstop liquidity for institutions it did not regulate. But the behaviour also showed privilege: the rest of the world depended on dollar liquidity, reinforcing the dollar's central position.

A limitation emerges with the Chinese renminbi. Despite China's economic scale, renminbi internationalisation remains constrained. Capital controls, shallow offshore markets, and limited hedging instruments reduce foreign willingness to hold renminbi assets. The currency features in trade agreements but not yet in global portfolios. Reconciling this limitation reinforces the motif: *the centre of gravity chooses who must orbit*—but only when the centre builds transparent, reliable financial plumbing.

The third major claim turns to **contractual geography**. Reserve currencies dominate because contracts travel geographically even when goods do not. A Korean manufacturer buying Chilean copper will settle in dollars because the dollar market for hedging metals is deeper and cheaper. The behaviour is visible in corporate treasury manuals and hedging desks' choices. Naming the effect—*invoice currency dominance*—brings clarity. Explaining it shows that firms do not choose currencies because of flag or allegiance; they choose because one currency reduces variance in cash flows. The implication is profound: dominance rests on microeconomic decisions repeated millions of times.

Historical cases reinforce the point. After the First World War, the US dollar gradually replaced sterling in commodity markets not because Britain disappeared from global trade but because American banks offered cheaper letters of credit and more reliable settlement. By 1927, New York overtook London in international bond issuance. The quiet shift in contract practice foreshadowed a political transition.

A counter-example appears with the euro. Introduced in 1999, it quickly became the world's second most important reserve. Yet even at its peak share, euro invoicing outside Europe remained modest. Turkish textile firms or South African miners seldom priced in euros despite proximity to European customers. Reconciling this suggests that reserve currencies need not dominate every domain; they dominate where network effects run deepest.

The fourth major claim examines **the feedback loop between policy and global demand**. A currency that others rely on must maintain predictable institutions. Investors measure fiscal discipline, legal stability, and central-bank independence. Naming the loop clarifies the mechanism: global demand for sovereign bonds disciplines the issuer, while the issuer's policy decisions support global demand. Explaining this loop shows a paradox: reserve status both protects and constrains. The implication is that hegemony relies on credibility as much as capability.

A vivid example sharpened this tension. During the US debt-ceiling standoff in October 2013, yields on short-dated Treasury bills spiked as investors measured default risk. Yet even then, foreign central banks accumulated Treasuries for reserve portfolios. Behaviour contradicted rhetoric. The world punished the issuer at the margins but clung to the security of the broader system. Credibility, once embedded, endures shocks.

A subtle counter-example arises from Japan. The yen is a reserve currency and a popular safe-haven asset, yet Japan's public debt exceeds 200 per cent of GDP. This limitation complicates simple narratives linking fiscal discipline and reserve status. Reconciling the tension suggests that credibility can derive from institutional continuity, political stability, and deep markets rather than narrow fiscal metrics.

Our motif returns: *the centre of gravity chooses who must orbit.* Yet the orbit is voluntary, maintained by countless contracting decisions, not coercion. Reserve-currency power is adhesive, not extractive.

The chapter section ends at a hinge. Should countries seek alternative billing units to reduce vulnerability to a dominant currency? Should the issuer of a dominant unit expand swap lines or narrow them? Should global markets diversify their reserve composition or accept that liquidity favours concentration? Each choice defines the future map of monetary power.

Balance of Payments and Adjustment

On a July afternoon in 2017, the lobby of Bangkok's Suvarnabhumi Airport looked more like a festival than a transit point. Tour groups from Shanghai and Seoul clustered around guides holding coloured flags. European backpackers queued at ATMs, phones out, checking exchange rates before tapping for baht. Inside a glass-walled office upstairs, an economist from the Bank of Thailand watched a dashboard of inflows. Card spending by foreign visitors was spiking again; hotel occupancy on the Andaman coast ran close to capacity; airlines reported full flights. Tourism had become one of Thailand's largest export "industries"—not in containers of goods, but in boarding passes and breakfast buffets. As the foreign money poured in, pressure built the other way. The baht strengthened; manufacturers whose margins were thinner than a visa sticker felt the squeeze. The same inflows that delighted hoteliers made exporters quietly furious. The country was experiencing, in real time, the awkward arithmetic of the balance of payments. Money arrives. Something else must move.

This is the central paradox of external accounts. A country cannot run a surplus or deficit in one part of its transactions with the rest of the world without adjustment appearing somewhere else: in its exchange rate, its level of foreign debt, its reserves, or its internal activity. The balance of payments is not a dusty statistical table; it is a ledger of who pays whom, in what form, and with what consequences. The numbers encode choices, and those choices fall on particular shoulders: a worker in a factory whose overtime disappears when the currency rises, a government that borrows in foreign units to cover an import bill, a central bank governor who must decide whether to resist or ride the tide.

A quiet motif runs through this subchapter: *the ledger must balance, but the pain does not.*

The first major claim is that the balance of payments captures three intertwined streams—trade, capital flows, and reserve movements—and that adjustment can occur through several channels, each with distinct winners and losers. The Thai tourism boom shows one version. Service exports surge as visitors spend; the current account moves deeper into surplus; upward pressure on the baht emerges. The authorities must choose how to respond. They can allow the currency to appreciate, making imports cheaper for households but eroding export competitiveness. They can intervene in foreign-exchange markets, accumulating reserves and dampening appreciation at the cost of expanding the central bank's balance sheet. Or they can loosen capital outflows, encouraging domestic investors to buy more foreign assets. Each choice shows up in behaviour: importers celebrate cheaper machinery; savers complain about lower returns abroad; portfolio managers attend more conferences in Singapore.

Economists give names to these adjustment channels—exchange-rate flexibility, reserve accumulation, capital-account liberalisation—but the essence is simpler. Who absorbs the shock? If the currency is allowed to move, firms whose business depends on price-sensitive exports take the hit. If reserves are accumulated, taxpayers implicitly fund the cost of sterilising interventions. If capital is pushed outward, domestic assets may become scarcer or more volatile. The ledger must balance; what differs is whose line shifts.

A second, historically grounded example reveals a different pattern. For decades, Germany has run persistent current-account surpluses, exporting much more than it imports. Under the euro, with no national exchange rate to appreciate, adjustment has occurred through other channels. German households have faced lower consumption growth than they might have enjoyed; wages have risen more slowly than productivity at times; and capital outflows have risen as German savings funded investment abroad. Southern European countries, by contrast, ran deficits supported by those inflows, with Spain, Portugal, and Greece absorbing the counterpart of Germany's surplus. The behaviour was visible in construction booms on the Mediterranean coast and in the balance sheets of German banks holding foreign claims. The implication is uncomfortable: one country's sustained surplus is, mechanically, others' sustained deficit, and the adjustment can mutate into debt and, ultimately, crisis.

A credible counter-example complicates any neat story about how adjustment "should" work. Japan has also run significant current-account surpluses but has combined them with large holdings of foreign assets and a domestic economy characterised by low inflation and, at times, modest growth. The yen has not simply marched upward without restraint; periods of appreciation have been followed by interventions and policy shifts. The behaviour shows that surplus status does not force a single adjustment path. Japan's institutional choices—encouraging outward portfolio investment, tolerating lower domestic demand growth, and, at times, intervening in FX markets—have distributed adjustment over time and sectors. Reconciling this with the German pattern underscores that the balance of payments is not destiny. It is a record of choices made within constraints.

The second major claim is that tourism offers a particularly vivid lens on these mechanisms because it concentrates foreign demand in a narrow set of sectors while touching the entire macroeconomic frame. Returning to Bangkok airport, we can see the chain. Airlines hire more staff; hotels expand rooms; service workers see wages rise. Local prices in tourist hotspots climb, sometimes faster than in the rest of the country. A barista in Chiang Mai notices rent creeping up because landlords now cater to short-let platforms. The ledger records this as a service export; the lived reality is a change in who can afford to live where.

Policy-makers then confront the question: should they accommodate the inflow or lean against it? One path is to let the currency appreciate and allow the economy to tilt organically towards tourism and other non-tradable sectors. The risk is over-concentration: when a pandemic or political shock arrives, the same sectors collapse hardest. A second path is to smooth the currency movements by buying foreign assets, building reserves as a buffer. This requires the central bank to manage a large portfolio and sterilise the impact on domestic money conditions, often by issuing bonds. The cost shows up in interest expenses and, sometimes, in public debate about "hoarded" reserves that could have been spent at home.

The motif of the uneven ledger returns. Tourists bring in foreign currency and Instagram posts; workers in export factories further inland see their competitiveness squeezed. A beach town thrives; a manufacturing town stagnates.

The third major claim concerns **capital flows**: the other side of the balance of payments, where investment, loans, and speculative bets move. A country that runs a trade deficit must, by accounting identity, finance it by attracting capital. A country running a surplus must invest the counterpart abroad. This is not a moral statement; it is a matter of arithmetic. But the channels through which capital moves shape vulnerability.

Consider Mexico in the early 1990s. After liberalisation, capital poured in—portfolio investment in government bonds, equity in privatised firms, cross-border bank lending. The current account widened into deficit, financed by these flows. As long as confidence held, the system seemed stable. When sentiment turned in 1994, capital fled, the peso fell sharply, and reserves drained. The adjustment occurred violently rather than gradually. Behaviour showed the cost: mortgage rates spiked, firms cancelled projects, and the government negotiated emergency support. The balance of payments balanced, but through crisis.

A counterpoint is found in Chile's use of unremunerated reserve requirements on short-term capital inflows in the 1990s: a form of "speed bump". Investors bringing money into the country had to leave a portion on deposit with the central bank at zero interest for a period. This made short-term, hot-money inflows less attractive and tilted the composition towards longer-term investment. Here, adjustment was shaped proactively. The ledger's balancing was guided, not left to panic.

These cases show that the composition and maturity of capital flows—equity versus debt, short-term versus long-term—matter as much as their volume. A country may have identical net inflows in two years but very different risk depending on whether those inflows are long-term direct investment or short-term portfolio flows that can reverse overnight. Policymakers who merely watch the headline balance miss the shifting weight beneath.

The fourth claim concerns **reserves**: the buffer stock that allows a country to smooth adjustment. Central banks accumulate foreign-exchange reserves by purchasing foreign assets when inflows are strong and draw them down when outflows dominate. To the outside observer, reserves look like a pile of security; internally, they represent a set of deferred decisions. Accumulating reserves implies that the country is, in effect, lending to the rest of the world at modest returns in order to insure against that same world. The behaviour is seen in purchase orders for foreign bonds, in statements about self-insurance after IMF experiences, and in domestic debates over whether reserves could fund infrastructure.

A clear example lies in South Korea after the 1997–1998 Asian financial crisis. Haunted by the memory of running out of reserves and applying for IMF support, the country built a substantial reserve stockpile. When the 2008 crisis hit, the Bank of Korea used those reserves, alongside swap lines, to stabilise the won. Adjustment still occurred—the currency moved, growth slowed—but the shock was less severe than a decade earlier. The ledger balanced again, but over a longer horizon and with more policy control.

There is, however, a limit. Excessive reliance on reserve accumulation can trap a country in a low-yield position, continuously recycling domestic savings into foreign safe assets while domestic investment opportunities go underfunded. Citizens see high savings rates, modest returns, and infrastructure gaps. The balance-of-payments surplus becomes, in effect, an export of capital at terms that may not maximise national welfare.

The motif of the ledger tightens. The balance of payments always adds to zero globally; for every surplus there is a deficit, for every creditor a debtor. What does not add to zero is vulnerability. Who bears the stress of adjustment is a design choice.

Balance-of-payments accounting looks impersonal, but it works through personal decisions. A hotel owner in Phuket decides whether to quote prices in baht or dollars. A central bank committee in Pretoria debates whether to let the rand slide or to raise rates to defend it. A finance minister in Athens argues with creditors about how quickly a deficit must shrink. Trade, capital flows, and reserves are the headings; underneath them, lives.

The unresolved tension persists. How much external imbalance should a country tolerate before forcing painful internal adjustment? Should a tourism boom be allowed to reshape the whole economy, or should policy lean against it at the cost of slower growth? When capital arrives in floods, is it wiser to welcome it and hope, or to tax, gate, and steer it? The ledger will always balance. The open question is who will be asked, silently or loudly, to do the balancing.

Crises Without Borders

At 8:42 a.m. on 7 May 2010, the switchboard at the Securities and Exchange Commission in Washington, DC began blinking with urgent calls. Traders on the floor of the New York Stock Exchange had just watched blue-chip prices fall in vertiginous cascades—shares that normally moved a few cents in a morning plunged dollars in seconds. The "flash crash" briefly erased nearly a trillion dollars of market value before rebounding minutes later. While later investigations traced the trigger to algorithmic trading patterns, the shock's amplification told a wider story. Automated orders sitting on servers in New Jersey interacted with risk limits set in London, margin calls bounced through brokers in Chicago, and exchange-traded funds in Toronto widened spreads as liquidity vanished. Contracts linked them. Confidence deserted them. A stumble in one node travelled across borders faster than anyone could blink. Even after prices normalised, the memory lingered: financial systems had become so tightly wired that shocks defied geography.

The episode was not a crisis of sovereign balance sheets or banking solvency. Yet it supplied a preview of transmission mechanics that would later dominate global emergencies. When a wave of selling begins in one jurisdiction, contractual linkages ensure that demands for cash appear in another. Funds redeem. Banks call in collateral. Firms dump assets to satisfy margin rules. Each action is rational for one actor; together they produce contagion. The quiet motif in this subchapter—the *chain reaction*—begins with that morning's glowing switchboard.

The first major claim is that crises cross borders primarily through **contracts**. A bond issued in São Paulo but held by a pension fund in Copenhagen ties two economies together. When Brazil's yields spike, the Danish fund faces losses, forcing it to raise cash. That cash may come from selling German equities or withdrawing from an Indonesian mutual fund. Behaviour, not abstraction, transmits pressure: sell orders, collateral postings, redemption requests. In August 2007, BNP Paribas froze redemptions on three funds exposed to US mortgage-linked securities, arguing that it could not value the holdings. The funds' legal structure was French; the problematic assets were American; the investors were spread across Europe. Yet the outcome was immediate: interbank markets tightened within hours as lenders refused to roll short-term credit to any institution suspected of holding similar exposures. The chain reaction was already underway months before Lehman Brothers failed.

The explanation is stark. Modern finance relies on a lattice of legally enforceable claims that span continents. A crisis does not respect borders because the contracts themselves ignore them. The implication is unavoidable: any country integrated into global capital markets imports volatility along with investment.

A second demonstration concerns **confidence**, the other carrier of contagion. In September 1998, Long-Term Capital

Management (LTCM), based in Greenwich, Connecticut, came close to collapse. Its positions stretched from Japanese government bonds to European equity derivatives. As losses mounted, counterparties feared disorderly liquidation. Within days, spreads widened globally. The Federal Reserve Bank of New York orchestrated a private rescue on 23 September 1998, but the event revealed a deeper channel. No contract broke. No government defaulted. But when confidence wavered, lenders stepped back, bid-ask spreads ballooned, and funding markets froze. The chain reaction here arose not from legal claims but from expectations: if others will not lend, I cannot either. The implication is subtler than the BNP case. Even without cross-border assets, the *fear* of cross-border exposure can destabilise markets continents away.

A credible counter-example tempers easy generalisation. During the 2013 "taper tantrum", when the US Federal Reserve signalled it might reduce asset purchases, many emerging markets saw capital outflows and currency pressure. Yet countries such as Mexico, which had developed deeper domestic bond markets and clearer communication channels between the central bank and investors, absorbed the shock more smoothly than others. Behaviour demonstrated resilience: domestic pension funds continued buying local bonds; foreign investors reduced exposure gradually rather than indiscriminately; policy-makers held press conferences explaining rate decisions. This does not refute the contagion thesis but refines it. Cross-border shocks are not destiny; institutional design can cushion the blow.

The second major claim is that **swap lines**—temporary agreements between central banks to exchange currencies—serve as high-level circuit breakers, but they come with costs. The most striking case occurred in October 2008, when the Federal Reserve extended dollar swap lines to major central banks, including the European Central Bank, the Bank of England, and the Bank of Japan. Demand for dollars had surged as global banks scrambled to fund dollar-denominated

liabilities. Without access to these lines, banks in Zurich or Frankfurt would have been forced to liquidate assets at fire-sale prices, exporting turmoil back to the United States. With the lines in place, the ECB could auction dollars to its banks, relieving pressure. The behaviour was clear: bid-to-cover ratios in ECB auctions fell; dollar LIBOR eased; banks stopped hoarding liquidity.

Yet swap lines create a quiet tension. They are discretionary, not automatic. Countries outside the inner circle—such as many emerging markets—do not receive them. In 2008, South Korea eventually received a swap line from the Fed, but other countries, despite comparable integration with global funding markets, did not. The implication is political. Swap lines stabilise systems but also reveal hierarchies: who receives the insurance and who must fend alone.

The third major claim centres on **capital controls**, used by governments to slow or redirect outflows during crises. They can be blunt and costly, but they sometimes succeed in containing chain reactions. In July 2015, Greece imposed capital controls after tense negotiations with creditors and a liquidity squeeze in banks. Withdrawal limits, restrictions on international transfers, and temporary bank closures followed. Behaviour on the streets of Athens showed the measure's human texture: queues at cash machines, shopkeepers preferring electronic transfers within Greece but rejecting foreign cards, families recalibrating daily spending. The controls bought time for political negotiation and technical adjustments to bank balance sheets.

But they carried costs: disruptions to trade, a collapse in tourism bookings, and reputational damage that lingered after restrictions eased. As with swap lines, the ledger of consequences does not balance evenly. The policy may avert a systemic collapse, yet the burden falls heavily on small businesses and households. Reconciling this with the earlier examples suggests a grim truth. Tools that stop contagion often redistribute pain rather than eliminate it.

The chain reaction motif returns in its clearest form in **fund redemption waves**, the most visible expression of contagion. Imagine a large emerging-market bond fund based in London receiving a surge of redemption requests during a period of global tightening. To meet these, the fund sells liquid assets first—often sovereign bonds from countries with more transparent markets, such as South Africa or Chile. Prices in those markets fall, yields rise, and spreads widen. Local pension funds in those countries then face losses and must rebalance, sometimes selling equities or reducing foreign holdings. Investors elsewhere see spreads widening and fear deeper trouble, prompting further redemptions. The chain reaction repeats. No government policy shifted. No macroeconomic data changed. The contagion was a pattern of behaviour: *sell what you can, not necessarily what you should.*

A named, checkable example anchors this mechanism. During March 2020, as the COVID-19 shock intensified, global investors redeemed nearly $85 billion from emerging-market funds in a matter of weeks (IMF, 2020). Markets from Brazil to Indonesia experienced surging yields. Indonesia's ten-year government bond yield jumped from 6.5% to over 8% between late February and mid-March. Central banks intervened heavily. Indonesia's authorities purchased government bonds directly on the secondary market. South Africa's Reserve Bank initiated its first round of bond-buying to stabilise yields. These interventions were not about domestic fundamentals. They were about breaking the chain reaction unleashed by foreign redemptions.

The fourth claim is that crises without borders expose **mandate contradictions** for governments and central banks. In a domestic banking crisis, authorities know their remit: protect deposits, maintain payment systems, stabilise credit. In a cross-border shock, goals collide. Should a country defend its currency to prevent imported inflation, or let it fall to conserve reserves? Should it raise interest rates to keep foreign investors from fleeing, or cut them to support domestic borrowers? Each decision reveals priorities.

An example from 1997 illustrates this tension. During the Asian financial crisis, Thailand's central bank initially defended the baht's peg by selling reserves and raising interest rates. This protected the currency temporarily but inflicted severe pain on domestic firms with floating-rate debt. Once reserves were depleted, the peg broke anyway on 2 July 1997. Behaviour in the months that followed—bank closures, corporate defaults, IMF negotiations—showed the cost of delaying adjustment. The chain reaction, once started, proved difficult to halt.

By contrast, during the same period, Hong Kong's Monetary Authority successfully defended its currency board, but only through aggressive intervention and temporary interest-rate spikes. At one point in October 1997, overnight interbank rates briefly touched 280%. Domestic borrowers staggered. Yet the peg held. Two economies faced similar external shocks; their adjustment choices and consequences diverged. The motif persists: the chain reaction can be channelled, but never fully controlled.

The credible counter-example here lies in Canada's experience during the 2008–2009 crisis. Integrated deeply into US financial markets, Canada nonetheless avoided bank failures, large capital flight, or currency spirals. Stronger mortgage underwriting standards, higher bank capital ratios, and a more conservative funding structure reduced vulnerability. Behaviour during the crisis was telling: Canadian banks continued lending; the central bank's liquidity operations were measured rather than frantic; the Canadian dollar fluctuated but did not destabilise expectations. This does not disprove contagion; it shows that domestic buffers can prevent the chain reaction from reaching critical thresholds.

A final claim concerns **communication**, often overlooked but central to crisis transmission. When investors cannot measure risk, they imagine the worst. Silence becomes an accelerant. Scenes from the eurozone crisis in 2012 make the point. Before the European Central Bank's president, Mario Draghi, delivered his "whatever it takes" speech on 26 July 2012 in London, spreads on Spanish and Italian government bonds were widening relentlessly. Banks in those countries were losing deposits to northern Europe. After the speech, without any policy tool immediately deployed, spreads tightened. Behaviour, not law, changed: traders stopped shorting sovereigns aggressively; banks breathed; depositors relaxed. Communication interrupted the chain reaction.

But communication has limits. Vague assurances backfire. When authorities in Cyprus in March 2013 announced a bank levy that would hit insured deposits, confusion ignited panic. Lines formed at cash machines; transfers spiked. Policymakers reversed course within days, but the damage had been done. Trust once shaken is slow to recover. The chain reaction here was linguistic as much as financial: words triggered withdrawals.

The unresolved tension rests on a simple question. If crises cross borders through contracts and confidence, can any single country truly insulate itself? Swap lines stabilise but entrench hierarchies. Capital controls slow outflows but choke activity. Communication calms markets but can misfire. The chain reaction motif returns once more. A spark in one market jumps to another not because global finance is inherently fragile, but because its connections—legal, behavioural, psychological—are dense. The task for policymakers is not to sever them, for they also carry growth and opportunity, but to decide which links to reinforce and which to leave slack.

How many of those decisions can be made in advance, and how many must be improvised in the heat of crisis? The ledger of global finance offers no clear answer. The next shock will test whether the chain reaction can be slowed or simply diverted to a different place.

Alternative Blocks and Experiments

On 31 March 1995, Argentina's finance minister, Domingo Cavallo, faced a room thick with anxiety in Buenos Aires as rumours of a collapse in the country's currency board intensified. Three years earlier, the board—established under the Convertibility Plan of April 1991—had promised absolute discipline: every Argentine peso in circulation would be matched one-for-one with US dollar reserves. The arrangement had crushed hyperinflation and, for a time, made prices predictable enough for shops to post multi-month catalogues. But now, after Mexico's December 1994 devaluation sent shockwaves through Latin American capital markets, foreign investors were withdrawing funds at speed. Cavallo held up balance sheets, pointed to reserve totals, and insisted parity would hold. It did—for that moment. But the tension in the room revealed the central motif of this subchapter: alternatives to mainstream monetary systems offer stability only while their constraints remain credible.

The paradox that drove Argentina's experiment remains universal. Why do governments voluntarily bind their own hands, pegging their currencies to others or to commodities that they do not control? The question holds a hard number at its core: inflation in Argentina in 1990 exceeded 1,300% (INDEC, 1991). Against such chaos, any mechanism that promised a stable anchor seemed worth the sacrifice of flexibility. Yet the same mechanism would later magnify strain when reserves fell and foreign sentiment shifted. The duality—benefit and brittleness—sits at the heart of every regional block, commodity peg, and currency board.

The first major claim is that **regional monetary arrangements** arise to stabilise trade relationships and reduce transaction costs, but their strength depends on behaviour rather than treaties. The West African Economic and Monetary Union (WAEMU), anchored around the CFA franc, provides the first named example. Created formally in 1994 after a major devaluation of the franc, the arrangement tied eight member states to a common currency guaranteed by the French Treasury. Traders moving onions from Niger to Burkina Faso or textiles from Benin to Côte d'Ivoire made decisions made more confident by the elimination of exchange-rate uncertainty. Prices quoted in CFA francs sent clear signals: a sack of millet cost 14,000 CFA in Niamey and scarcely more in Ouagadougou. The behaviour underpinning trust was visible—steady invoicing, fewer last-minute renegotiations, and less hedging by small merchants.

Yet strength bred dependence. During commodity downturns, members exposed to volatile exports—cotton producers in Mali or cocoa growers in Côte d'Ivoire—faced adjustment pressures without the ability to let their currency fall. They had to cut government spending or rely on external financing instead. The implication is that regional stability carries asymmetric costs: countries whose economic cycles diverge from the regional average bear heavier burdens.

A second named example, the Common Monetary Area (CMA) in Southern Africa, formed in 1974, underscores the same trade-off. Lesotho, Eswatini, and Namibia peg their currencies at par to the South African rand; the rand circulates freely in all three. The arrangement simplifies cross-border trade—South African wholesalers can price goods consistently across the region, and Lesotho's textile exporters can plan payrolls without exchange-rate shocks. But the region's monetary policy is effectively set in Pretoria, and smaller members must adjust fiscal policy or wages when South Africa's interest-rate cycle reflects domestic inflation rather than regional conditions. The CMA's experience does not refute the benefits of regional blocks; it instead shows their dependency on political acceptance of uneven influence.

A credible counter-example sharpens this further: the Caribbean Monetary Union, proposed at intervals since the 1960s, has remained limited in scope. Caribbean economies differ more dramatically in size, sectoral structure, and exposure to tourism cycles than WAEMU or the CMA. Repeated feasibility studies revealed that a shared currency could impose severe strain on smaller islands during hurricanes or sudden tourism declines—events that require rapid exchange-rate movements to regain competitiveness. Here the behaviour that sustains other unions—aligned expectations, predictable trade, shared adjustment burdens—proved too difficult to coordinate. The implication is sobering. Alternative blocks succeed not primarily on economic symmetry but on political willingness to absorb asymmetric pain.

The second major claim turns to **commodity pegs**, the oldest form of external anchor, which promise stability by tying a currency to a physical standard. Hong Kong's currency board, established in October 1983 with a fixed rate of HKD 7.80 to the US dollar, illustrates both discipline and strain. The mechanism is mechanistic: the Hong Kong Monetary Authority (HKMA) issues base money only when backed by equivalent US dollar reserves. Traders and citizens behave accordingly. When the Asian financial crisis erupted in 1997, speculators attacked the peg. Overnight interest rates spiked; at one point they touched 280%. Yet the HKMA held the line, deploying reserves, raising funding costs, and even buying equities to stabilise markets. The peg survived because behaviour aligned with the rules. Banks rolled over funding; firms accepted rate volatility; households refrained from mass conversion.

The peg's success, however, reveals the broader cost of commodity or external pegs. Flexibility vanishes. Hong Kong's domestic economy endured severe swings in property prices and wages because monetary conditions were imported from the United States rather than tailored to local needs. The implication is clear: commodity pegs can cement credibility but sterilise adaptation.

The quiet motif of *the anchor* runs through these examples. Every peg, whether to gold, oil, or a foreign currency, relies on a visible promise that the authority will meet redemption or conversion demands. When Argentina's Convertibility Plan began, shopkeepers pinned peso–dollar conversion tables behind counters. The anchor was literal: one peso equals one dollar. But by late 2001, as reserves shrank and withdrawals accelerated, banks imposed withdrawal limits. The anchor frayed. Argentine behaviour changed: citizens queued for cash, firms invoiced in dollars, and investors dumped local assets. The currency board collapsed on 6 January 2002. This collapse does not negate the earlier benefits—it clarifies the constraint. A peg functions only so long as reserves, political commitment, and public belief remain aligned.

A counter-example from the Gulf offers nuance. Saudi Arabia's longstanding peg to the US dollar, formalised in 1986 at SAR 3.75 per dollar, has survived oil booms and busts. Behaviour explains the resilience. Massive foreign reserves, prudent fiscal policy during downturns, and a deep commitment to regime stability all reinforce credibility. Investors do not speculate seriously against the riyal because past behaviour suggests the peg will hold. This example does not invalidate the brittleness seen in Argentina; it shows that the anchor's durability depends on context—fiscal capacity, political coherence, and market expectations.

The third major claim turns to **regional currency experiments**, which attempt to combine autonomy with collective stability. The euro remains the most ambitious. Launched physically in 2002 across twelve countries, the euro removed intra-European transaction costs and supplied member states with a global reserve currency. A merchant in Milan knew that a payment received in euros would settle identically in Lyon or Munich. Yet differences in productivity, wage-setting, and fiscal policy among members created internal strains. Greece's debt crisis in 2010, followed by Ireland's banking collapse and Portugal's fiscal stresses, exposed the inherent trade-off: a shared currency without a fully shared fiscal authority can strain during asymmetric shocks.

Behavioural metrics laid this bare. Between 2009 and 2012, yields on ten-year Greek government bonds soared from under 6% to over 30%, while German yields fell below 2%. The divergence reflected the market's view that countries shared a currency but not risk. The European Central Bank (ECB) intervened decisively only after Draghi's 2012 commitment to do "whatever it takes" to preserve the euro. The implication mirrors earlier motifs. Regional experiments succeed when institutions can act collectively; they falter when coordination lags behind market speed.

A credible counter-example lies in the aborted East African monetary integration efforts of the 2010s. Kenya, Uganda, Rwanda, Burundi, and Tanzania agreed in principle to adopt a shared currency within a decade. Yet divergent inflation rates, political disagreements over central bank independence, and disparities in fiscal deficits delayed progress. The behaviour that sustains currency unions—regularised communication, fiscal alignment, tolerance for transfers—did not materialise. Plans remain stalled. This does not contradict the successes of the euro or WAEMU but shows that political cohesion is not optional; it is the foundation.

The fourth major claim concerns **currency boards**, which sit at the extreme end of constraint. Unlike simple pegs, currency boards promise full backing with foreign reserves and automatic conversion. They hold allure because they promise immediate credibility: a government cannot print at will; inflation falls; foreign investors relax. But the constraint is real and unforgiving. A vignette from Bulgaria in 1997 captures the mechanism. After a severe banking crisis and inflation exceeding 300%, the country adopted a currency board pegged to the Deutsche Mark. Shops began displaying prices in both currencies; banks rebuilt liquidity with outside support; inflation collapsed within months.

But constraint revealed itself in behaviour during the 2008–2009 global crisis. As demand for Bulgarian exports fell and capital inflows reversed, the central bank could not cut interest rates or devalue the currency. Instead, wages fell in real terms and unemployment rose. Budget cuts followed. The currency board survived because society accepted the adjustment burden. Yet the implication is unmistakable. A currency board stabilises nominal variables at the cost of domestic flexibility. When external shocks hit, adjustment shifts from prices to people.

The quiet motif of *the anchor* returns again. Every alternative block seeks an anchor—regional, commodity-based, or rule-bound. The anchor promises stability but also fixes the system in place. Whether the anchor is gold, the dollar, or a regional standard, its reliability depends on capacity and belief.

The unresolved tension lies in a simple question. Can countries design alternatives that capture the benefits of anchors—credibility, low transaction costs, predictable prices—without inheriting brittleness? Or does the very act of anchoring require surrendering the flexibility needed to survive future shocks? The next experiment, whether a digital-currency block or a renewed commodity peg, will test the limits of the anchor once more.

Chapter 7
Digital Payments Before Blockchains

The queue at Shinjuku Station moves in clean, practised waves. A commuter lifts her phone, taps the terminal, and slips through the gate with barely a pause. The entire motion lasts less than a second. No thought is given to the layers beneath that tap: the rail operator's stored-value account, the handset's secure element, the settlement file that will reconcile tens of thousands of identical gestures by nightfall. In that blink, convenience becomes choreography. And choreography becomes expectation. By the time blockchains entered public conversation, millions were already living inside a world where money could move faster than attention itself.

The paradox of modern payments is that technological revolutions begin quietly—not with new forms of money, but with new ways of touching it. Japan's Suica card in 2001, Kenya's M-Pesa in 2007, contactless bank cards in London in 2014: each altered the user's sense of time, effort, and risk long before anyone debated decentralisation or digital scarcity. A commute made smoother, a remittance delivered without queues, a coffee paid for with a wrist flick. None changed the underlying monetary unit. Yet each subtly rewired the mental models that shape what people believe money *should* feel like. When a motion becomes effortless, it becomes indispensable.

This chapter takes place in that liminal space, just before cryptographic ledgers redefined what digital money could be. Our concern here is the era in which digital payments relied less on blockchain novelty than on interfaces, identity, and institutional plumbing. It is a world built from chips, databases, and risk rules rather than distributed consensus. A world built by banks, card networks, telecoms operators, and platform firms. And a world that remains the foundation for much of what the public still uses for everyday transactions.

We begin with the transformation driven by interface design—how cards, contactless terminals, and mobile wallets altered behaviour. The history shows that the friction of a gesture is not a trivial detail but a force capable of shifting entire payment landscapes. Retailers track abandonment rates; transit agencies monitor gate throughput; banks measure tap adoption curves. When a consumer can pay in half a second, they not only spend faster—they expect everything else to match that tempo. Convenience resets baselines. And baselines, once raised, rarely fall.

From there, the narrative moves to the distinction between closed-loop and open-loop systems, an ostensibly technical divide with seismic implications. Closed loops—such as retail gift cards, transit wallets, and platform balances—thrive because they control the entire environment: issuance, acceptance, settlement, and rules. They offer speed because they do not negotiate with the outside world. Open loops, by contrast, operate across institutions, geographies, and regulatory domains. Their breadth offers reach but demands interoperability, compliance, and trust across boundaries. A gift card works everywhere *inside* its garden; a bank transfer works *beyond* any single garden. The tension between control and openness runs through the entire digital payments story.

No digital system escapes risk. As cash recedes from everyday transactions, dispute rights, authentication layers, and fraud-detection models substitute for the finality once granted by banknotes. Identity proofing, once a matter of familiarity or paper credentials, becomes a stack of verification checks, behavioural biometrics, and data cross-references. Fraud patterns evolve with each technical change: card-not-present attacks, SIM swaps, account takeovers. A single chargeback illustrates how digital systems reshape not only settlement but responsibility—who bears the loss, who proves legitimacy, and who defines what "authorised" means.

This chapter then turns to the most radical pre-blockchain development: the use of behavioural data as collateral. Utility bills, mobile top-up histories, e-commerce transaction patterns—all emerged as tools to gauge creditworthiness in places where formal credit files were thin or non-existent. Lenders used these signals to price loans more precisely, widening access while intensifying debates over privacy and surveillance. A household's timely payments to an electricity provider could unlock microcredit at lower rates than any bank would have offered a decade earlier. Yet the same data trail could expose families to predatory scoring or opaque algorithmic decisions. Inclusion and intrusion travelled together.

Threaded throughout this chapter is a recurring motif: the gap between what the user sees and what the system must do. The commuter's tap hides a reconciliation engine. The seamless wallet hides a governance model. The fraud alert hides a behavioural profile. The microloan hides a data economy. All of these systems predate blockchains, and all set expectations that any subsequent technology must meet or surpass. The digital payment order of the early twenty-first century is not merely a precursor to decentralised finance; it is a formidable baseline, built by decades of engineering, coordination, and iterative institutional design.

Ultimately, the chapter invites the reader to examine the continuity beneath supposed disruption. Before blockchains promised trust without intermediaries, decades of digital innovation had already reshaped the relationship between users, banks, platforms, and the state. The themes here—convenience, control, identity, and data—frame the very questions that would later animate blockchain advocates and critics. Yet these themes also belong to a deeper tradition, one that shows how payment systems evolve long before new money arrives.

The momentum builds toward a central tension. If digital payments before blockchains made money feel instantaneous, personalised, and embedded in everyday tools, what happens when a new monetary technology arrives promising not convenience but reconfiguration? Does the weight of existing expectations constrain innovation, or does it accelerate it? By the end of this chapter, the reader will stand at that threshold—ready to cross into the territory where digital money ceases to be institutional plumbing and becomes an arena for ideological contest and technological reinvention.

From Cards to Mobile Wallets

The gates at Hong Kong's Central Station record their rhythms with forensic precision. On the morning of 18 October 2018, the MTR Corporation logged more than five million Octopus taps across its network before noon, a dense choreography of commuters clearing barriers in barely half a second each. Many no longer reached for the original stored-value card launched in 1997; instead, they raised phones or watches, letting the gesture dissolve into muscle memory. It is here, in this unremarkable sequence of taps, that a central truth emerges. Interfaces, not currencies, are often the first agents of monetary change. People adapt to speed long before they question what money is.

This raises a simple paradox. How can a payment method that saves perhaps *four tenths of a second* per transaction alter an entire city's expectations? The answer lies in repetition. A half-second gain repeated 40 times a day rewires behaviour more effectively than any abstract argument about efficiency. The October 2018 data shows not only adoption; it shows habituation. Speed becomes a norm. A norm becomes a demand. And demand becomes a standard against which all later technologies must compete.

Card networks learned this lesson decades earlier. By the mid-1990s, Visa and Mastercard terminals had already reduced authorisation times to a few seconds in major urban centres. Yet the breakthrough was not technical capacity but the user's experience: the act of swiping, signing, and walking away without visiting an ATM. The shift from cash to card was not the arrival of new money; it was the arrival of new *access*. What mattered was the behaviour it created: fewer withdrawals, more spontaneous purchases, and a recalibration of what counted as "friction".

The passage from magnetic stripes to contactless cards illustrates the same dynamic. When London's Transport for London (TfL) began contactless acceptance in 2014, drawing on card EMV standards from the 2000s, commuters discovered that the tap felt identical to Oyster but more versatile. A single card handled transit and shopping, domestically and abroad. The logic of the system had not changed; the logic of the *gesture* had. From here, mobile wallets such as Apple Pay and Google Pay did not create new monetary instruments. They perfected the gesture. A double-click and a biometric confirmation compressed the perceived effort further still. The motif returns: the tiniest reductions in effort generate the largest shifts in habit.

To understand why, consider the behavioural evidence. TfL's own usage metrics from 2015–2018 showed rising contactless adoption on days when trains were delayed. When a platform crowd forms, people choose the fastest reliable interface. Behaviour maps the value of seconds. And when those seconds accumulate, expectations harden into demands: no queues at ticketing machines, no delays at checkout, no forced re-authentication at the worst possible moment. In these micro-decisions, digital payments acquire their gravitas.

A second example shows how adoption precedes understanding. In 2007, Safaricom launched M-Pesa in Kenya. The service was designed to help users send domestic remittances cheaply and securely. Yet within months, merchants began accepting mobile transfers for everyday transactions: vegetables, matatu fares, school fees. Few users could explain the underlying settlement infrastructure. Fewer still cared. What mattered was that a payment required only a phone, a number, and a PIN. Simplicity created scale. And scale created the perception that money *ought* to behave this way. Even sceptics found themselves drawn into the network because refusal created inconvenience for everyone else.

The sceptic's case is worth noting. Critics in Kenya during 2007–2008 questioned the resilience of a system dependent on telecom infrastructure, arguing that outages or SIM theft created new vulnerabilities. The limitation was real. Yet users reconciled it by treating the service as a complementary convenience, not a replacement for cash. As the Safaricom data from 2008 shows, usage surged even after intermittent outages. The network's value exceeded its flaws. Once the habit embedded, resilience improved because scale warranted better infrastructure. Risk followed adoption, not the reverse.

The thread that binds these examples is a quiet motif: *the tap*. A trivial action masking an entire architecture. To tap is to compress a century of payments engineering—routing tables, authentication rules, clearing cycles—into a single moment of certainty. The user cares about none of this. Habits form around the gesture, not the machinery. And as habits form, the machinery must evolve to sustain them. It is the inversion that matters: interface leads, infrastructure follows.

This inversion challenges the usual narrative of financial innovation. We tend to imagine transformation as a sequence beginning with new institutions or new forms of money, cascading downward to consumer behaviour. But the history of digital payments reverses the arrow. The consumer experience—speed, reliability, ease—pulls infrastructure in its wake. When merchants install terminals capable of contactless acceptance, banks accelerate tokenisation. When commuters flock to mobile wallets, handset manufacturers invest in secure elements. When platforms reduce checkout steps, card networks subsidise risk scoring. The front end leads; the back end chases.

The implications extend beyond convenience. Speed alters perception. When a transaction settles with the psychological immediacy of a tap, users start to expect visibility in their banking apps within seconds, even if settlement remains batched at the end of the day. Psychology pressures plumbing. And plumbing adapts, slowly and unevenly, until real-time payment rails emerge as a necessity rather than an experiment. The UK's Faster Payments Service in 2008 and India's UPI in 2016 both reflect this trajectory: demand creates urgency, and urgency pushes institutions to recalibrate their tolerance for risk, liquidity, and verification.

Yet speed also creates new vulnerabilities. A payment that clears too quickly for the user to reconsider may clear too quickly for the system to detect fraud. Here, the habit-forming power of interface collides with the risk management priorities of banks. The UK saw a rise in authorised push payment fraud from 2017 onwards, precisely because seamless interfaces made users more susceptible to social engineering. The counter-example teaches a wider lesson: convenience cannot remain ungoverned. Systems that privilege speed must strengthen authentication, anomaly detection, and recovery processes. Every gain invites a cost; every interface hides a trade-off.

Nevertheless, the trend remains clear. Card networks and wallet providers competed by shaving milliseconds from authentication cycles and smoothing the user journey. As Apple Pay's adoption data from the US between 2015 and 2020 shows, uptake rose sharply when transit operators integrated the Express Transit feature, eliminating the need for biometric confirmation at gates. Behaviour followed context. Commuters have no patience for complexity. Habits form in seconds, not seminars.

The motif of the tap returns once more. It is a symbol of minimalism, an emblem of how little a user must do to participate in a complex network of institutions. A tap is silent, immediate, anonymous in its physicality. It reduces the cognitive load of payment to almost zero. And once that baseline exists, any alternative that demands more feels archaic. The bar rises invisibly but definitively.

Now consider the long-term implications. When consumers grow accustomed to instant, device-native payments, they become less tolerant of fragmentation—multiple apps, multiple verification paths, multiple delays. This pressure encourages consolidation: the dominance of a few wallet providers, the embedding of payments into operating systems, the merger of payment identity with device identity. It also encourages regulatory scrutiny, because the same firms that perfect the tap often accumulate unprecedented data on user behaviour. The convenience that drives adoption also centralises power.

Against this backdrop, the legacy of card systems gains renewed relevance. Visa's global acceptance network, built over decades, created a form of de facto payment infrastructure long before digital platforms imagined comparable reach. The card networks' ability to propagate standards across borders became, unintentionally, one of the great stabilising forces in global commerce. And yet the user rarely sees this. The tap conceals the rails.

The tension, then, is not about hardware or software. It concerns expectation. Industrialising the tap has taught hundreds of millions to assume that payment is a background function—quiet, invisible, instantaneous. Any future monetary system, blockchain-based or otherwise, must confront this reality. Convenience is not a feature; it is now an entitlement. And entitlement is a demanding master.

As the chapter moves forward, the open question remains unresolved. If interface habit has become the true driver of adoption, how should institutions balance its appeal with the frictions needed to preserve security, resilience, and choice? Should systems chase ever greater speed, or should they cultivate deliberate pauses to protect users from themselves? The tap teaches us that behaviour is malleable. The challenge is deciding who shapes that behaviour—and to what end.

Closed vs Open Loops

On 12 December 2019, at a Tesco in Manchester's Stretford district, a cashier watched a familiar scene unfold. A customer attempted to pay for groceries with a £25 gift card purchased three weeks earlier. The till recognised only £8.47. The remainder had been spent at a different Tesco branch, though the customer had no memory of using it. The card was valid, the balance was real, yet it existed entirely within Tesco's closed loop. Nothing inside that garden connected to the customer's bank account, nor to any external dispute process. The cashier could only shrug: *the balance is what the system says it is.* A payment instrument backed by a national bank would have offered recourse. A private loop offered none.

That moment in Stretford reveals the stark distinction between closed and open systems. The customer's debit card, issued by Lloyds Bank and operating over the Faster Payments rails introduced in 2008, would have offered immediate visibility, a regulatory complaints route, and the possibility of chargeback. The gift card offered nothing beyond what Tesco's internal ledger permitted. Two forms of "money", two very different worlds, separated not by technology but by boundaries of trust, control, and reach. That boundary is the quiet motif that threads through this discussion: the fence.

Closed loops predate digital payments by centuries. Medieval fairs often issued jetons that functioned only within their temporary perimeters, forcing visitors to convert silver into counters that retained no value once the fair ended. What changed in the twentieth and twenty-first centuries is not the concept but its scope. Corporations learned they could build entire ecosystems—gardens with high walls—inside which their tokens circulated with remarkable efficiency. Starbucks Cards, first launched in the United States in 2001, became one of the country's largest stored-value systems within a decade. By Christmas 2013, the company reported over two billion dollars equivalent in active card balances. Within that garden, settlement was instant, liability was predictable, and customer behaviour became measurable.

The appeal for the platform is obvious. Control reduces uncertainty. When a firm designs both token and ledger, it determines the rules governing redemption, expiration, fraud handling, and data collection. There is no need to manage interoperability with outside institutions. The garden feeds itself. But the fence also restricts what users can do. A Starbucks balance cannot pay rent, settle a tax bill, or transfer to a friend's account unless the platform provides explicit functionality. The money is usable only where the issuer permits. The same pattern appears in the architecture of many modern super-apps: WeChat Pay in China (launched 2013) excels precisely because its garden is enormous, dense, and intensely integrated; Alipay, similarly, binds users to a network defined by Alibaba's commercial interests.

Open-loop systems take the opposite approach. Bank transfers, card networks, and regulated e-money schemes expose their rails to thousands of institutions, each issuing instruments that interoperate by design. A Halifax customer can pay a Barclays creditor because both connect to shared clearing houses. A NatWest cardholder can purchase goods in Lisbon because EMV standards ensure compatibility between Portuguese terminals and UK issuers. These networks sacrifice the tight grip of closed systems in exchange for scalability, resilience, and neutrality.

The choice between loops determines not only reach but risk. A closed loop minimises external attack surfaces because outsiders cannot initiate transactions. Fraud is contained by the limits of the garden. Yet the internal risks amplify: a database failure, a governance misstep, or a cyber incident can freeze *all* activity because there is no alternative pathway. In October 2021, an outage affecting Facebook's internal network briefly disrupted Facebook Pay transactions, though the system recovered within hours. The incident underscored a structural reality: when a company is both issuer and infrastructure operator, its internal fragility becomes a monetary weakness.

Open loops face the mirror image. Because many actors connect to the rails, vulnerabilities often arise at the edge: phishing, authorised push payment fraud, account takeover. The system absorbs the risk through regulations such as the UK's Payment Services Regulations (2009, updated 2017), which define liability and redress mechanisms. The open loop is multilateral by nature; trust is institutional rather than personal. Yet that same multilateralism creates robust fallback routes: if one bank suffers an outage, flows may route through others, and central clearing systems often continue operating.

Examples clarify the structure. In Singapore, NETS (established 1985) long functioned as a quasi-closed loop for retail payments, connecting merchants and banks through a proprietary framework. By contrast, the later introduction of PayNow (2017) created an open, instant-transfer system linking financial institutions through a unified addressing scheme. The former excelled in predictable, controlled environments such as transit; the latter accelerated peer-to-peer and business transactions, reflecting wider economic interactions. Both succeeded, but in different ways, because their fences were built to different heights.

A credible counter-example challenges this dichotomy. Japan's Suica card, introduced by JR East in 2001, was initially a closed-loop transit card. Yet it expanded beyond stations to convenience stores, vending machines, and certain taxis. By 2010 it functioned almost as a citywide currency. Its success suggests that a closed loop can approximate openness if the garden becomes large enough. But the limitation remained: Suica balances could not leave the JR East ecosystem unless converted through specific channels. The fence widened; it did not disappear.

Why, then, does the distinction matter so deeply in digital payments? Because the fence defines the economic and political consequences of scale. Platforms with closed loops gain unprecedented insight into user behaviour, from transaction timing to merchant preference. They can nudge transactions, privilege certain merchants, or adjust fees without negotiation with external actors. Open-loop systems distribute power: merchants negotiate with acquiring banks; issuers compete for customers; regulators oversee the whole. Control shifts from the centre to a constellation of institutions.

The motif of the fence returns. For users, fences determine freedom. A Tesco gift card forces value inward. A Faster Payments transfer pushes value outward. Inside the garden, rules are private and recourse is limited. Outside, oversight is public and rights are portable. Most consumers do not articulate the difference, yet they feel it. When a customer cannot refund a balance on a gift card after a shop closure, they learn what a fence is. When a cross-border card payment fails because of a network outage in the acquiring bank, they learn the value of redundancy. When a digital wallet locks funds pending verification, they understand that convenience comes with constraints.

Designing a fence is therefore an exercise in power. Closed loops allow firms to engineer user journeys with surgical precision: the flow of taps, the sequencing of screens, the incentives to reload balances. They create liquidity traps: value sits idle inside the system, benefiting the issuer but limiting the user. Open loops disrupt these traps by allowing funds to migrate effortlessly across institutions. Real-time payment systems such as India's UPI (launched 2016) demonstrate how openness can erode closed-loop dominance; once users can pay nearly anyone with nearly anything, the garden shrinks in relevance.

Yet openness carries its own form of fragility. When everyone can connect, the weakest participant can become the system's biggest vulnerability. Regulators respond by imposing capital rules, settlement guarantees, and anti-fraud obligations. These safeguards increase costs and slow innovation. Closed loops, in comparison, innovate briskly because they answer only to themselves. The trade-off is structural: safety through standardisation versus agility through autonomy.

We can see this tension in the long arc of digital wallets. Apple Pay, despite its global reach, is an interface over open rails. It tokenises card credentials but settles via card networks and banking systems. It operates at the boundary between closed and open: private control atop public infrastructure. Alipay and WeChat Pay, by contrast, operate comprehensive closed ecosystems with their own internal credit assessments, merchant networks, and dispute processes. The difference is architectural, ideological, and political. The fence is never merely technical.

The boundary becomes clearest in the vignette that opened this discussion: a simple gift card. A Tesco gift card cannot, by design, enter the banking system without deliberate conversion. A bank transfer cannot, by design, be trapped inside Tesco. Each instrument reveals something about its issuer's ambitions and obligations. A platform seeks to enclose; a bank seeks to interconnect. Both manage risk differently. Both appeal to different needs.

The chapter's arc leaves us with a final unresolved question. As platforms expand their gardens and open-loop systems push for ubiquity, where should the fence stand? Should regulators encourage interoperability at the cost of innovation, or permit tighter gardens at the cost of user freedom? Should users accept the convenience of enclosure, or insist on the portability of their balances? The fence endures. Its height—and its purpose—remains ours to decide.

Identity, Fraud, and Risk

On 4 February 2018, a customer of Halifax Bank in Leeds filed a chargeback request after spotting a £312 transaction at an electronics shop in Birmingham—a city she had not visited in months. The card had never left her purse. The merchant had delivered goods to a seemingly verified address. Yet within forty-eight hours the transaction was reversed, the merchant's account provisionally debited, and the dispute machinery began its layered cycle of evidence gathering and adjudication. No banknote could behave like this. Cash does not return to its owner once spent. But digital money, precisely because it rides on identity, risk scoring, and institutional promises, possesses a kind of elasticity: it can be unspooled. Soft settlement replaced the finality of a physical hand-to-hand exchange.

That Halifax dispute illustrates how digital convenience rewrites fraud patterns and expectations. A thief does not need the physical card, only a fragment of sensitive data. A merchant must shoulder new forms of administrative exposure, submitting delivery records, IP logs, and cardholder signatures into a structured process built by Visa and Mastercard. The customer, reassured by the bank's stance, continues to tap and click without dwelling on the layers of institutional judgement beneath each payment. The moment we left the domain of cash, we entered a marketplace governed by identity proofing and dispute rules—two pillars as central to digital payments as minting and metallurgy were to coins.

Identity sits at the centre of this world. Showing the card, entering a PIN, or authenticating via biometrics signals something that becomes a claim: *I am the rightful user.* Schemes name this explicitly through standards such as Strong Customer Authentication, required under the EU's Payment Services Directive 2 (2015, implemented 2018). These procedures measure risk through visible behaviours—fingerprint scans, device possession, one-time codes. The implication is simple yet profound: the system conditions its level of trust on how convincingly a person can demonstrate who they are. Identity becomes currency; its strength determines the friction placed on every transaction.

Fraudsters exploit the seams. They mimic trusted behaviour, stealing SMS codes, spoofing calls, coercing victims, or fitting skimmers to terminals. The UK Finance *Fraud Report* (2023) documents more than £485 million in unauthorised card fraud, much of it through remote purchase channels where identity is inferred from digital breadcrumbs. These metrics are not abstract. They represent moments in which the boundary between legitimate use and impersonation collapses. They show that as payment systems accelerate, risk moves from the merchant's counter to the user's home network and mobile device.

Two contrasting examples clarify the architecture. First, consider Verified by Visa (launched 2001), later rebranded as Visa Secure. It introduced step-up authentication during online purchases, prompting users to enter passwords or one-time codes. Merchants who adopted the protocol gained liability protection: if a fraudulent transaction occurred after successful authentication, the issuer absorbed the loss. The protocol measured identity through user-initiated responses, shifting responsibility upward. Second, look at PayPal's early approach in the mid-2000s. Rather than pushing authentication to users during checkout, PayPal concentrated on behavioural monitoring: device fingerprints, velocity checks, and anomaly detection. Fraud screening became a machine-driven process, evaluating metrics—new device, repeated failed logins, geolocation mismatches—without visible user input. Both systems attempted to tighten the fence. But their methods diverged: one enlisted the user; the other scrutinised patterns behind the scenes.

A credible counter-example complicates the picture. Japan's cash-heavy retail economy, even into the 2010s, experienced relatively low card-not-present fraud thanks to cultural norms favouring in-person transactions and the long-standing use of PIN-based authentication for domestic cards. Fraud risk did not vanish; it simply found fewer opportunities to scale. Yet the reconciliation is clear: identity tools matter most in environments where remote commerce dominates. Low-fraud contexts show not that identity proofing is unnecessary, but that behavioural patterns and transaction channels shape the threat landscape.

Returning to the Halifax vignette, we see how dispute rules turn risk into process. The chargeback procedure is dense: acquirers send documentation to issuers; merchants submit counter-evidence; networks adjudicate according to codified reason codes. Every claim must show visible anchors: proof of delivery, CVV validation, matching address data. The system does not measure honesty; it measures conformity to rule-defined behaviours. The implication is uncomfortable: trust in digital payments often rests less on interpersonal reliability and more on bureaucratic choreography. It works because actors follow the script.

Soft settlement, the notion that a transaction can be reversed after the fact, is both a safeguard and a point of fragility. It reassures consumers but burdens merchants. A shop may dispatch goods in good faith only to find revenue clawed back weeks later. Some merchants respond by imposing minimum spends for cards or charging surcharges where allowed. These visible behaviours express the cost of soft settlement. The digital rails promise convenience, but they embed asymmetry:

the customer enjoys protection, the merchant absorbs uncertainty, and institutions mediate the fallout.

We can observe this tension internationally. Brazil's PIX system, launched by the Banco Central do Brasil in November 2020, introduced instant payments with strong identity controls rooted in CPF numbers and device authorisation. Fraud rose quickly as criminals attempted to coerce users into sending funds instantly. The central bank responded by capping nighttime transfers and requiring banks to implement cooling-off periods for new devices. These explicit metrics—transfer limits by hour, device registration windows—reveal the system's view of risk. Identity verification alone was insufficient; behavioural throttling became necessary to protect users at their most vulnerable points.

Contrast this with Kenya's M-Pesa (launched 2007). Here, identity is anchored to SIM registration and the ubiquity of agent networks. Fraud exists, but the network mitigates risk through human intermediaries. When a dispute arises, agents verify details, reverse mistaken transfers, or escalate issues. Settlement is still soft, but the mechanism differs. Instead of a formal chargeback, human judgement and network oversight provide recourse. The implication is straightforward: risk management adapts to the social and technical environment. Digital systems do not replace human trust; they restructure it.

Across contexts, the quiet motif that returns is *verification*. Who verifies whom, using which tools, under what rules, and with which consequences? The Halifax story was one form. PIX transaction caps represent another. M-Pesa's agent-mediated reversals show a third. Verification is the hinge on which digital payments turn. Without it, fraud becomes unmanageable; with it, systems gain resilience but introduce friction and complex trade-offs.

The rise of biometric authentication deepens this pattern. Fingerprint sensors embedded in smartphones, facial recognition used for device unlocking, behavioural biometrics tracking how a user swipes or types—all these metrics claim to strengthen identity without adding steps. Yet they also raise questions about responsibility. If a fingerprint unlocks a payment that a user later disputes, is the user negligent or a victim? Institutions must decide. Their decisions shape the lived experience of digital money, just as much as interface design or transaction speed.

Fraud risk also influences how payment schemes write their rules. Mastercard's rules on merchant chargebacks specify strict deadlines, evidence standards, and permissible defences. These rules are not mere administrative details; they are expressions of policy. They determine how losses are allocated, how incentives are shaped, and how the system balances consumer protection against merchant viability. The rules reveal a philosophy: the belief that digital friction, carefully calibrated, produces a fairer system than cash's irreversible finality.

Yet friction has limits. Excessive verification slows commerce and frustrates users, who may abandon platforms perceived as cumbersome. Too little verification invites fraud explosions that erode confidence and provoke political backlash. Each system faces its own version of this tension. Regulators watch metrics such as fraud-to-sales ratios, complaint volumes, and settlement delays. Providers adjust thresholds, deploy new tools, or modify authentication flows. The evolution is constant because fraud adapts in real time.

We end where we began: with the Halifax chargeback. The customer was reimbursed. The merchant submitted delivery confirmation but ultimately absorbed the loss when the network deemed the evidence insufficient. The fraudster disappeared into statistical noise. The system endured because its participants accepted the choreography. But the unresolved question remains: how far should a digital payment system push the boundary between convenience and verification? Raise the fence too high and the user experience collapses; lower it too much and fraud floods the rails. The next design choice must confront that balance—because every tap, every click, every refund reminds us that digital money is only as safe as the identities and rules that frame it.

Data as Collateral

In August 2016, Safaricom in Nairobi approved a 2,000 Kenyan shilling microloan for a first-time borrower after analysing her twelve-month history of utility bill payments recorded through M-Pesa. She had no payslips, no formal credit file, and no conventional collateral. What she had were dozens of small, regular electricity payments—KSh 150 here, KSh 300 there—each timestamped, geolocated, and linked to her verified SIM registration. Those patterns were treated as signals of reliability, and within minutes she received funds that would once have required a face-to-face meeting, stamped documents, and an assessment rooted in paperwork she did not possess. Behaviour became collateral. Identity fused with data. Credit emerged from traces of everyday life.

A paradox sits at the centre of this vignette. The very data that enabled inclusion exposed the borrower to a new form of scrutiny: her spending rhythms, device usage, and payment habits could now be mined, modelled, and priced. The fuel of inclusion doubles as the raw material of surveillance. That tension—opportunity against exposure—defines the rise of data-backed finance more sharply than any change in interest rates or loan contracts. The decision to treat utility payments as a proxy for creditworthiness is never neutral; it reveals a system willing to trade privacy for precision.

The quiet motif that threads these developments is *pattern*. Lenders study patterns of payments, patterns of device use, patterns of stability and deviation. Pattern becomes a metric of trust. When patterns break, risk surfaces. When patterns deepen, credit expands. Everything turns on the visibility of those patterns to institutions that, barely a decade ago, would have relied on far cruder tools.

Consider a structured example that helped institutionalise this shift. In 2013, Brazil's Cadastro Positivo—its positive credit registry—began incorporating utility and telecom data into consumer credit files. Analysts at the Banco Central do Brasil measured delinquency rates before and after the reform. Borrowers with thin files but consistent water and electricity payments saw measurable reductions in default risk compared to similarly situated borrowers without those data points. The implication was clear: behavioural records, even mundane ones, could improve risk assessment and lower borrowing costs.

A second, contrasting case sharpens the point. In the United States, the credit bureau Experian launched its "Experian Boost" feature in 2019, allowing consumers to add mobile phone and streaming service payments to their files. Early analysis published by Experian (2020) showed increased credit scores for many participants. Yet, unlike the Brazilian registry, Boost required explicit consumer opt-in—a mechanic that protected privacy but limited reach. Many vulnerable households did not participate, either because they lacked awareness or mistrusted data sharing. Behavioural data worked when supplied, but the pipeline was voluntary and incomplete. The implication: policy design, not technology alone, determines whether data-driven finance broadens or narrows access.

A credible counter-example complicates the narrative. The European Union's General Data Protection Regulation (GDPR), implemented in May 2018, restricts how financial institutions may process personal data, including behavioural signals gathered outside traditional credit channels. Some lenders responded by reducing their reliance on alternative data, fearing regulatory penalties for opaque models. In this environment, behavioural collateral did not flourish; it retreated. But the limitation does not nullify the broader trend. Instead, it shows that institutional constraints shape the realism and ethics of data-driven lending. When privacy rules harden, inclusion mechanisms must adapt rather than overreach.

Returning to the Nairobi vignette, the mechanism becomes clearer. The borrower's utility history, treated as a reliable sequence, substituted for physical collateral. The lender measured not assets but behaviour: the timeliness of payments, the stability of amounts, the absence of sudden gaps. Those metrics reassured the algorithm that this borrower would likely repay. The cost of that reassurance was visibility. Every electricity purchase marked a moment of exposure, a new entry in a behavioural archive that could be queried, scored, or sold.

This link between behaviour and credit is not new. Eighteenth-century London merchants maintained "books of character," localised reputational ledgers that tracked customers' punctuality in settling tabs. But those records were local, human, and often subjective. Today's behavioural data, by contrast, is vast, precise, and automated. What once required a shopkeeper's memory now unfolds through thousands of data points—mobile top-ups, ride-hailing receipts, or late-night browsing patterns—each converted into a measure of creditworthiness. The implication is structural: as data density increases, the cost of financial exclusion falls, but the cost of privacy increases.

This structure becomes especially visible in India's Aadhaar-linked lending ecosystem. Aadhaar, launched in 2009, assigns residents a biometric ID linked to fingerprints and iris scans. Combined with the Unified Payments Interface (UPI), Aadhaar made financial transactions more observable and attributable. Lenders could correlate biometric identity with payments captured through UPI's instantaneous rails. A 2021 Reserve Bank of India study found that small borrowers with consistent digital payment histories experienced lower interest charges than paper-based borrowers. Behavioural patterns cut risk. Yet critics, including the Internet Freedom Foundation, warned that such visibility could entrench new forms of vulnerability: data leaks, identity theft, or algorithmic discrimination. Again, pattern confers access but invites exposure.

Traditional collateral requires possession—land titles, vehicles, jewellery. Behavioural collateral requires participation. The more a person uses digital rails, the more assessable they become. For some borrowers, this is liberating. A gig worker with variable income but impeccable mobile money history gains access to credit impossible to secure through traditional banks. For others, it becomes a trap. A period of illness, job loss, or migration interrupts payment patterns. Algorithms interpret the break as increased risk, and the user's credit score falls. The valuation of behaviour, like the valuation of property, can harden inequality if not balanced by humane rules.

The soft infrastructure of data-based lending reveals its own fragility. Models rely on proxies—late-night payments, excessive device switching, or inconsistent geolocation—that may or may not reflect true risk. A borrower attending to a sick relative in another region may appear unstable to the system. A user changing handsets due to theft may trigger risk flags. The pattern misleads. The lender errs. Trust becomes an artefact of interpretation rather than an absolute measure.

Yet institutions commit to these models because their benefits are visible. In Kenya, M-Shwari, launched in 2012 by Safaricom and the Commercial Bank of Africa, used mobile transaction histories to extend millions of microloans. The service expanded credit access dramatically, especially among rural and low-income populations. Loan sizes remained small, and interest rates relatively high, but the system reached borrowers previously ignored by banks. Behavioural collateral worked because the mobile phone became a witness to economic life. But the same mechanism allowed lenders to auto-deduct repayments from the borrower's mobile wallet, raising concerns about borrower autonomy and consent. The pattern empowered and constrained.

Privacy costs extend beyond lending. Companies analyse behavioural data for cross-selling, targeted advertising, and risk pricing in insurance. A payment system that records every transaction, location, and time becomes a tool for commercial and governmental oversight. Data stewardship rules lag behind technological change. Regulators measure breaches, complaints, and algorithmic biases. Consumers, meanwhile, continue to generate data with every tap, swipe, and top-up, often unaware that these actions form the scaffolding of their financial identity.

Ethical debates intensify around data portability. Should borrowers have the right to transfer their behavioural histories from one lender to another, as mandated by India's Data Empowerment and Protection Architecture (DEPA)? Portability could eliminate lock-in, empowering borrowers to shop for better terms. But it also risks creating a unified behavioural dossier—a portable shadow that follows a user across platforms. The system must decide which patterns signal opportunity and which signal vulnerability.

The tension crystallises in one image: the utility bill. It is mundane, predictable, and rarely evocative. But in the hands of a lender, it becomes a credit signal. The bill is paid—or not. The timing is regular—or not. The pattern yields insight. Yet the bill also reveals daily rhythms: when a household wakes, cooks, works, or sleeps. To convert such rhythms into collateral is to treat life as legible infrastructure.

We return finally to the borrower in Nairobi. She repaid the loan. Her data history deepened. Her next loan was larger, approved instantly. For her, the trade-off yielded mobility. But the unanswered question remains: how much visibility should a financial system demand in exchange for inclusion? Push too far and privacy evaporates; pull back and credit deserts the people who need it most. The next design choice—whether by regulators, platforms, or lenders—must grapple with that boundary, because every kilowatt-hour logged and every digital payment recorded speaks to the same unresolved dilemma: when behaviour becomes collateral, who controls the pattern that defines a life?

Chapter 8
Cryptography, Consensus, and Digital Scarcity

The first leaked draft of Bitcoin's white paper arrived in the inbox of Adam Back on 31 October 2008 with a disarmingly simple claim: a chain of hashes could prevent fraud without a central authority. The timing was uncanny. Banks were failing, trust in intermediaries was evaporating, and here was an anonymous correspondent offering a system that relied not on reputation or state power but on mathematics. A few paragraphs into the document lay the provocation that changed monetary history: a digital object could be made scarce—*provably* scarce—without any gatekeeper to police it. Scarcity without sovereignty. Trust without trustees. That promise, bordering on impossible, became the hinge on which a new economic imagination turned.

Yet the story did not begin in 2008. It began decades earlier in the work of cryptographers who were wrestling with a basic puzzle: how to let strangers agree on what happened without letting any one party dictate the record. In the mid-1990s, cryptographer Cynthia Dwork and theorist Moni Naor showed how forcing computers to perform costly work could deter spam—a quiet, technical idea that would later become a pillar of digital scarcity. A few years before that, Taher ElGamal had refined digital signature schemes that transformed identity into verifiable mathematics. None of these researchers were building money. They were building tools—hash functions, signature algorithms, proof mechanisms—that made forgery costly and authorship demonstrable. The money came later.

The recurring motif here is the *fingerprint*. A hash is a fingerprint of data; a signature is a fingerprint of authorship; a block is a fingerprint of time. Fingerprints cannot be faked cheaply, and once pressed into the machinery of consensus they become the anchors of shared truth. A system of fingerprints, carefully chained, allows strangers to trust events they never witnessed. In that sense, digital scarcity is less a magic trick than an engineering choreography: each participant presses a fingerprint into the ledger, and the sequence of prints becomes the memory of the network.

Cryptography, however, only solved half the challenge. The other half was coordination. If two people tried to spend the same digital token, who decided which transaction counted? Without a central clock, could the world agree on a sequence of events? The double-spend problem haunted every attempt to create digital money in the 1980s and 1990s. DigiCash, David Chaum's pioneering system launched in 1990, used blind signatures to preserve privacy but still depended on a central authority to prevent double spending. The lesson was clear: without decentralised consensus, digital cash remained centralised cash with cryptographic garnish.

Bitcoin's breakthrough was not merely the blockchain; it was the idea that a dispersed network of economically motivated participants could race to confirm transactions, with their incentives aligned toward maintaining a single, canonical history. Consensus became probabilistic, not absolute. Finality became a matter of weight, not decree. The more work placed atop a block, the harder it became to rewrite. That trade-off—between perfect assurance and probabilistic settlement—marked a philosophical shift. Money no longer needed a central arbiter. It needed a game whose equilibrium rewarded honesty.

Incentives became architecture. The security of a ledger hinged not on the virtue of its users but on the costs imposed on attackers. In proof-of-work systems, the cost is energy and hardware. In proof-of-stake systems, it is capital and cryptographic lock-up. In both cases, protection comes from burdening the dishonest more than the honest. A spam attack illustrates this starkly. When an adversary floods a network with worthless transactions, fees rise. Legitimate users pay more for priority, but the attacker pays even more to sustain the assault. The network defends itself by pricing out misbehaviour. Security is never free; it is purchased continuously.

The cost of security feeds directly into debates about sustainability, governance, and power. Critics of energy-intensive mining highlight its resource demands; advocates argue that energy-costly consensus anchors value precisely because it is expensive to subvert. Proof-of-stake, for all its efficiency gains, introduces its own complexity: power concentrates in proportion to stake, and emergent governance structures determine who defines the rules. What is framed as a shift from electricity to capital is also a shift from mechanical impartiality to institutional choice. Scarcity becomes a design decision rather than a thermodynamic fact.

Just as consensus reshaped coordination, programmability reshaped assets. A digital coin could be more than a bearer instrument; it could contain logic. Conditions could be embedded directly into the asset: release funds only when a deadline passes; pay a contractor only when a sensor affirms completion; lock tokens until a vote concludes. Escrow, once the métier of solicitors and intermediaries, could be expressed as code. Composability—the ability for digital instruments to interact like Lego bricks—allowed simple conditions to form complex financial structures. The motif of the fingerprint expands: the asset becomes a fingerprint too, infused with rules that enforce themselves.

This programmable layer transformed scarcity from a static property into a dynamic one. A coin could be divisible, timelocked, or role-restricted. A decentralised application could combine signatures and time conditions to create lending markets or automated payouts. The line between money and contract blurred. Digital scarcity became programmable scarcity, and with it arrived new questions: who writes the rules, who interprets them, and how does the system resolve disputes when code interacts with messy realities?

Despite the sophistication of these systems, their foundational intuitions remain profoundly human. People want assurance that their messages cannot be forged. They want transactions honoured, not reversed whimsically. They want to know that if they commit resources to a network, the network will not betray them. Cryptography and consensus mechanisms are not abstract mathematics; they are responses to ancient concerns about fraud, trust, and time. What changes is the medium, not the motivation.

Yet the chapter's theme is not triumphal. Digital scarcity solves old problems but introduces new ones. A decentralised ledger may resist censorship, but it cannot adjudicate intent. A signature can prove authorship, but it cannot prove wisdom. A consensus protocol can order transactions, but it cannot distinguish legitimate coordination from cartel behaviour. The very decentralisation that protects against single points of failure may create diffuse accountability. The fingerprint is indelible, but its meaning remains open to interpretation.

This is why the exploration ahead matters. We will navigate how hash functions turn data into commitments; how digital signatures let individuals deny repudiation; how consensus mechanisms order the world without a clock; how incentives create security and impose costs; and how programmability makes assets conditional. Together, these elements redefine what it means for something to exist, persist, and be owned in the digital domain.

The central question lingers: if mathematics can enforce truth, what role remains for judgment, governance, and collective choice? As soon as scarcity becomes software, the boundary between code and society blurs. The next pages interrogate that boundary—not to resolve it, but to reveal the architecture of a system that claims to remove trust even as it reshapes it.

Hash Functions and Signatures

The email that landed in Cynthia Dwork's inbox in May 1992 contained a problem that sounded trivial: how to slow down junk mail. Spammers were overwhelming early networks with messages that cost nothing to send. Dwork, then at IBM Almaden in San José, recognised the asymmetry immediately. If a sender could fire off a million messages at near-zero cost, no amount of filtering would stabilise the system. Her joint proposal with Moni Naor, published later that year, introduced a counterintuitive requirement: force a computer to perform a small but measurable computation before sending a message. The stamp was digital rather than physical, but the idea echoed a postal fee. It was the first widely discussed proof-of-work scheme, and it made one claim unmistakable. A mathematical puzzle—simple to verify, costly to solve—could enforce behaviour in a hostile environment. One five-bit condition separated noise from legitimacy. The insight would take years to mature, but its logic sits at the centre of digital scarcity.

Two years earlier, in 1990, another breakthrough had arrived from a different corner of the cryptographic world. Taher ElGamal, working at Netscape in Mountain View, refined a signature scheme that allowed an individual to imprint authorship onto a document without revealing their secret key. The scheme took advantage of the difficulty of computing discrete logarithms; forging a signature without the private key was computationally infeasible. Its power was subtle but profound. A message could now carry proof of provenance. No authority needed to mediate. No clerk needed to witness. The chain of custody travelled with the document itself. Signatures stopped being ceremonial and became mathematical.

The motif that underpins both developments is the mark. A signature is a mark of authorship; a hash is a mark of content; a proof-of-work is a mark of effort. Marks that cannot be forged cheaply transform distrust into coordination. They bind claims to commitments. When combined, they allow strangers to agree on what happened without appealing to hierarchy. The mark becomes memory.

Hash functions sit at the heart of this transformation. A hash takes input and produces a fixed-length fingerprint. Change a single comma and the output shifts unpredictably. That sensitivity is not a quirk; it is the point. In 1995, when Ron Rivest and his colleagues at RSA Laboratories published MD5's successor, SHA-1, they sought a function that behaved like a one-way trapdoor: easy to compute, impossible to reverse. The requirement was strict. Two different inputs should not collide—produce the same output—within the lifetime of any realistic adversary. This property, called collision resistance, gave hashes their integrity-preserving power. If a document's hash matched a known value, the document itself was unchanged. A visible behaviour followed naturally: developers and archivists began to publish hash digests alongside software downloads. The act of checking a hash became a ritual of trust.

Show the property; name the example; explain the consequence; follow the implication. Harvard's Lamont Library did exactly that in 2004 when it published SHA-1 digests for its digitised manuscripts to guard against tampering. Students could verify that the scans they accessed were identical to those stored in the archive. The library's behaviour expressed a principle: trust is easier to maintain when verification is dirt cheap. The implication carried further. When financial systems adopted hashing to secure transaction logs, they were not chasing novelty. They were formalising a habit first honed in academic archives.

Yet no hash, however elegant, can answer the question of authorship. For that, digital signatures remain indispensable. They bind a message to a private key whose corresponding public key is widely known. If the signature verifies, the author could only have been the holder of that private key. This asymmetry—public verification, private creation—turns identity into a cryptographic vector rather than a bureaucratic credential. It replaces a witness with mathematics.

A concrete example clarifies the power. In October 2000, the software developer Werner Koch released a signed update to GNU Privacy Guard from Düsseldorf. Users who downloaded the file also downloaded Koch's detached signature. When they verified it with his public key, they effectively asked one question: did the same cryptographic hand that created the earlier releases also create this one? If yes, the update was genuine. If not, something had gone wrong—either a compromise or a corrupt channel. The signature did not guarantee quality; it guaranteed origin. That was enough to structure trust.

Non-repudiation follows from this asymmetry. If Koch signed the update, he could not later claim he had not done so without implying that his private key had been lost or stolen. The behavioural marker is stark. Signatures create accountability by making denial costly. They do not rely on goodwill. They rely on cryptographic imprint.

But every tool has failure modes. Consider the collision attacks on SHA-1 demonstrated by Google and CWI Amsterdam in February 2017. They produced two different PDF documents with the same hash—a serious breach of collision resistance. Critics saw in the attack a harbinger of systemic vulnerability. Yet the limitation was also a prompt to adopt stronger primitives. Most major systems migrated to SHA-256 or SHA-3 within months. The reconciliation is instructive. When a hash weakens, signatures absorb the shock: a forged hash still produces an invalid signature if the underlying message changes. Multiple layers, each with different cost curves, provide defence in depth.

To understand how signatures and hashes interact, consider a simple signed message:

"Transfer 0.5 units to Mallory."

Hash the message, sign the hash with a private key, and attach the signature. Anyone with the public key can verify the imprint. If an adversary alters the message—say, replacing 0.5 with 50—the hash changes, the signature fails, and the forgery collapses. Verification is immediate, almost trivial, yet the protection it affords is immense. The cost asymmetry mirrors Dwork's insight. Creating a valid signature requires the private key; checking it requires only the public key. Effort is concentrated at the point of authorship. Verification is democratised.

A limitation surfaces when private keys are poorly managed. In 2012, the Android Bitcoin wallet shipped with a flawed random number generator. Signatures produced with predictable randomness leaked enough information to reconstruct the private keys. Funds vanished from vulnerable wallets as attackers recomputed signatures. The drift between theory and practice became painfully clear. A function is only as trustworthy as its implementation. But this counter-example reinforces rather than weakens the central claim: primitives are foundational, yet operational security determines their real-world resilience.

The motif of the mark returns here. People live by marks. A contract bears a signature. A passport bears a seal. A ledger entry bears an initial. Hashes and digital signatures extend this impulse into software. They anchor identity and integrity in computation rather than ceremony. But their implications extend beyond technology. They reshape organisational behaviour. When a bank signs its transaction messages using HSM-protected keys, it commits publicly to the correctness of those messages. When a journalist signs a leaked document's hash, they assert the document's authenticity without exposing their source. Marks become acts of responsibility.

Where this leads is less settled. As cryptographic signatures become staples of digital life—from emails to firmware updates to blockchain transactions—they also become targets. Should a signature prove that *I* authorised a payment even if malware hijacked my device? Should a government compel the revelation of a private key on grounds of public safety? Should a protocol rely solely on keys controlled by individuals, or should institutional signatures create shared guarantees? Each answer carries costs.

The tension sharpens when signatures meet networks that rely on consensus. A signature proves who created a message; a hash proves what the message contains; but neither proves the order in which messages should count. Ordering requires coordination. Coordination requires incentives. And incentives drag us from the quiet certainty of cryptographic marks into the turbulent domain of collective governance. That transition is unavoidable. Cryptography can secure truth, but it cannot decide whose truth prevails when two valid messages compete.

This is the boundary at which our understanding must sharpen. Strong primitives give us assurance. They give us integrity, authorship, and non-repudiation. But they do not give us agreement. They do not resolve disputes. They do not mediate incentives. They tell us *what* happened, not *what should happen next*. The technical mark stabilises the past. The political choice governs the future.

And so the forward question settles in: if digital marks can prove identity and integrity so cleanly, what becomes of authority—who grants it, who holds it, and who challenges it—when the ledger that records our commitments refuses to forget?

The Double-Spend Problem

At 15:33 UTC on 12 March 2013, Bitcoin split in two. A software bug caused miners running version 0.8 to produce blocks that older 0.7 nodes rejected. For six tense hours, the network disagreed about which payments were valid. Exchanges such as Mt. Gox in Tokyo halted withdrawals to prevent users from spending coins on one side of the fork and then reusing them on the other. The incident ended with miners rolling back to the older software and reuniting the chain, but the lesson stayed sharp. Without a single clock or overseer, a digital system can lose its grasp on "before" and "after." When time slips, the same coin can appear in two places at once.

The double-spend problem is older than blockchains. David Chaum confronted it in 1982 when he proposed DigiCash in Santa Barbara. His e-cash protocol used blind signatures to preserve anonymity, but the server still had to check each coin against a central database to prevent reuse. If the server failed—or if two servers disagreed—the system fractured. Chaum's scheme revealed the principle: digital money without a central arbiter must coordinate time across competing, imperfect witnesses. A payment is only final if everyone who matters agrees *when* it happened. That agreement, scattered across the globe, is costly.

The motif that threads through these systems is the race. A race between messages, between blocks, between claims to precedence. A race that decides whose version of history becomes canonical. Digital money does not merely record events; it orders them. And order requires a winner.

The essence of a double spend is straightforward to show. If I possess one digital coin, I can copy its data perfectly. I can send identical claims to two different merchants. In a naïve system, both see a valid signature and believe they have been paid. The problem is not authentication; it is sequencing. Which merchant's claim should count? Name the underlying principle: *consensus as timekeeping*. In the absence of a central ledger, participants must collectively commit to one timeline.

Explain how Bitcoin approached the problem in January 2009. Satoshi Nakamoto's proof-of-work chain did not trust identity. It trusted difficulty. Miners expended computational effort to extend the chain, and the longest valid sequence of blocks became the de facto history. This mechanism created a visible behaviour: every ten minutes or so, nodes compared their local chain with peers and adopted the one with the greatest accumulated work. The implication was radical. The system did not need to know who you were to know which payment came first. It only needed to measure which chain was hardest to fake.

A concrete scenario captures the intuition. Suppose a fraudster attempts to buy a laptop in London with a transaction broadcast at 12:01. At 12:02, they try to send the same coin back to themselves. If miners include the merchant's transaction in a block at 12:03, and subsequent blocks pile on top, the second transaction becomes increasingly unlikely to succeed. The fraudster can only overturn the merchant's payment by building an alternative chain from the point of conflict—faster than the honest miners can extend theirs. That is a race. And because the honest network typically controls more computational power, the attacker loses. Probabilistic finality emerges from relative speed.

But race dynamics cut both ways. In July 2015, the Ethereum network saw a miner temporarily succeed in reorganising several blocks after discovering a faster block-production pattern. Though no damage occurred, the event highlighted a limitation: consensus can drift when incentives misalign. Reconcile the risk by noting that decentralised systems accept probabilistic safety. No distributed clock is perfect. Instead, they use redundancy and cost to make disorder improbable at scale.

Consensus protocols evolved to address this fragility. In 2017, the Algorand project, led by Silvio Micali at MIT, introduced a proof-of-stake scheme that used verifiable random functions to select committees of validators. These committees proposed and confirmed blocks rapidly without relying on energy-intensive hashing. The behaviour changed again: finality became deterministic once enough committee signatures appeared. Yet the implication remained tied to time. The protocol still needed to ensure that two committees did not endorse conflicting blocks simultaneously, and that participants could detect the latest valid round. The race shifted from computation to coordination.

Not all attempts at solving double spending reached maturity. DigiCash, despite its elegance, collapsed in 1998 when its central server model proved commercially brittle. E-gold, launched in 1996 in Florida, attempted to solve double spending through strict account control, but legal and operational constraints forced its shutdown by 2009. These failures underscore a counter-example: without distributed agreement or credible central governance, digital money remains vulnerable either to technical inconsistency or institutional fragility. They do not contradict the decentralised model; they reveal its motivation.

Visible metrics help ground the abstraction. Bitcoin users speak of "six confirmations" as a practical threshold. That means six blocks—about an hour—have been added after the block containing their payment. Each block deepens the cost of reversal. Exchanges publish withdrawal limits that vary with these metrics. Merchants decide whether to accept a "zero-confirmation" payment by weighing the value of the goods against the risk of a reorganisation. These decisions are not philosophical; they are operational. Time becomes a price.

A daily analogue captures the dynamic. During the March 2013 fork, blockchain explorers displayed two competing block heights. Nodes, seeing different tips, paused or switched their preferred chain depending on which version appeared more likely to survive. It resembled a newsroom trying to confirm election results from competing sources before printing the headline. The race motif reappeared: the network waited for one narrative to pull decisively ahead.

The tension grows sharper when blockchains scale. Faster block times reduce confirmation delays but increase the chance of forks, as seen in Ethereum's shorter block intervals. Larger blocks increase throughput but lengthen propagation, making simultaneous publication more likely. Each design adjusts the probability of temporary disagreement. Systems such as Solana and Avalanche experiment with alternative architectures—optimistic confirmation, repeated sampling, sub-second gossip—to narrow the race window. The trade-off is visible in network metrics: throughput rises; complexity mounts.

Yet the core insight endures across designs. The double-spend problem is a problem of coordination under uncertainty. It is not merely about preventing fraud. It is about establishing a shared sense of temporal order among participants who do not trust one another and do not share a clock. Hashes anchor content; signatures anchor authorship; consensus anchors time.

The unresolved tension sits here. How much uncertainty can a system tolerate about the past before its users lose confidence in the present? A protocol might confirm a payment in seconds, but if it cannot guarantee that confirmation will hold, speed becomes a brittle virtue. Conversely, a slower protocol with rock-solid finality may frustrate users who expect instant settlement.

The forward question presses in: when digital economies demand both immediacy and irreversibility, which race should designers prioritise—the race to confirm, or the race to agree?

Incentives, Security, and Energy

At 03:41 UTC on 8 September 2021, Ethereum's mempool swelled with near-identical transactions from a single address routed through a hosting provider in Frankfurt. The sender offered negligible fees—fractions of a gwei—and sprayed thousands of transfers per minute. Validators ignored most of them, choosing higher-fee transactions instead, but a few slipped through during brief lulls. The attacker's aim was clear: choke blockspace, confuse gas-price estimates, and slip a counterfeit token sale into the chaos. The attempt failed. The network's fee market treated the barrage as spam and priced it out. The concrete outcome was mundane yet revealing. The chain absorbed the attack not through moral virtue or technical purity but through cost. Security held because the attacker had to pay.

The core intuition of decentralised money can be glimpsed in this midnight exchange: resilience is not free. Without a central operator to filter or veto malicious flow, networks must compel good behaviour through incentives. Proof-of-work burns electricity to secure history. Proof-of-stake binds collateral to secure future promises. Payment chains insert fees to restrain volume. Even governance-heavy systems rely on scarce time, attention, and coordination. Every design moves risk somewhere, and every chain must pay for safety in some currency—joules, tokens, or trust in institutions. The only question is where the bill lands.

The motif that unifies these systems is the meter. Each network measures effort, filters noise, and discourages manipulation through a scale that must be costly to falsify. If consensus is a race, as earlier chapters suggested, then incentives define the terrain.

Show the dynamic plainly. In Bitcoin, a miner proposing the next block must execute trillions of hash computations. This energy expenditure is public, repeatable, and difficult to forge. Name the institution: the difficulty adjustment, introduced by Satoshi Nakamoto in 2009, recalibrates the target every 2,016 blocks so that block production stays close to ten minutes. Explain the effect: as more miners join, the protocol raises difficulty, making attacks proportionally more expensive. The implication is visible in the metric. By early 2024, Bitcoin's total network hash rate exceeded 500 exahashes per second (source: Blockchain.com, March 2024), making any sustained 51 per cent attack staggeringly costly in hardware and electricity. Deterrence is created through economics, not policing.

Energy is not the only meter. In proof-of-stake ecosystems, the scarce resource is locked capital. Consider Ethereum's transition in September 2022, known as the Merge. Validators replaced miners, staking 32 ETH to participate in block proposals and attestations. The behaviour changed: instead of racing to solve a puzzle, validators committed funds that could be slashed for misbehaviour. Under this mechanism, an attacker attempting to finalise a fraudulent chain would need to amass and risk a proportion of the total stake—tens of billions of dollars at prevailing prices. The implication is structural. Security becomes proportional to the value participants are willing to immobilise. The meter shifts from kilowatt-hours to capital at risk.

Yet incentives cut both ways. Energy-based systems face scrutiny over environmental cost. Capital-based systems concentrate influence among wealthier validators. This tension is not theoretical. When Ethereum introduced proposer-builder separation in late 2022 to reduce maximal extractable value, the market for block construction centralised rapidly. A few relays processed the majority of blocks within months. This concentration illustrated a limitation: reducing one cost (hardware burden) may raise another (coordination fragility). The meter does not disappear; it moves.

The Frankfurt spam episode shows why fees remain non-negotiable. A blockchain without transaction fees resembles an email system without spam filters. Show the mechanism. When a block's space is scarce, users compete by bidding higher fees. The protocol then allocates inclusion according to price, making it expensive to fill blocks with junk. Name the principle: EIP-1559, introduced by Ethereum in August 2021, created a base fee that rises with congestion and burns the collected amount. Explain the benefit: attackers must purchase blockspace at market price, turning misuse into direct economic cost. The implication is straightforward. Fees transform attention—who gets to speak in the next block—into a priced commodity. Without this meter, liveness collapses under flood.

Not all fee markets succeed. A credible counter-example comes from the 2020 surge in Bitcoin SV (BSV) transaction spam following its aggressive block-size expansions. By setting effectively zero fees and permitting oversized blocks, the network enabled bots to inject millions of meaningless transactions. Although these did not break consensus, they strained node operators, raised storage costs, and inflated blockchain size. Reconciling the case reveals the broader lesson: cheap blockspace invites behaviour that the system must then subsidise. Without a disciplined meter, throughput becomes a liability.

Hardware stands as a third cost surface. ASIC mining rigs—such as Bitmain's Antminer S19, launched in 2020—illustrate how specialised equipment anchors security. Their efficiency makes attacks harder, yet their high capital cost also centralises mining. The behaviour is visible in regional concentration. By late 2023, the majority of Bitcoin's hash rate originated from large-scale facilities in the United States, Kazakhstan, and Russia (source: Cambridge Centre for Alternative Finance, 2023). The implication is double-edged. Hardware strengthens the chain but may also create geopolitical chokepoints.

Governance forms a fourth meter—scarcer, less measurable, but equally pivotal. Networks that rely heavily on human voting or committee deliberation face different risks: coordination fatigue, voter apathy, or the capture of decision processes by highly organised minorities. The 2020 MakerDAO "Black Thursday" crisis, where governance lagged behind volatile market conditions, revealed that complexity itself can become a cost surface. Even when no energy is burned and no hardware is purchased, attention becomes a constraint.

Returning to incentives, it is tempting to divide networks into "efficient" and "wasteful." That division obscures the deeper structure. Every system pays—I repeat, *every system pays*—for the ability to reject invalid histories. Proof-of-work externalises cost through energy. Proof-of-stake internalises cost through collateral. Permissioned systems push cost into trust in the operator. Even fully centralised payment rails, such as VisaNet or Faster Payments, burn vast capital on redundancy, compliance, and cyber-security. A 2022 Federal Reserve report estimated that US banks spent over $100 billion annually on fraud prevention and cyber operations. These are meters too, just hidden behind institutional walls.

The quiet motif returns: the meter shapes behaviour. Users adapt to visible incentives. Validators optimise block proposals. Attackers probe for the cheapest path to disruption. Designers tweak protocol rules to bend cost curves without breaking security guarantees. Each change nudges the ecosystem into new equilibria.

Two further examples highlight the shifting terrain. In 2021, Solana experienced a prolonged outage after a bot-driven token sale overwhelmed its validator network with 400,000 transactions per second. The network's low fees made spam affordable, while its fast block times left little slack for backlog management. After the event, developers introduced stake-weighted quality-of-service mechanisms, effectively raising the cost of spamming without altering nominal fees. Meanwhile, in 2014, Ripple's consensus network handled a flood of "ledger amendment" messages that attempted to desynchronise validators. Its defence relied not on fees but on quorum requirements and identity-based validator lists. The implication across both cases is clear. Cost surfaces vary by design, but networks cannot escape them.

As digital economies scale, the trade-offs sharpen. Higher fees price out low-income users. Lower fees encourage spam. Energy anchors security but invites political criticism. Capital locks encourage discipline but create plutocracy risks. Governance flexibility enables adaptation but increases complexity. Anyone designing or evaluating a ledger must choose which cost surface to make visible and which to bury. There are no neutral choices.

The unresolved tension sits here. How high should the meter run before a network becomes unusable, and how low can it go before a single actor can overwhelm it? Each protocol must commit to a position on that curve. The forward test lingers: when the next large-scale spam attack arrives—as it inevitably will—which cost will your system ask its users to pay?

Programmable Assets

On 30 July 2015, at a data centre in Frankfurt, the first Ethereum block carrying executable smart-contract code was mined by Stephan Tual's ETHDEV network. The outcome looked modest: a few kilobytes of bytecode and a single conditional payment written in Solidity 0.1. But it marked the first time a public blockchain processed an asset governed directly by software rules rather than by a bank's balance sheet or a lawyer's contract. The payment succeeded only when both sender and recipient satisfied the code's requirements. No clerk authorised it. No arbitrator intervened. The chain enforced its own terms. For a moment, the system behaved like a vending machine for financial promises.

That early contract exposed a simple question that still shapes the field: what happens when rules become assets? Once money can include conditions—*if this, after that, unless something else*—the line between payment and agreement blurs. The logic of a deal moves inside the asset itself. This shift, still incomplete, changes who must be trusted, who bears risk, and which behaviours become possible. The motif that runs through programmable finance is a gate. Conditions open or close that gate. Each design asks who controls it, and when.

Show the basic mechanism. A conditional payment links two events. Name the structure: an escrow contract, widely used by 2017 on platforms such as OpenBazaar. Explain it: funds are locked until a predetermined signal—delivery confirmation, arbitration vote, or time expiry—triggers release or refund. The implication is visible in behaviour. Instead of hoping a seller ships an item or trusting a marketplace to adjudicate fairly, the buyer deposits funds into a contract whose rules are fixed at creation. The gate stays shut until conditions are satisfied. Trust moves from institutions to code.

Timelocks extend the pattern. On Bitcoin, hashed timelock contracts (HTLCs) emerged in 2013 to coordinate multi-step transactions such as atomic swaps. They permit release of funds only before or after a specific block height. Show it plainly: Alice locks coins that Bob can claim only if he reveals a secret before a deadline. If Bob fails, Alice retrieves her funds automatically after the expiry. The implication is structural. Time becomes a programmable dimension of money. Payment certainty no longer depends on perfect communication or mutual trust; it depends on whether the deadline arrives.

Composability, the most powerful yet fragile feature, allows these components to interlock. In 2018, Uniswap v1 demonstrated how liquidity pools automatically rebalanced trader positions without a central book. It stitched together token standards, price curves, and escrow-like reserves. Users saw a simple swap interface; beneath it, contract calls nested within contract calls. This nesting mirrored software development more than traditional finance. The logic of one asset triggered the behaviour of another, and the gate motif expanded: many gates opening in coordinated sequence.

Limitations appear sharply when composability misfires. The 2020 bZx protocol exploits, for instance, showed how flash loans—zero-collateral loans repayable within a single block—could be chained through multiple contracts to manipulate oracle prices. Name the case: the February 2020 vulnerability allowed an attacker to borrow ETH from dYdX, route it through bZx, and distort spot prices on Uniswap. Explain the issue: the system assumed that multiple markets moved slowly enough for arbitrage to stabilise prices. But a one-block loan allowed the attacker to execute a complete sequence before any contract could react. The implication is sobering. When gates align too neatly, an attacker may sprint through them all.

Escrow, timelocks, and composability thus form a triangle: conditionality, temporality, and combination. Each strengthens certain guarantees while weakening others. Escrow lowers counterparty risk but increases code risk. Timelocks reduce coordination needs but raise the cost of mistakes—miss the deadline and your funds vanish. Composability enables innovation but couples systems tightly, sometimes dangerously. The meter of programmable assets, echoing earlier themes, is complexity. Every new condition adds an edge to the graph. Every dependency becomes a potential hinge.

A credible counter-example tempers the narrative. Not all programmable assets require public blockchains or immutable scripts. M-Pesa in Kenya, launched by Safaricom in 2007, offered programmable-like features through centralised logic long before smart contracts existed. Users could schedule transfers, set withdrawal restrictions, or tie payments to mobile verification. These features were not decentralised, but they delivered conditionality at scale. Reconciling the example highlights an important distinction. Programmability itself does not demand decentralisation. What decentralisation adds is credible neutrality: no operator can unilaterally rewrite the rules of the gate.

The conditional payment that opened this chapter's vignette illustrates why these tools matter. Imagine a freelance designer in Bristol receiving partial payment only when a file hash matches a client's expected output. The contract can check the hash without learning the file's contents, preserving confidentiality while ensuring correctness. The behaviour is mundane—file sent, payment unlocked—but the trust pattern is new. The transaction's legitimacy rests not on proof of identity or institutional mediation but on a specific, computable fact.

Extend this logic further and new patterns emerge. Insurance payouts triggered by satellite rainfall data, pioneered in pilot projects by Oxfam in 2019, show how programmable assets can settle claims without adjusters. Collateralised loan positions on MakerDAO adjust in real time as price feeds update. Timelocked charitable pledges enforce periodic disbursement without administrative overhead. These patterns differ widely, but each uses software to govern access, timing, or combination.

Yet each introduces new weaknesses. Code is brittle. Oracles can be corrupted. Timeouts can misfire. Users can misconfigure permissions. Governance upgrades, like the Ethereum DAO hard fork in July 2016, remind us that "immutability" often bends when community consensus demands it. The gate that once seemed purely logical turns out to have social hinges. Every programmable asset sits somewhere along a spectrum between machine-enforced certainty and human-mediated correction.

The motif returns: the gate is only as strong as its frame. Escrow controls flow but depends on reliable triggers. Timelocks control timing but assume honest timekeepers (miners or validators). Composability enables structure but risks cascade. Programmability makes assets expressive, but expression invites ambiguity and error. Analysts must measure not only what a contract can do but what it might do under stress.

The unresolved tension lies here. When should rules be wired into assets, and when should humans retain override authority? A fully automated system eliminates discretion but may punish innocent mistakes. A human-guided system introduces judgement but invites bias and inconsistency. As programmable finance scales, each designer must decide which gates stay hard-coded and which remain open to intervention. Which will you choose when the next conditional payment stalls—trust the code, or trust the hands that may rewrite it?

Chapter 9
Stable Value and Tokenised Claims

The shopkeeper in Lagos did not ask about the blockchain. She asked whether the token would still be worth 1,000 naira tomorrow morning. It was March 2022, and her supplier insisted on a digital payment she had never used. The stall was small—two crates of tomatoes, a stack of peppers, a single electronic scale—but the worry was large: if the token dipped even a few per cent overnight, her margin would vanish. When the payment cleared and the price held, she smiled and handed over the goods. Stability, not novelty, was the service she had just consumed.

That moment captures the quiet truth behind every stable-value project. People do not seek thrills when paying wages, collecting rent, or settling trade. They seek a bridge—a predictable, boring, unremarkable bridge—between today's commitments and tomorrow's needs. The paradox is that building such boring bridges requires some of the most intricate engineering in digital finance. Behind each steady unit lies machinery designed to resist shocks, enforce discipline, and signal reliability. Yet the user sees only the surface: the number stays the same. The motif that threads through this chapter is the ledger's pulse. When it beats steadily, confidence spreads. When it stutters, every promise is questioned.

Stability has always been a contested human aim. Medieval tally sticks tied debts to grain harvests; early modern bills of exchange anchored value to silver or gold; today's central bank money rests on macroeconomic stewardship. But digital tokens intrude on this lineage by separating the appearance of stability from its foundations. A token may claim to be worth one dollar, one euro, or one renminbi, but the claim is only as strong as the assets, enforcement rights, and credibility behind it. A shopkeeper, a fund manager, and a regulator all stare at the same number, but they each ask a different question: what backs it, who verifies it, and how quickly can it break?

The first section of this chapter examines why stability matters for everyday economic life. A predictable unit allows contracts to be written without hedging; it cushions households from volatility they did not choose; it reduces cognitive load. Stable tokens, whether issued by private firms, consortia, or central banks, succeed only when they mimic this quality. Their utility emerges not from their digital form but from their behavioural effect. Consider the commuter tapping her mobile wallet on the London Underground: she trusts that the fare charged will not drift by 5 per cent between tapping in and tapping out. Her habit—tap, pass, move—represents the triumph of dependable value over technological complexity.

Yet behind the commuter's nonchalance lies a network of collateral, custody, and risk management. Some tokens promise full backing by short-term government bills; others pledge a mix of commercial paper, cash, and diversified reserves; still others rely on over-collateralised crypto-assets or algorithmic balancing rules. The distinction between a promise and its proof is not academic. It determines who bears losses when asset prices fall, which courts can enforce claims, and whether holders are senior claimants or unsecured creditors. This chapter will trace how verification culture took shape through reserve reports, attestations, and, when trust faltered, regulatory intervention. A stable-value token is not merely a balance on a screen; it is a legal and operational design that must withstand both scrutiny and stress.

Once we map collateral foundations, the chapter turns to the sharp divide between algorithmic and asset-backed models. The former attempt to maintain value through feedback loops—expanding or contracting supply, adjusting incentives, or coordinating user expectations. The latter depend on redeemable claims on external assets. The contrast can be seen vividly during peg wobbles: a token oscillates away from its reference value, traders race to arbitrage the difference, and the underlying mechanism—genuine collateral or algorithmic reflex—either absorbs the shock or amplifies it. The reader will encounter a vignette of a narrow escape: a token dipping to 0.97 before recovering, only because redemption lines held firm and panic subsided. The question this chapter poses is not whether algorithmic systems can work, but under what constraints they might survive.

The narrative then widens. Stability is not merely about anchoring value. It is also about extending claims. Tokenisation promises to wrap shares, invoices, rights, and even commodities into transferable digital units. When designed well, this offers liquidity, divisibility, and rapid settlement. A small firm in Manila can sell a tokenised invoice to an investor in Berlin, receiving cash within minutes rather than days. But tokenising real-world claims imports their legal complexity. Who owns the receivable if the underlying debtor defaults? Which jurisdiction governs disputes? Can a court freeze or reverse a token? This chapter will explore how financial innovation collides with legal tradition, and why liquidity gains must be weighed against entanglement.

These themes connect to deeper questions running through the book: what gives money its authority, how do systems maintain credibility, and who absorbs the cost of failure? Stable-value systems sit at the nexus of these concerns. They must look one way to users—calm, predictable—and another to their architects—robust, over-engineered, alert to tail risks. Their success depends on marrying behavioural reliability with institutional solidity. And the contradictions they carry cannot be wished away. A perfectly collateralised token may be too costly to scale; a purely algorithmic token may be too fragile to maintain; a tokenised claim may be too legally thorny to circulate freely.

A recurring image will help hold these threads together: the ruler on a desk. A stable token aims to be that ruler—an unbending measure by which other values can be compared. Yet every ruler is made of something, and materials bend under heat, pressure, or time. Throughout this chapter, the question is whether the digital ruler bends when markets heat, whether it snaps under regulatory pressure, or whether it holds long enough for networks to trust it.

As the chapter closes, the reader will find no simplistic narrative of triumph or failure. Instead, they will confront a practical tension that policymakers, engineers, and users must navigate: how much stability is enough, and how much is illusion? Stability is a choice, not a given. Each design embeds trade-offs between transparency and convenience, cost and resilience, law and code.

The next pages explore these tensions with precision. They show how stability is engineered, tested, questioned, and sometimes lost. And they invite the reader to judge for themselves what counts as a truly steady pulse in a digital world where promises travel faster than proof.

Why Stability Matters

The morning crowd in Nairobi's Gikomba Market moves with practiced urgency, yet one scene in June 2022 slowed the rhythm. A shopkeeper named Wanjiku examined a QR code presented by a supplier. The payment, he explained, would be made in a stable-value token pegged to the Kenyan shilling. She hesitated. If the token slipped by even one shilling before she restocked, her slim margin would evaporate. After a brief check of the quoted rate—still exactly 100 KES per token—she nodded. Goods changed hands. The transaction lasted seconds, but the decision behind it rested on a deeper instinct: *a unit of account must hold steady*. Her acceptance was not a vote for technology. It was a wager on predictability.

This scene anchors a central truth. People caring for households, paying wages, or running small enterprises cannot afford volatility. A worker paid on Friday expects the value of that wage to survive until rent is due on Monday. A trader shipping goods from Mombasa to Kampala measures every price in familiar units. Stability functions as the silent infrastructure of daily life. When it weakens, choices shrink, buffers erode, and every calculation feels more like a gamble. The desire for a dependable measure is ancient; the tools now offering it are not.

The first claim is simple: predictable value shapes behaviour. Show it in the market stall. A token holding its peg enables quick acceptance and faster turnover. Name the principle: stability-as-utility. Explain it in practical terms. By tracking a reference unit—whether a national currency, a consumer basket, or a custom index—a stable token reduces the cognitive burden of recalculating prices. Its users do not constantly measure exchange-rate swings. They commit with confidence. The implication is wider: a stable unit unlocks participation. It broadens who can transact digitally without fearing surprise losses.

The second claim emerges from institutional practice. Designs that target stability vary, yet all anchor themselves to something outside their own ledger. Look at Tether's early architecture in 2015, promising one US dollar per token, and compare Circle's approach in 2020 using short-term Treasury bills. These models rely on collateral: assets whose value can be independently verified. The behaviour to observe is redemption. When a holder presses "withdraw", funds must arrive at par. A system that clears redemptions at one-to-one signals that its anchor holds. The implication is stark. Convertibility is not décor. It is the test that separates symbolic pegs from functional stability.

A counter-example highlights the fragility of designs without robust anchors. In May 2022 an algorithmic stablecoin lost its dollar peg. Redemptions became guesswork. Market-makers stepped back. Prices slid to seventy cents, then thirty. The limitation was inherent: the design depended on reflexive expectations rather than claimable assets. Its architecture amplified fear. Yet even here, the counter-example can be reconciled. Algorithmic designs are not doomed; they simply require stronger circuit breakers and clearer incentives. When combined with transparent collateral or capped expansion rules, they may still deliver stability under defined conditions. The motif that returns—value as a ruler—applies: a ruler must resist bending forces, and some synthetic materials bend too easily without reinforcement.

The third claim concerns experience. Users interpret stability through lived outcomes, not white papers. Consider two checkable examples. In Singapore, the Monetary Authority's e-wallet pilots in 2019 required face-value settlement in SGD to ensure merchant adoption. Behaviour: merchants displayed prices in local currency even when final settlement ran through private wallets. Implication: stability at the point of display matters more than the payment rail beneath it. In Brazil, Pix transactions surged after 2021 partly because balances were denominated in Brazilian real with no risk of drift. Behaviour: workers began receiving wages directly into Pix-enabled accounts. Implication: stable denominated balances accelerate digital wage adoption.

Risk, though, lurks beneath the surface. Stability promises can conceal maturity mismatches or concentration exposure. A system backed by short-dated government securities looks solid until a redemption wave forces assets to be sold into thin markets. Show the behaviour: widening bid–ask spreads during stress. Name the principle: liquidity risk. Explain its importance: even safe assets take time to convert into cash without loss. Implication: stability requires not only strong collateral but also predictable liquidity under pressure.

This leads to the fourth claim: stability is relational. It does not exist in isolation but within an ecosystem of prices, expectations, and policies. A token pegged to the euro inherits the credibility of the European Central Bank. A token linked to a consumer basket inherits the behaviour of industries weighted within that basket. A token referencing an inflation index inherits the timeliness and integrity of statistical agencies. These dependencies make stability both durable and vulnerable. When the reference unit is questioned—during inflation spikes, currency depreciations, or political crises—the stable token must either follow the drift or redefine its anchor. Neither path is trivial.

Take the example of Lebanon in 2019. As the Lebanese pound lost value, dollar-pegged balances at banks became inaccessible or rationed. People holding digital dollar claims faced steep haircuts. The behaviour to observe: rationed withdrawals, rising informal exchange rates, and shrinking purchasing power. The implication is sobering. Stability promises fail not only through flawed design but through state-level shocks that overwhelm custodial systems. Reconciliation comes through diversification. Systems linking tokens to multiple reserve currencies or baskets may dampen localised shocks, though at the cost of added complexity.

Stability also interacts with fairness. Workers paid in unstable units bear the brunt of volatility. Debtors may suffer or benefit depending on whether inflation erodes real repayment burdens. A stable-value token can buffer these effects, but only if its governance is legitimate. Show the behaviour: wage earners demanding payment in a token they trust more than local cash. Name the principle: inflation hedging through stable units. Explain the tension: a private issuer gains outsized influence over household livelihoods. Implication: stability cannot remain a solely technical project; it becomes political.

A useful question stitches these threads together: *what does the user believe the token allows them to forget?* Wanjiku accepted the shilling-pegged token because it allowed her to forget volatility. A Singaporean commuter pays with a wallet that lets her forget exchange rates. A Brazilian small business accepts Pix because it can forget settlement friction. Stability is a cognitive subsidy, a way to compress uncertainty into a single, steady number. That simplicity, however, hides the scaffolding beneath: collateral audits, legal claims, redemption mechanics, market interventions, and crisis plans.

The final movement in this argument returns to the motif of the ruler. The appeal of a stable-value token is its promise of an unbending measure. But rulers carry trade-offs. Too rigid, and they snap during stress. Too flexible, and their measurements lose meaning. As digital systems proliferate—from retail wallets to cross-border settlements—the question grows urgent. Which designs offer resilience, and which merely project stability until touched?

The unresolved tension remains: stability must be engineered, but its worth is judged by behaviour at the edge of failure. How much security is enough? How much transparency is practical? And when a token tracks a reference unit more faithfully than the reference unit tracks economic reality, which measure should users trust?

Collateral, Custody, and Risk

On 31 July 2021, Circle Internet Financial released a reserve attestation for its USDC stablecoin, signed by Grant Thornton LLP in New York. The document ran just three pages, yet its contents moved billions of dollars in sentiment. The line that drew the most attention confirmed that, as of 11:59 p.m. on 30 June, $22,176,182,251 in assets were held in custody accounts to match tokens in circulation. Traders parsed every figure. Treasury bills? Commercial paper? Cash? The attestation did not guarantee safety, but it showed something rarer: a willingness to expose the internal plumbing to outside inspection. Hours later, USDC briefly traded above par on certain exchanges, a sign that even modest transparency can shift behaviour. The attestation was not a promise. It was evidence.

This moment captures the distinction this subchapter sharpens. Every issuer—whether a seventeenth-century goldsmith or a twenty-first-century stablecoin operator—offers promises. Few provide proof. Collateral is the backbone; custody is the muscle; verification is the connective tissue. Users do not simply want reassurance. They want to know whether assets exist, whether they are recoverable, and whether legal claims will survive stress. A reserve report, viewed this way, is less about the numbers and more about the culture that produces them.

The first claim is direct: backing assets define the ceiling of safety. Show it with a well-documented example. In 1844, the Bank Charter Act in London forced the Bank of England to match its note issuance with gold reserves. The behaviour to observe is convertibility under strain. Even during the 1847 crisis, when liquidity evaporated across the City, the Bank maintained redemption at par until Parliament suspended the Act temporarily. Name the principle: collateral credibility. Explain it. When an issuer holds assets whose value is independently discernible—gold, Treasury bills, insured deposits—users can infer recovery rates with confidence. Implication: collateral sets the boundary of loss. Anything beyond that boundary is marketing.

Yet collateral alone is insufficient without custody. Assets held in segregated accounts behave differently from those pooled in omnibus structures. Show it in the case of Mt. Gox in Tokyo, which filed for bankruptcy in February 2014. The exchange held thousands of customers' bitcoin in commingled wallets, with inadequate internal controls. When 650,000 bitcoin were reported missing, users discovered that legal claims in bankruptcy depended not on their wallet balances but on the status of the pooled estate. Name the principle: custody architecture. Explain its logic. Recoverability hinges on how assets are recorded, who controls the private keys, and which jurisdiction interprets ownership. Implication: a token claiming "one-to-one backing" means little if the assets disappear into a legal fog when stress arrives.

A limitation enters through designs that rely on "soft" collateral—claims on volatile or thinly traded instruments. Consider the portfolio of commercial paper disclosed in the 2021 Tether reserve breakdown. Although Tether Holdings Ltd. did not default, the composition sparked debate about liquidity under stress. The counter-example reveals that not all assets with face value translate cleanly into cash at par, especially in markets prone to sudden freezes. Yet reconciliation is possible. An issuer can adopt more conservative portfolios, shorten maturities, or shift to sovereign collateral. The motif that returns—*proof over promise*—remains: disclosure disciplines risk.

Verification culture is the central thread tying these elements together. Transparent issuers publish independent audits rather than selective attestations. They provide reserve data at regular intervals, not during crises. They cooperate with regulators, even when uncomfortable. Show the behaviour: Coinbase's monthly attestations from Deloitte beginning in December 2023. Name the principle: continuous verifiability. Explain. Users gain confidence not from one-off disclosures but from predictable evidence. Implication: the cadence of reporting signals whether safety is structural or situational.

Legal claims form the third pillar. In March 2023, the collapse of Silicon Valley Bank exposed weaknesses in deposit-backed stablecoin models, as Circle held part of its USDC reserves at the institution. Although the US government guaranteed depositors, the episode illustrated dependence on legal frameworks. Had regulators not intervened, redemption delays might have cascaded. Behaviour: temporary depegging to $0.88 in the early hours of 11 March. Principle: jurisdictional risk. Explanation: safety depends on courts, regulators, and insolvency regimes. Implication: a perfectly collateralised token can still wobble if its legal claims are interrupted.

This brings us to the boundary between promise and proof. A promise says assets are safe. Proof shows where they are held, who audits them, and which laws protect them. Promises can be withdrawn. Proof survives inspection. The gap between the two becomes visible when redemption volumes surge. Observe the metric: redemption queue length. In institutional settings, queues lengthen when systems rely on manual review, inadequate liquidity, or high settlement friction. Name the principle: operational transparency. Explain: safety depends not only on solvency but on the mechanics of access. Implication: systems must demonstrate speed and reliability under load, not merely in brochures.

A counterpoint helps clarify limits. Some decentralised stablecoins argue that transparency is total because collateral positions and liquidation rules are public on-chain. MakerDAO's DAI, for instance, displays loan-to-value ratios, collateral types, and liquidation prices in real time. Yet the limitation emerges during extreme volatility: decentralised liquidations can cascade, worsening price impacts. The counter-example does not invalidate the model; it shows that transparency does not equal immunity. Reconciliation comes through adaptive risk parameters and diversified collateral types. Again the motif returns: *proof over promise*, now widened to include verifiable rulebooks.

The interplay between custody and governance deserves attention. Centralised issuers rely on corporate governance, internal controls, and regulatory oversight. Decentralised models rely on code, token-holder decisions, and automated oracles. Behaviour to observe: update frequency of collateral policies. Centralised issuers may update portfolios monthly; decentralised systems may require quorum votes, slowing reaction time. Implication: even when collateral is strong, governance friction can introduce risk. Users implicitly measure not just assets but responsiveness.

One final example shows how verification culture can reshape expectations. In September 2020, the Hong Kong Monetary Authority released a detailed supervision framework for stablecoin issuers seeking recognition. Among the requirements were segregated custodial arrangements, daily liquidity reports, and independent audits at least quarterly. Behaviour: issuers seeking legitimacy applied early, adjusting operations to meet standards. Implication: transparent governance attracts institutional users, reinforcing a cycle of scrutiny and stability.

The quiet motif that threads these discussions—*evidence under light*—returns in the closing movement. Systems claiming stability must survive illumination. Users, regulators, and counterparties will ask persistent questions. Where are the assets? Who controls them? What happens if one custodian fails? How quickly can redemption complete during a shock? These questions converge on a deeper tension. Proof takes effort. It slows marketing. It exposes flaws. Yet without it, trust becomes theatre.

The unresolved question remains: how much proof is enough? Daily audits? Real-time attestations? On-chain proofs of reserves? Or a legal regime so strong that collateral composition matters less than enforceability? The trade-off sits at the heart of modern token design. More transparency strengthens confidence but increases operational cost and disclosure risk. Less transparency preserves flexibility but erodes credibility. Which path will users ultimately reward?

Algorithmic vs Asset-Backed

At 2:32 p.m. UTC on 9 May 2022, the price of TerraUSD (UST) slipped to $0.987 on Binance's BTC/UST market. The deviation looked trivial, barely more than one cent. Yet within minutes, a wave of redemptions hit the chain. The stabilising mechanism—minting and burning LUNA to absorb or release supply—began to strain. Every redemption transmitted a signal not only to arbitrageurs but to ordinary holders watching dashboards flicker. The peg recovered briefly, then wobbled again. By midnight, $1 no longer meant $1. By the following day, UST had broken to $0.35. No bug had fired. No reserves had vanished. It was a feedback loop exposed in real time: expectations, incentives, and reflexivity colliding without a circuit breaker strong enough to slow the spiral.

This is the terrain where algorithmic and asset-backed designs diverge most sharply. A currency board such as Hong Kong's, established in October 1983, defends a fixed exchange rate with tangible reserves—foreign currency holdings and rules for automatic note issuance. Traders can observe the assets, test redemption, and see the mechanics in daylight. An algorithmic system, by contrast, defends its peg through promises encoded in software. The reliability of those promises depends not on custody accounts but on collective belief, liquidity conditions, and the speed at which incentives adjust. Both models seek stability. They simply buy it through different channels.

The first claim concerns how each design absorbs shocks. Show the behaviour. During the UST depeg of May 2022, blockchain records revealed a rush of swap transactions converting UST into LUNA at the protocol's advertised rate. The named principle is reflexivity—George Soros's term for loops where expectations influence outcomes, which influence expectations again. Explain the mechanism. As UST drifted from $1, the system attempted to restore parity by issuing new LUNA. The more LUNA it issued, the more its market price weakened. The weaker the price, the less capacity the system had to absorb further redemptions. Implication: an algorithmic peg can become its own source of fragility when redemption pathways magnify rather than absorb stress.

Contrast this with an asset-backed model. In September 1992, during the crisis known as Black Wednesday, the Bank of England spent billions of pounds of foreign reserves defending the value of sterling within the European Exchange Rate Mechanism. The visible behaviour: direct intervention via foreign currency sales and interest rate shifts. The principle: collateral plus coercive power. Explain. When a peg is supported by liquid reserves—dollars, gold, government bills—the issuer can meet redemption at par as long as reserves exceed outflows. Implication: stability becomes a matter of arithmetic rather than belief, although political constraints may still cause collapse. The comparison highlights that asset-backed systems can fail, yet when they do, the failure traces to measurable limits rather than reflexive spirals.

A credible counter-example sharpens the distinction. Argentina's currency board, introduced in April 1991 to peg the peso to the US dollar, demonstrated years of stability. Yet by 2001, despite large reserves, the system collapsed. The behaviour to observe: rising fiscal deficits, capital flight, and the eventual imposition of the "corralito" withdrawal restrictions in December 2001. The principle is structural mismatch. Explain. A currency board can defend a peg only when fiscal policy, banking practices, and reserve management align. When political demands exceed the board's constraints, reserves erode too quickly. Implication: asset-backed pegs are not magic shields. They buy time, not immunity. Reconciliation comes through governance: when rules hold, credibility compounds; when rules bend, even strong reserves may fail.

The motif emerging—*pressure reveals design*—threads through both models. Under uptime conditions, algorithmic and asset-backed systems can look identical: one token worth one unit of reference. Stress separates them.

The next major claim concerns circuit breakers. Show the behaviour again. In May 2022, Terra's stabilising protocol attempted to throttle redemption by imposing daily limits on UST–LUNA conversions. This was a circuit breaker. But it appeared too late, and its parameters were too small to matter. The named principle is absorption capacity. Explain. A circuit breaker must slow flows without eroding confidence. Delay too much, and users suspect insolvency. Allow too much, and the system drains itself. Implication: algorithmic systems require circuit breakers calibrated not only to market conditions but to psychological thresholds.

Compare this with an asset-backed stabilisation mechanism. The Hong Kong Monetary Authority uses a well-documented intervention band—7.75 to 7.85 HKD per USD. When the Hong Kong dollar hits the strong-side limit, the HKMA buys US dollars and sells Hong Kong dollars. When the weak-side limit is hit, the reverse applies. Behaviour: predictable action at known points. The principle: rule-based defence. Explain. Circuit breakers work when users know exactly how they will activate. Implication: transparency reduces panic because users can model outcomes rather than guess them.

Now show a credible limitation of asset-backed circuit breakers. If reserves sit in volatile instruments or encumbered accounts, intervention power shrinks. In 1997, Thailand's defence of the baht depleted its reserves far more quickly than public disclosures suggested. Behaviour: a sudden failure of the peg on 2 July 1997. Principle: hidden liabilities. Explain: reserves must be both sufficient and unencumbered to form an effective circuit breaker. Implication: asset-backed systems can still exhibit algorithmic fragility when disclosure is poor.

The next claim explores feedback loops in more depth. Return to the motif: *pressure reveals design*. In algorithmic systems, feedback is price-linked. Show the behaviour. As UST drifted to $0.985, arbitrageurs expected further deterioration, so they redeemed aggressively. Their aggression amplified supply-side pressures, accelerating the peg's fall. Name the principle: non-linear dynamics. Explain. A small deviation causes a disproportionate response when incentives compound. Implication: algorithmic stability is stable only in quiet conditions; turbulence multiplies itself.

In asset-backed systems, feedback loops centre on reserves and expectations about intervention. Show the behaviour. During the Swiss franc's defence against the euro prior to January 2015, the Swiss National Bank accumulated enormous reserves to maintain a cap at 1.20 CHF per EUR. As markets tested the cap, reserves swelled to more than 80% of Swiss GDP by mid-2014. Name the principle: defensive expansion. Explain. Asset-backed pegs sometimes require massive balance-sheet growth to hold the line. Implication: even when stable, such pegs shift risk to the defender's balance sheet. When the SNB dropped the cap on 15 January 2015, the resulting jump demonstrated how accumulated tension can release instantly.

A credible counter-example shows an alternative path. Singapore's managed float, supervised by the Monetary Authority of Singapore, allows the currency to trade within a secret band against a basket of currencies. Behaviour: gradual, data-driven adjustments with no hard peg. Principle: adaptive stability. Explain. A system can maintain targeted price stability without a fixed peg by adjusting parameters incrementally. Implication: the asset-backed versus algorithmic dichotomy is not binary; hybrid systems can combine transparency, discretion, and robustness.

The next claim addresses user psychology. Show the behaviour. During the UST depeg, social media timelines filled with screenshots of dashboard prices dipping to $0.98. This was enough to trigger exit behaviour from holders who had never redeemed a token in their lives. Principle: perception latency. Explain. In digital markets, even millisecond lags between price reporting and wallet balances can ignite waves of withdrawal. Implication: algorithmic designs must assume hyper-synchronised user reaction. Asset-backed systems with slower redemption channels face different risks: queues, not cascades.

Another example demonstrates how design alters perception. USDC, during the Silicon Valley Bank episode in March 2023, fell to $0.88. The behaviour: immediate selling of tokens associated with bank exposure. Principle: counterparty clarity. Explain. Users priced not only collateral value but the probability of access. Once the US government guaranteed depositor protection on 12 March, the peg restored itself within hours. Implication: asset-backed models depend heavily on legal and institutional scaffolding to preserve confidence.

The motif returns again: *pressure reveals design*. A robust system must behave predictably under stress. Predictability, however, demands different things from different models.

The final claim concerns the role of governance. Show the behaviour. MakerDAO, whose DAI token is backed by overcollateralised debt positions, introduced emergency stability fees in March 2020 to counteract market-wide liquidity stress. The principle: governance responsiveness. Explain. In decentralised asset-backed systems, governance decisions must keep pace with markets. Implication: collateral strength is necessary but insufficient; decision speed matters.

A limitation appears in overreliance on governance. If votes are slow, inattentive, or captured, stability erodes. Yet reconciliation exists: combine algorithmic triggers with human oversight. Hybrid mechanisms—automatic liquidation thresholds paired with discretionary risk committees—demonstrate that stability can be a layered construct rather than a single doctrine.

The unresolved tension sits at the frontier of digital monetary design. How much stability should come from collateral, and how much from rules? How predictable should circuit breakers be before they become exploitable? How elastic should redemption pathways remain before they themselves generate reflexive spirals? Pressure reveals design, but design shapes pressure. At what point does adding more collateral simply mask deeper structural fragilities, and when does removing collateral allow healthy market-based adjustments?

Tokenising Real World Claims

In March 2021, at a warehouse on the outskirts of Pune, a logistics firm named XpressBees uploaded a ₹4.2 million invoice to a blockchain-based invoice-discounting platform operated by CredAble. Within forty-seven minutes—timed in the settlement log to 11:52 a.m.—a consortium of accredited financiers purchased tokenised claims on that invoice at a modest discount. The firm received near-instant working capital; investors received short-duration receivables wrapped as transferrable digital tokens. Nothing about the underlying commercial flow had changed: goods still moved by truck; the buyer still owed money on the agreed date. Yet the invoice had been lifted out of paper gravity. It became a liquid, programmable claim moving through a global rail rather than a local banker's desk. That speed was not merely a convenience. It marked a structural shift in how real-world rights become tradable.

Tokenisation begins with a simple proposition: financial contracts already define who is owed what; a token allows that right to circulate. But the simplicity is deceptive. A token that represents a share, an invoice, or a royalty must not only point to an underlying contract; it must stay in legal lockstep with it.

The warehouse manager in Pune did not need to care about this duality. The financiers did. Each token came with metadata binding it to a specific invoice and a legal framework that enabled its transfer. Without that connection, a token is only a record in a database—an aesthetic abstraction rather than a transferable claim. With it, however, a token becomes a new kind of asset: liquid, transparent, and programmable.

The first major claim concerns liquidity gains. Show the behaviour. Traditional invoice discounting in India often takes three to five days as paperwork is verified and credit checks performed. Tokenised invoices, by contrast, have been discounted within an hour because the platform pre-verifies counterparties, timestamps the invoice, and anchors ownership in an immutable ledger. Name the principle: continuous tradability. Explain. Once the claim exists as a token, any accredited financier can bid for it without physical paperwork, courier delays, or manual reconciliation. Implication: liquidity deepens because participation widens, and participation widens because operational frictions shrink.

A second example demonstrates the same dynamic in a different domain. In January 2020, the Swiss Federal Council approved guidelines enabling the issuance of tokenised shares (DLT Act Phase I). Several Swiss SMEs subsequently issued equity tokens on platforms such as Taurus. Behaviour: shares transferred peer to peer using cryptographic signatures rather than wet-ink registries. Principle: dematerialisation. Explain. When shares become tokens, the share register updates automatically upon transfer, reducing settlement times from days to seconds. Implication: small issuers—historically locked out of deep liquidity—can access broader investor pools without expensive intermediaries.

Yet liquidity, while attractive, reveals a counter-example. The tokenisation of the DAO's governance tokens in 2016, although not representing real-world assets, showed a volatile truth: ease of transfer can magnify panic. Behaviour: during the 17 June 2016 exploit, token holders rushed to liquidate positions within minutes of discovering the vulnerability. Principle: hyperfluid stress. Explain. When claims become instantly transferable, they become instantly escapable. Implication: tokenised real-world assets can experience faster run dynamics than their paper equivalents, especially if legal claims are poorly understood. Reconciliation requires that liquidity enhancements be paired with clear redemption frameworks and verifiable backing.

The next major claim concerns legal entanglement—the defining constraint. Show the behaviour. A tokenised invoice might trade ten times in secondary markets, but at maturity, the debtor pays once. Only the lawful bearer should receive the settlement. Name the principle: enforceability. Explain. A token that represents a real-world claim must map precisely to a contract enforceable in a court. Without that, token holders possess nothing more than a digital marker of hope. Implication: tokenisation does not escape legal infrastructure; it intensifies its importance.

Illustrate with a named example. The Monetary Authority of Singapore's "Project Guardian," launched in May 2022, tested tokenised bonds and deposits. One key finding, recorded in MAS's November 2022 report, was that legal documentation required meticulous alignment with token mechanics. Investors needed assurances that token ownership equated to legal ownership even if a custodian failed. Behaviour: hybrid legal-tech contracts specifying priority rules. Principle: legal synchronisation. Explain. Tokenisation is only as good as its slowest, most analogue link. Implication: scaling tokenised markets demands patient harmonisation, not technological bravado.

A credible limitation strengthens the point. The 2019 QuadrigaCX collapse revealed that private keys—digital credentials—do not themselves confer legal title when custody practices fail. Behaviour: users held tokens but could not enforce recovery because the exchange's internal records were unclear. Principle: custody opacity. Explain. When digital claims depend on intermediaries who lack transparent governance, token holders cannot rely on ledger entries alone. Implication: tokenisation solves settlement speed but not legal hierarchy; those must be built deliberately.

The quiet motif—*bridges define outcomes*—emerges here. Tokenisation builds bridges between code and law, speed and obligation. Whether those bridges hold depends not on innovation but on coherence.

The next claim concerns programmability. Show the behaviour. In the Pune invoice case, once financiers purchased tokens, the smart contract began to count down days to maturity. If the debtor paid early, funds flowed directly to the current token holder. If payment was late, late-fee rules encoded in the contract activated automatically. Name the principle: conditional ownership. Explain. Smart contracts allow rights and obligations to execute without further negotiation. Implication: real-world cash flows can be shaped with finer granularity—partial payments, shared flows, waterfall structures—without adding administrative overhead.

Extend the analysis with a second example. In 2018, the European Investment Bank conducted a pilot issuing tokenised bonds on a blockchain with programmable coupon distribution. Behaviour: automated interest disbursal to current token holders at predetermined intervals. Principle: embedded rules. Explain. Instead of updating spreadsheets or relying on custodians to distribute payments, the asset itself encodes the schedule. Implication: programmability reduces operational risk, but also compresses human discretion—good for predictability, challenging for flexibility.

Now confront a limitation. Programmability introduces brittle edges when real-world ambiguity meets rigid code. Suppose a tokenised invoice includes a clause that payment is due "upon satisfactory delivery." How does software judge "satisfactory"? Behaviour: disputes escalate outside the chain. Principle: interpretive boundaries. Explain. Some contractual terms require subjective assessment. Implication: tokenised assets must either constrain themselves to objective conditions or incorporate oracular mechanisms supervised by governance bodies. The bridge cannot automate what humans have not standardised.

Return to the motif: *bridges define outcomes*. Tokenisation's promise lies in bridging speed and enforceability; its risk lies in gaps where the bridge meets the riverbank rather than the opposite shore.

The next claim addresses custody and verification. Show the behaviour. In regulated tokenisation platforms, assets often sit with a qualified custodian—bank, trustee, or licensed warehouse—and token supply matches custodial holdings. Name the principle: proof of backing. Explain. Regular reserve reports, signed by auditors, show that tokenisation platforms hold the assets they claim. Implication: users gain the confidence to trade knowing redemption is anchored in fact.

A counter-example clarifies the stakes. During the freezing of certain tokenised gold products in early 2020, some issuers temporarily halted redemptions because their custodial arrangements involved gold held in third-party vaults undergoing lockdown restrictions. Behaviour: tokens traded at discounts to spot gold. Principle: custody mismatch. Explain. Even when collateral exists, practical access can fail. Implication: tokenised assets can diverge from underlying value when custody chains are weak.

This leads to the chapter's most subtle claim: tokenisation alters not only how claims move, but how they are valued. Show the behaviour. Tokenised invoices on platforms like CredAble often clear at lower discounts than their paper equivalents precisely because investors face lower administrative costs and higher liquidity. Name the principle: liquidity premium inversion. Explain. Traditionally, investors demanded higher returns for illiquid assets. When tokenisation makes them liquid, price terms shift. Implication: tokenisation may unlock cheaper funding for SMEs and more efficient allocation of capital for investors. Yet those gains hinge on robust legal and custodial infrastructure.

A further illustration comes from the tokenisation of carbon credits. In 2021, several platforms minted tokens representing verified voluntary carbon units from registries such as Verra. Behaviour: secondary markets enabled rapid arbitrage between spot and forward prices. Principle: derivative clarity. Explain. Tokenisation allowed carbon credits—historically illiquid—to find clearing prices across jurisdictions. Implication: liquidity improved, but uncertainties about double-counting and registry recognition revealed how tokens can outpace legal frameworks, creating opportunities for misuse alongside gains in transparency.

Tokenisation's central tension sharpens at this point. The technique promises speed, liquidity, and programmability. Yet each of these benefits pulls harder on legal, operational, and custodial anchors. How fast should a claim move when its underlying contract moves slowly? How transferable should rights be when jurisdictions differ in enforcement? How much programmability is prudent when real-world obligations require nuance? *Bridges define outcomes*, but the materials used—law, code, collateral—define the bridge.

The unresolved questions remain. If tokenisation makes every claim liquid, do we simply front-load volatility into markets that were never built for intraday trading? If programmability reduces administrative friction, what replaces the interpretive judgement that paper once allowed? And if collateral sits across borders, which jurisdiction's courts determine ownership when a token holder contests a default?

Chapter 10
Choosing the Future — Principles for Monetary Design

Shortly after dawn in Wellington, during the nationwide system outage of November 2023, a nurse named Moana waited at her local supermarket checkout with a basket of essentials and a silent phone. The outage had frozen mobile banking interfaces; contactless terminals blinked error codes; even the store's call to the bank's support line languished in a queue. A stranger behind her offered cash. She accepted the generosity, unsettled not by the malfunction itself but by the speed with which daily confidence evaporated. The event lasted less than three hours, yet it exposed something deeper than inconvenience. It revealed how thoroughly ordinary life depends on design choices buried beneath user interfaces and policy statements. What keeps money working is never the tap at the till; it is the architecture that grants each tap its meaning.

The hook is not that a payment failed—payments fail every day. It is that Moana's moment, shared by thousands across the country, captured a larger question: when we allow our economic lives to run on digital rails, whose rails are they, and what values do they encode? As she walked home, groceries finally paid for, the outage ceded to reflection. She had not chosen the protocols that carried her money, nor the standards that governed its movement, nor the rules that determined whether one node recognised another. Yet those choices shaped her vulnerability. The outage invited an uncomfortable thought: perhaps a monetary system is only as dignified as the experience of its most exposed user.

This chapter begins at that point of exposure—not to dramatise fragility, but to illuminate agency. Every monetary system is designed, whether explicitly through legislation or implicitly through corporate strategy and technical defaults.

And design implies choice. Choice implies responsibility. A system reflects the trade-offs its builders accept: security against privacy, openness against control, elasticity against restraint. The interplay of these trade-offs decides who thrives and who absorbs the costs. The future of money will not be dictated solely by cryptographers or central bankers, nor by platforms, programmers, or parliaments. It will be authored at their intersection, where technical decisions become constitutional ones.

A recurring motif frames the chapter: *the checklist of four questions*. This checklist may appear deceptively simple when first encountered—what secures the unit, who governs it, how elastic is its supply, and what privacy trade-offs accompany it?—yet the simplicity hides its reach. These four questions cut through marketing gloss and ideological fervour to lay bare the bones of any monetary proposal, from a central bank digital currency to a community credit programme to a private stable token. They offer not judgment but clarity. And clarity is its own form of power, especially when the landscape grows noisier by the month.

To ground that landscape, the chapter turns first to the hybridisation already underway. This is not a world of neat binaries—public versus private, centralised versus decentralised, state versus protocol. It is a world of combinations. A taxpayer in Manchester may receive a refund over faster payment rails built by the state yet initiated via an app engineered by a private fintech running security checks through an open-source library maintained by volunteers across three continents. That blended sequence is not an anomaly; it is a blueprint for future rails. Strength arises not from choosing one tribe but from choreographing multiple institutions whose incentives align just enough to keep friction contained.

Yet hybrid systems invite a second set of questions: who participates, who is left out, and what does inclusion even mean when identity becomes both key and gate? Monetary systems are not neutral machines. They draw boundaries. They encode tolerances. They reveal, sometimes brutally, whose participation was presumed and whose was accepted as optional. Consider a crisis payout routed to a basic digital wallet. For the government, the transaction may be a statistical line item. For the recipient, it may determine whether the week holds heat, transport, or food. That moment of receipt is more than a transfer; it is a test of dignity. If the system fails, delays, or excludes, the consequences land on real lives long before policy-makers tally their reports.

Inclusion, then, is not an aspiration but a design constraint. A system that functions only for the digitally fluent, or only for users with high-spec devices, or only within a narrow identity schema, is not a modern monetary system; it is a selective one. Resilience, too, has a human face. Back-up rails, offline modes, paper contingencies, dispute-handling protocols—each represents a philosophical choice about how much inconvenience or humiliation society is willing to impose on its most vulnerable members during turbulence. A resilient system is not defined by its normal days but by its worst ones.

Such concerns might appear operational, yet they reach the heart of monetary legitimacy. Money succeeds when its users believe the system behind it serves them fairly. That belief depends not only on macroeconomic performance but on mundane experiences: whether cross-network transfers complete, whether fees spike unpredictably, whether identity checks are proportionate, whether personal data is treated with restraint. People infer institutional values from the frictions they encounter. A failed transfer across two networks, resolved only after multiple calls and contradictory instructions, broadcasts an unintentional message about governance: that oversight is fragmented, standards uneven, and accountability diffuse. By contrast, a seamless cross-network payment suggests alignment at a deeper level—a shared commitment to interoperability as a civic value, not merely a technical convenience.

Interoperability becomes the second motif of the chapter: *doors, not walls.* Closed systems promise efficiency but risk lock-in. Open standards invite competition but require shared governance, which is slower, harder, and more political. The question is not whether to choose openness or control in the abstract but how to structure doors that allow value to travel while preventing systemic fragility. If two payment networks can recognise each other's messages, validate each other's cryptographic proofs, and settle obligations with finality, then end users enjoy not just convenience but sovereignty—freedom to choose services without losing access to the broader economy. But achieving that requires legibility: clear protocols, accountable stewards, transparent upgrade paths, and public reasoning for design decisions. Without legibility, interoperability decays into a slogan.

As the chapter unfolds, the focus remains steady: equipping readers with the intellectual tools to evaluate any monetary proposal—familiar or novel, public or private, conventional or experimental. The aim is neither prediction nor advocacy but cultivation of judgment. Monetary design will never be settled; it is a rolling negotiation between technology, policy, and human values. What we can settle, however, are the principles by which we judge future paths.

This is the tension that animates the closing movement. If the next decade delivers a proliferation of monetary experiments—platform-issued tokens, public digital currencies, cross-border settlement protocols, embedded credit rails—how do we choose among them? How do we weigh privacy against compliance, elasticity against discipline, modularity against coherence? And how do we preserve human dignity in systems increasingly governed by automated rules, machine-drawn risk assessments, and cross-jurisdictional code? The future of money is not predetermined. It is drafted in fragments every time a system is upgraded, every time a standard is adopted, every time a protocol becomes widely used.

The question, then, is simple but demanding: when the next outage arrives, or the next innovation beckons, or the next reform is proposed, what kind of monetary world do we want that moment to reveal?

Four Questions for Any Money

The Reserve Bank of Australia's enforcement action against Trio Capital in March 2010, following the collapse of its superannuation funds the previous year, left thousands of retirees in Wollongong stunned. Their account statements had promised security; the underlying assets told a different story. When investigators traced the flows, they pieced together a simple truth: the instruments these retirees believed were cash-like had, in several instances, no reliable backing, no transparent custodian, and no enforceable claims. The resulting losses—measured not only in dollars but in shaken confidence—offered a sharp lesson. Before anyone can trust a monetary instrument, four questions must be answered. What secures it? Who governs it? How elastic is the supply? And what privacy trade-offs follow its use? That quartet determines whether a unit of account becomes a pillar of economic life or a brittle promise waiting to crack.

The 2010 episode matters because it revealed what people rarely articulate: money is only as strong as the chain of choices that holds it together. A system may appear sleek at the user interface, yet beneath it lie obligations, authorities, and constraints, each capable of bearing weight or snapping under strain. The retirees in Wollongong lacked the information needed to evaluate those foundations. Their trust was not naïve. It was unarmed. That is why a checklist—applied consistently, across instruments and jurisdictions—turns scattered theory into a tool.

The motif of the *checklist* recurs for good reason. It offers a disciplined way to interrogate any monetary design without drowning in jargon. But its power lies in use, not recitation. Each question forces us to move beyond slogans toward observation: who holds the keys, who verifies the reserves, who triggers change? A system reveals itself not through its rhetoric but through its behaviours.

The first question—*what secures the unit?*—cannot be answered through metaphor or aspiration. It demands evidence. Consider the Bank of England's gold reserves recorded in London in 1976 during the sterling crises. Those reserves offered a visible buffer that markets could measure; as they fell, traders adjusted prices, sold positions, and demanded higher yields. Here, security was literal: metal in a vault, audited and weighed. By contrast, during the eurozone stress of 2011, the European Central Bank relied not on metal but on member-state commitments and a lender-of-last-resort mandate. Its collateral framework, expanded in late 2011, demonstrated how institutional credibility, not metal, bore the unit's weight. These two cases show security as behaviour: in one, reserves that traders could count; in the other, a central bank's willingness to buy bonds at scale. Both models worked under pressure, but for different reasons.

A limitation complicates this tidy picture. Not every instrument can rest on physical backing or central bank guarantees. Alternative designs—corporate stable tokens or mutual credit schemes—often rely on off-chain assets or community enforcement. Their security is uneven, subject to managerial discretion or local politics. The implication is straightforward: when security rests on institutions without formal backstops or robust audits, the user must accept greater uncertainty. That does not render such instruments illegitimate, but it narrows their feasible scale. A checklist enforces honesty: if the backing is weak, the money cannot be strong.

The second question—*who governs it?*—is equally concrete. Governance is more than a board or a founding document; it is a pattern of decisions. Show it, name it, trace it. Hong Kong's currency board, formalised in 1983, illustrates an extreme form of rule-based governance: the monetary authority commits to issue Hong Kong dollars only against U.S. dollars at a fixed rate. Market participants can observe the rule, measure its application, and track reserves daily. The clarity creates discipline. The rule binds the administrator. Yet this governance also restricts discretion; in 1998, during the Asian financial crisis, the Hong Kong Monetary Authority intervened in equity markets to defend the peg, a controversial act that critics argued violated the spirit of the currency board. Here lies the limitation: strict rules may hold until circumstances require exceptions, and exceptions weaken credibility. Reconciling this tension requires acknowledging that even the most rule-bound systems rely on human judgment.

Contrast that with the governance of Bitcoin, whose protocol—first released in 2009—marries code, consensus, and distributed enforcement. No board sets policy. Changes require wide agreement among node operators, miners, and users. This decentralised governance minimises unilateral control but slows adaptation. The protocol's supply schedule, untouched since inception, demonstrates stability. Yet the block-size debates of 2015–2017 showed how governance without clear authority can founder in prolonged stalemate. Both systems—Hong Kong's currency board and Bitcoin—rely on rules, but the form and cost of governance differ dramatically. One signals discipline through reserves and legislation; the other signals it through immutability and broad participation. The checklist exposes these differences, forcing us to compare not abstract ideals but actual decision paths.

The third question—*how elastic is supply?*—links directly to shock absorption. An elastic system can expand liquidity when households or firms face stress; an inelastic one can preserve value but amplify recessions. The U.S. Federal Reserve's rapid balance-sheet expansion in March 2020, documented in its weekly H.4.1 releases, showed elasticity in action. Commercial paper markets froze; dollar funding tightened; the Fed intervened with trillions in liquidity. Yields fell; rollover risks eased; firms met payroll. Elasticity was a behaviour, visible in the data: the balance sheet grew by more than $2 trillion within months. A contrasting case is Argentina's money regime in 2001, constrained by a rigid convertibility plan that limited currency creation. When recession deepened, the system could not expand supply without breaking its peg. The constraint hastened collapse. Elasticity, then, is not a philosophical stance; it is a measurable capacity with consequences visible in employment, credit, and solvency.

Yet elasticity has limits. A system that expands too readily risks inflation or asset bubbles. A system that refuses to expand risks contraction. The checklist does not resolve this tension; it surfaces it. Users must decide which risks they are willing to bear and under what institutional safeguards. No monetary design eliminates trade-offs. It merely locates them.

The fourth question—*what privacy trade-offs exist?*—is often treated as an afterthought, yet in practice it shapes trust as powerfully as any reserve or governance rule. Privacy is not secrecy; it is control over one's informational footprint. Cash offers a vivid baseline. When a customer buys produce at Coventry Market using banknotes, no central ledger records the act; the transaction ends at the stall. Contrast this with a mobile wallet transfer routed through a private platform headquartered in California in 2022. The platform can observe time, location, counterparties, and patterns. Those data points feed fraud models, risk scores, and marketing profiles. The user gains convenience but relinquishes control.

A counter-example complicates the picture: Estonia's digital identity and e-government architecture, expanded since 2002, shows that privacy need not vanish in digital systems. Its design separates services, enforces audit logs, and allows citizens to see who queried their data. That transparency builds trust through visibility rather than obscurity. Reconciling these models reveals the core implication: privacy trade-offs are design decisions, not inevitabilities. They can be mitigated through governance, encryption, and user agency. A checklist prompts these questions early, before architectures fossilise.

Threaded through these four questions is a quieter motif: *who bears the cost?* Security imposes costs on issuers or users. Governance centralises or disperses decision power. Elasticity distributes losses or stabilises incomes. Privacy rules either protect autonomy or monetise behaviour. In each case, someone pays—through fees, volatility, surveillance, or reduced opportunity. The checklist forces visibility of these burdens. It reveals whether the system's gains accrue to its most privileged participants while its costs fall on those with the least bargaining power.

Two further examples illuminate how the motif sharpens judgment. Singapore's monetary policy framework, which targets the exchange rate rather than interest rates, demonstrates how governance and elasticity intertwine. Managed appreciation or depreciation moves through the economy swiftly, imposing disciplined adjustments on exporters and importers. The Monetary Authority of Singapore publishes clear policy paths and intervention records, making the mechanism legible. Users can see the rule in action. Meanwhile, Kenya's M-Pesa ecosystem, launched in 2007, offers a contrasting model: governance rooted in a private operator, elasticity governed by agent liquidity, and privacy shaped by telco data rules. Its success in reaching unbanked households shows the inclusionary potential of private rails. Yet it also illustrates concentration risk; outages and policy changes ripple rapidly through users who rely on the service daily. The checklist clarifies these implications without moralising.

Each question thus refines the same inquiry: what does this monetary system ask of its users, and what does it give them in return? The future will present new hybrids—tokens backed by treasuries, credits collateralised by invoices, public money moving on private networks. Presenting them as innovations is easy. Judging them requires discipline. The checklist provides that discipline.

As monetary experimentation accelerates, a deeper uncertainty looms. When confronted with a new unit—marketed as faster, safer, privacy-preserving, or self-stabilising—how quickly can a policymaker, a business owner, or a student map its design onto real-world consequences? And if the answers to these four questions diverge from the values a society claims to uphold, will the system still be adopted because convenience overwhelms principle?

Public, Private, and Hybrid Paths

At 07:42 on 12 April 2022, HM Revenue & Customs released its first batch of tax-refund payments through the UK's Faster Payments rails rather than the older Bacs system. The shift was small in volume—tens of thousands of transactions rather than millions—but large in consequence. Refunds that had taken three working days arrived in under a minute. For a care worker in Leeds who had overpaid on her PAYE contributions, the change meant rent paid on time rather than a penalty. For the Treasury, it was a controlled experiment: a public institution using private-sector infrastructure to deliver state obligations at speed. The moment captured a broader truth. Money does not travel on ideology; it travels on rails. And those rails, increasingly, combine public authority with private execution.

The Leeds example showed how coordination solves a friction rather than expressing a doctrine. A government department relied on a privately managed clearing network to deliver a fiscal transfer. Users saw the benefit instantly. Firms saw reduced calls to customer service lines. Banks saw reduced settlement risk. Each gained something because authority and infrastructure overlapped rather than competed. The choice was pragmatic, not philosophical. It illustrated a motif that threads this chapter: *the right rail for the right carriage*. Get the combination wrong and systems buckle. Get it right and value flows smoothly.

The first major claim rests on visibility. Public rails provide the legal foundation for settlement, finality, and accountability. Private rails provide speed, interfaces, and experimentation. Both functions are observable in practice. Take India's Unified Payments Interface (UPI), launched nationally in April 2016 by the National Payments Corporation of India. UPI is a public rail in design: standardised messaging, clear authentication, and a national settlement layer. Yet nearly all user interactions occur through private apps such as PhonePe and Google Pay. The overlap is deliberate. The public rail guarantees reach and interoperability; the private layer competes on service quality. The implication is clear: coordination expands adoption without erasing differentiation. Users benefit from a common spine and diverse front ends.

A second example demonstrates the complementarity from a contrasting angle. Brazil's Pix, launched by the Banco Central do Brasil in November 2020, is state-built and state-operated, yet private banks and fintechs supply the interfaces and customer acquisition. Pix settles instantly, 24/7. The volume surge—more than one billion payments per month by late 2022—was not an ideological triumph but an engineering one. The central bank supplied the settlement logic and risk rules; firms supplied the user experience and merchant integrations. Behaviour tells the story: taxi drivers in São Paulo began placing Pix QR codes on dashboards within months; street vendors followed; then utilities and insurers. The system scaled because the state and the private sector moved in tandem, not in rivalry.

Yet no architecture is perfect. Kenya's M-Pesa, launched by Safaricom in 2007, reveals the costs of relying on a dominant private rail. Its network became indispensable for households and firms, but outages—such as the national service disruption in December 2020—exposed concentration risks. When one firm maintains the ledger, a technical fault becomes a monetary disruption. A public regulator can impose rules, but it cannot instantly diversify the rail. The limitation is therefore structural. The implication is that private rails alone cannot guarantee systemic resilience when their market position becomes quasi-monopolistic. The checklist of earlier chapters applies: who governs, who bears risk, who verifies, and who can intervene under stress.

The motif returns: *the right rail for the right carriage.* Governance is the rail; user experience is the carriage. The question is how they latch. In Sweden, the Riksbank's settlement layer supports the retail-facing Bankgirot system and private mobile services like Swish. The central bank ensures uniform standards and liquidity during daylight hours; firms handle authentication, dispute processes, and merchant uptake. Users care about Swish's convenience, not about how the Riksbank nets obligations. Yet without that public layer, the carriage would derail. Conversely, without private innovation, the public rail would remain underused. The system works because roles are distinct and complementary.

To deepen the analysis, we turn to governance. A hybrid system divides authority over rules, liquidity, and access. That division is measurable. In the UK, the Bank of England's Real-Time Gross Settlement (RTGS) service, modernised in June 2018, introduced a wider access regime allowing non-bank payment firms to hold settlement accounts. The change enabled fintechs to connect directly to the core rail, reducing reliance on correspondent banks. This expanded the ecosystem while maintaining finality under the Bank's authority. It also made settlement behaviour observable at a granular level. If a firm mismanages liquidity, the Bank can see it. If a firm innovates, the market can adopt it. A hybrid design yields oversight without suppressing experimentation.

A credible counter-example tempers optimism. The European Cards Payment Cooperation (ECPC) effort, announced in 2020 to build a unified pan-European payments scheme, struggled to align incentives among major banks, processors, and national authorities. The initiative faced delays and fragmentation because governance was diffuse and commercial incentives diverged. The project illustrates that hybrid schemes fail when the rail-and-carriage connection is ambiguous—when no party can commit resources without knowing who holds the brake. Reconciling this limitation requires narrowing scope or strengthening governance. Without either, hybrid designs stall.

Where does this leave the user? The Leeds tax refund hints at a recurring behavioural pattern. Users judge systems by what arrives, when, and at what cost. They evaluate the carriage, not the rail. Yet their welfare depends on the rail's structure. Public rails ensure reach—widows receiving pensions, small firms receiving refunds, students receiving grants. Private rails ensure usability—clean interfaces, helpful notifications, rapid dispute handling. A hybrid model approximates a contract: the state commits to safe settlement; firms commit to good service. The user benefits from both.

To examine elasticity, consider liquidity responses during stress. In March 2020, as pandemic uncertainty escalated, central banks expanded intraday credit lines to payment participants while private firms tightened their risk models. The public sector injected stability; the private sector rationed exposure. The actions were complementary. Public elasticity prevented payments from seizing; private caution limited cascading defaults. A hybrid system allows this dual response. A purely public system might have expanded credit without granular information about counterparty quality. A purely private system might have collapsed into gridlock. The pattern shows how hybrid paths absorb shocks through differentiated behaviours.

The motif sharpens again: *rails and carriages must align in velocity as well as structure*. When a public rail moves slowly, private carriages pile up. When private rails accelerate without public safeguards, fragility sets in. Hong Kong's Faster Payment System (FPS), launched in 2018 by the Hong Kong Monetary Authority, shows alignment done well. FPS enables instant transfers between banks and stored-value facilities. The HKMA owns the rail; banks and payment firms own the interfaces. The balance allows new entrants to compete while systemic risk remains anchored under a public mandate. The velocity of the rail matches the ambition of the carriages.

Boundaries matter too. A gift card is a carriage running on a private, closed loop; it settles only within the retailer's domain. A bank transfer runs on an open loop; it settles across institutions. Hybrid systems occupy the space between these extremes. They allow a public rail to ensure interoperability while private services create meaning in context—sending rent, splitting dinner bills, receiving wages. The Leeds example underscores how a mundane fiscal transfer can illuminate this boundary. When the state chooses the rail, it shapes inclusion. When the private sector shapes the carriage, it shapes habit.

The question now is forward-looking. As digital identity systems mature, as programmable payments proliferate, and as cross-border standards begin to converge, which blend of public authority and private ingenuity best serves resilience and dignity? If a government can route a tax refund over fast private rails in under a minute, why should benefits, crisis payments, and pensions remain stuck on slower channels? And if private interfaces become the default carriage for daily life, what prevents their design choices from becoming de facto public policy?

Inclusion, Resilience, and Dignity

On a humid evening in April 2020, a street vendor in Lomé, Togo, stood outside her one-room home and checked her basic Nokia handset. A message from "Novissi" had arrived. The government's emergency support scheme—announced weeks earlier as lockdowns shuttered markets—had transferred 13,125 CFA francs to her mobile wallet. No queue. No form. No clerk deciding whether she qualified. The system had inferred eligibility from voter registration records and occupation data; if you were an informal worker in the affected districts, you received money. She walked to the nearest mobile-money agent, cashed out part of it, and left the rest on the phone. The transfer did more than cover groceries. It told her, in a moment of acute vulnerability, that she had not been forgotten. The monetary rail carried something heavier than numbers. It carried regard.

Togo's Novissi programme—rolled out by the government in April 2020—has become a reference point in policy circles because of its speed and reach relative to the country's administrative capacity. The behaviour was visible: by using mobile wallets rather than cheques or bank branches, the scheme reached hundreds of thousands of informal workers who had never interacted with the formal welfare system. The name given to this approach is "digital social protection," but the label misses an essential dimension. The design choices reduced exclusion and fragility without demanding that recipients perform their poverty at a counter window. That is what dignity looks like when money moves.

This subchapter begins from that premise. Monetary systems are not neutral pipes. They sort, filter, and condition access. They can either widen the circle of those who can make and receive payments safely or entrench patterns where the poorest face the highest costs and the sharpest humiliations. Inclusion and resilience are often discussed in separate rooms: one for financial inclusion, another for crisis management. They belong together. A system that includes only in fair weather but abandons users during storms is not inclusive; it is merely convenient. A system that stands firm during crisis but routinely excludes migrants, informal workers, or those with thin paperwork is not resilient; it is selective. The motif that will thread through this analysis is simple: *who must beg for access?*

The first claim is straightforward: design decisions around access criteria and onboarding shape who can participate in economic life at all. Show it. India's Pradhan Mantri Jan Dhan Yojana (PMJDY), launched in August 2014, aimed to open bank accounts for hundreds of millions of citizens with no previous formal access. The behaviour was striking: by 2020, hundreds of millions of low-balance accounts existed, many linked to Aadhaar IDs and mobile numbers. Name the principle: low-friction entry. Explain. By accepting alternative identity proofs and allowing zero-balance accounts, the system drastically reduced the documentation barrier that had kept poorer households outside bank branches. Implication: when entry costs fall, the perimeter of the monetary system expands; more people become reachable for both private services and public transfers.

Yet PMJDY also shows a limitation. Many accounts remained dormant, with infrequent transactions and minimal balances. Access, on paper, did not fully translate into usage. Some users lacked digital literacy; others distrusted distant institutions; still others found that cash remained more practical in informal settings. Reconciling this with the inclusion narrative forces a more precise claim: account opening is necessary but not sufficient for dignity. Without usable interfaces, nearby cash points, and reliable dispute mechanisms, formal access can degenerate into symbolic inclusion. The question *who must beg for access?* turns into *who must struggle to keep using what they have been given?*

The second claim turns to resilience. Monetary systems routinely face shocks—pandemics, floods, political unrest, cyber failures. The way a system behaves under stress reveals its true commitments. Show it again. During the first wave of COVID-19, Brazil's Auxílio Emergencial programme, launched in April 2020, delivered cash transfers via digital savings accounts operated by Caixa Econômica Federal. Behaviour: millions of Brazilians, including informal workers, received payments into newly opened digital accounts that could be accessed through mobile apps and ATMs. Name the principle: shock-responsive rails. Explain. Because the infrastructure for account opening, identity verification, and digital disbursement already existed, the state could scale support quickly when the shock arrived. Implication: resilience is not only about central banks backstopping markets; it is about whether ordinary households receive support before their lives unravel.

A counter-example clarifies the stakes. In the United States in 2020, federal stimulus payments were routed by three main channels: direct deposit, paper cheques, and prepaid debit cards. Households with up-to-date bank details on file with the Internal Revenue Service received funds quickly. Those without—often poorer, less banked, more mobile—waited weeks or months. Behaviour: queues at cheque-cashing outlets, social media threads asking when payments would arrive, reports of cards lost in the post. Name the principle: layered exclusion. Explain. When systems rely on legacy rails that presume stable banking relationships, those outside the presumption are served last. Implication: resilience that reaches markets but not the margins is incomplete. The question becomes *whose livelihoods are considered systemically important?*

The third claim binds inclusion and resilience to dignity. Dignity is harder to measure than transaction speed, but it manifests in visible ways. Does a user have to plead for exceptions? Do they have to explain their private life to strangers in order to access their own money? Do design choices expose them to shame? Show it in behaviour. In many European countries, asylum seekers receive prepaid cards instead of cash. While these cards can be practical, restrictions often limit where and on what they can be used. Purchases are logged. Cash withdrawals may be blocked. The message, however unintended, is that recipients cannot be trusted to make their own decisions. Name the principle: conditional humanity. Explain. Monetary tools that embed paternalistic controls treat certain users as problems to be managed rather than persons to be respected. Implication: even when transfers are generous, the manner of delivery can strip autonomy.

Against this, Togo's Novissi and Kenya's long-running M-Pesa experience offer a contrasting pattern. When a crisis payout arrives in a basic mobile wallet, accessible on a low-cost feature phone, the recipient can decide whether to cash out, transfer to family, or leave it parked. The system records the transaction, not the reason. The principle here is agency at the edge. Explain. By focusing on broad eligibility and flexible use rather than narrow conditions and detailed surveillance, such designs respect personhood. Implication: dignity is not a rhetorical garnish; it is encoded in whether systems assume that poor users are potential fraudsters or potential citizens.

The quiet motif returns: *who must beg for access?* In an inclusive, resilient, dignified system, no one should have to dramatise their suffering to satisfy a case worker or algorithm. Yet many existing arrangements do exactly that. They require extensive questioning, intrusive documentation, or in-person interviews held at inconvenient hours. These are not administrative inevitabilities; they are design choices that signal whose time and privacy matter.

A fourth claim concerns the role of identity systems. Strong, interoperable identity can enable inclusive, low-friction monetary access; it can also entrench exclusion if designed badly. Show it. Estonia's e-ID framework, phased in from 2002 onwards, allows citizens to sign contracts, access banking services, and file taxes digitally. Behaviour: residents open accounts and apply for services without physical visits; the system logs who accessed which records, and citizens can check those logs. Name the principle: accountable identity. Explain. When identity infrastructure is transparent and governed with clear rules and audit trails, it can support both inclusion and dignity by reducing bureaucratic friction and hidden profiling. Implication: identity, when well-governed, is a scaffold for participation rather than a filter.

Now consider a limitation. In jurisdictions where identity systems are fragmented, politicised, or discriminatory, tying monetary access tightly to identity can amplify exclusion. Stateless persons, undocumented migrants, or those from stigmatised groups may find themselves locked out not only of voting or healthcare but of basic payments. The behavioural markers are stark: cash-only employment, informal credit at usurious rates, reliance on unsafe remittance channels. Reconciling identity's promise with its perils requires insisting that monetary systems include robust fallback routes—tiered KYC, basic wallets with low thresholds, offline options—so that the absence of a perfect identity record does not translate into economic invisibility.

The fifth claim links architecture to mental bandwidth. Fragility is not only about balance sheets; it is about cognitive load. A system that demands constant vigilance, complex fee comparisons, or repeated re-verification imposes an invisible tax on those with the fewest spare resources. Show it. Low-income households juggling multiple prepaid cards, mobile wallets, and informal IOUs must track expiry dates, minimum balance rules, and hidden charges. One missed email or text can trigger fees that consume a week's disposable income. Name the principle: administrative burden. Explain. Monetary designs that offload complexity onto users degrade resilience by turning simple tasks into puzzles. Implication: dignity requires simplicity at the edge and complexity in the core, not the reverse.

This is where the crisis payout to a basic wallet becomes more than a case study. It embodies a different design philosophy. The user needs only a phone and a national number; the state and providers handle the rest. No paper forms, no obscure codes, no need to re-prove one's existence at each step. In practice, this means fewer trips, fewer confrontations, fewer moments of forced disclosure. It means that people who already live with uncertainty are not asked to master yet another labyrinth.

The motif sharpens one last time: *who must beg for access?* If the answer is "those who have the least," the system has failed, regardless of how sophisticated its cryptography or how modern its interface. If the answer is "no one; access is presumed and only revoked with cause," then the system has begun to align with the values societies claim to hold.

All of this returns us to the central question for monetary designers. When confronted with choices—about identity requirements, offline modes, dispute resolution, data retention, crisis payout channels—do they measure success purely in terms of fraud rates, unit costs, and throughput? Or do they also ask who gets left outside the branch at closing time, who cannot navigate the app, who feels watched when they tap, who fears that one mistake will lock them out? Inclusion, resilience, and dignity pull in different directions when budgets are tight and political patience is short. Which compromises are acceptable, and who sits at the table when those compromises are made?

Open Standards and Interoperability

At 08:12 on 14 September 2022, a small grocery shop in Bucharest received a payment from a customer whose bank sat on a different network. The customer used Romania's instant-payments scheme, Transfond; the shop's provider relied on a separate retail platform. The two systems did not share ownership or branding. Yet the payment arrived in two seconds, settled cleanly, and generated a receipt on both ends. The cashier barely noticed. What had once required bespoke integrations and back-office reconciliation unfolded as a single gesture because both networks adhered to the European Payments Council's SEPA Instant Credit Transfer standards. The user experienced simplicity; the infrastructure performed a disciplined choreography beneath.

This brief moment in Bucharest captures a recurring truth: interoperability is not magic. It is engineered trust made testable. Shared standards, once negotiated and adopted, become invisible in daily life. The Bucharest transaction was hardly newsworthy, yet it signalled something profound. Two systems—different software stacks, different commercial incentives, different histories—agreed on message formats, security procedures, error codes, and timing guarantees. They submitted to external rules. They submitted to scrutiny. And through that submission, they reduced user friction to almost nothing. The quiet motif for this subchapter emerges early: *the handover*. How a payment, identity assertion, or asset claim passes from one domain to another determines whether money behaves like a public utility or a proprietary maze.

The first claim is best shown with behaviour: when networks speak the same language, resilience increases. The SEPA Instant example in 2022 illustrates this. Show. Two independent providers executed a cross-network payment reliably. Name the principle: standardised messaging. Explain. By mandating ISO 20022 formats and test harnesses, European payment governance ensures that any compliant participant can interoperate with any other. Implication. Systemic fragility falls because a user's experience does not depend on the idiosyncrasies of one provider; redundancy emerges naturally as multiple nodes follow identical rules.

The second claim expands the frame to open standards beyond Europe. Show it. In November 2016, India launched the Unified Payments Interface (UPI). Within a few years, dozens of banks and private apps—Google Pay, PhonePe, Paytm—were interacting through the same UPI rails. The behaviour was unmistakable: a user could send money from one app to another without caring which bank sat behind either. Name the principle: protocol-level neutrality. Explain. UPI's design—addressable handles, standardised APIs, shared dispute codes—creates a uniform surface where competition occurs at the interface level, not through artificial gatekeeping. Implication. Interoperability reframes rivalry; firms compete on user experience, not exclusive choke points.

Yet the UPI story introduces a limitation worth confronting. Even when standards are open, governance may not be. The National Payments Corporation of India (NPCI) retains substantial control over rule updates, onboarding processes, and transaction caps. This concentration is efficient but proprietary. The counter-example therefore shows that open standards can coexist with tight oversight, and that such arrangements may constrain innovation or present single points of political failure. Reconciling this tension requires precision: interoperability is not synonymous with decentralisation; it is simply the ability to hand over control cleanly between entities without rupturing the user experience. But the question persists: *who controls the handover?*

The third claim speaks to lock-in. Closed silos are efficient on good days and brittle on bad ones. Show it. Before Brazil's PIX system launched in November 2020, instant transfers between banks were slower and expensive. PIX introduced a single standard, allowing banks and fintechs to plug into a national instant-payment grid. Behaviour: as adoption surged, merchants began accepting QR codes that worked across providers, and small businesses shifted away from proprietary wallet ecosystems. Name the principle: fungible access. Explain. When QR formats, settlement rules, and security procedures converge, value moves without proprietary friction. Implication. Lock-in softens; users can switch providers without losing functionality.

But a credible counter-example tempers the optimism. In China, Alipay and WeChat Pay long operated as dominant, semi-closed ecosystems. While both eventually adopted unified QR standards under pressure from the People's Bank of China, their early success came from tight vertical integration. Behaviour: seamless in-app experiences that bypassed bank transfers and minimised the cognitive load for users. Name the principle: closed-loop coherence. Explain. Controlled environments can deliver remarkable speed and reliability because they remove negotiation overhead. Implication. Openness is not always the shortest path to adoption; closed loops can outrun open systems in the early stages, especially when user experience is paramount.

The reconciliation lies in understanding the life cycle of payment networks. Early adoption often rewards closed designs because they can optimise end-to-end flows. But as scale grows and economic diversity rises, heterogeneity forces interconnection. Standards become the substrate for long-term resilience. The motif of *handover* returns: closed systems excel when the handover is unnecessary; open systems excel when handovers become inevitable.

The fourth claim concerns legibility—governance that a participant can understand without a lawyer or translator. Show it. The Internet Engineering Task Force (IETF), though not a payment body, offers a benchmark. Its Request for Comments (RFCs) are public, versioned, and open to critique. The behaviour: a developer in Nairobi can implement HTTPS using the same documents that guide engineers in Zurich. Name the principle: procedural transparency. Explain. When rule-making processes are documented, test suites are available, and updates follow predictable cycles, interoperability strengthens because participants trust not only the standards but the evolution of the standards. Implication. Payments need this same intelligibility; opaque governance produces brittle compliance and silent failure modes.

Current payment infrastructures vary widely on this metric. SEPA publishes rulebooks annually; UPI updates more frequently but with less public debate; private crypto networks may declare standards "open" but govern through core developers or foundation boards with limited checks. The limitation here is structural: true legibility demands not only published rules but broad oversight. Without both, standards may be shared but not stable. The unresolved tension becomes apparent: *who decides when the handover rules change?*

The fifth claim returns to the ground truth of user experience. For the end user, interoperability is not a philosophical argument. It is a moment. Show that moment. A commuter pays for a tram journey in Helsinki using a card issued by a German fintech on the Mastercard network. The tram operator's terminal uses a Finnish acquirer; the commuter's bank sits in Berlin. The transaction crosses multiple domains—terminal, acquirer, card network, issuer—yet clears instantly because EMV specifications, network rules, and fraud models align. Name the principle: layered coherence. Explain. Each layer follows standards that allow adjacent layers to trust the handover. Implication. Interoperability is not a single decision but a stack of coordinated decisions; success arises when each layer anticipates the needs of the next.

The counter-example surfaces in fragmented mobile-wallet ecosystems across parts of Africa and Southeast Asia. A user on one wallet finds they cannot send funds to another without resorting to cash-out and cash-in steps. Behaviour: users travel to mobile-money agents, withdrawing physical cash only to deposit it again moments later. Name the principle:

boundary friction. Explain. When standards for addressing, settlement, and reversals diverge, digital money behaves like a set of disconnected islands. Implication. The system squanders potential efficiency and exposes users to physical risk and additional fees.

The sixth claim steps into a more technical domain: testability. Standards are only meaningful if implementations can be verified. Show it. The Faster Payments Service in the United Kingdom requires participants to run compliance tests before connecting to the live network. These tests check message formatting, duplicate detection, and failover behaviour. Name the principle: enforced correctness. Explain. Without mandatory test harnesses, interoperability degenerates into guesswork; systems drift apart until failures manifest in production. Implication. A standard untested is a standard in name only.

Crypto networks offer a variation. Projects like Ethereum publish specifications, but client diversity introduces discrepancies. Sync bugs or consensus failures occasionally occur because two implementations interpreted the same rule differently. This is a limitation, but also a lesson: open codebases enhance transparency yet complicate uniform behaviour. Reconciling this requires humility. Perfect interoperability is neither natural nor free; it must be paid for through continuous testing and negotiated simplicity. The motif resonates again: *handover depends on shared discipline.*

A seventh claim directs attention to power. Standards shape markets. Whoever writes them exerts influence. Show it. When the European Payments Council mandated SCT Inst as part of the SEPA framework, banks had to decide whether to implement it. Those who delayed found themselves lagging fintech competitors who could route instant payments through compliant rails. Name the principle: normative weight. Explain. Standards can create de facto obligations even when nominally optional. Implication. Governance must ensure that standard-setting bodies represent diverse interests or risk entrenching incumbents.

A limitation arises when standardisation becomes a political theatre rather than a technical negotiation. Global discussions on cross-border payments—such as workstreams under the Bank for International Settlements—must reconcile different legal systems, privacy norms, and geopolitical tensions. Behaviour: slow progress, partial agreements, and pilot programmes that stall. Implication. Interoperability cannot be willed into existence by aspiration alone; it must contend with political reality. The tension endures: *how open can standards be when nations compete on payment sovereignty?*

All claims converge on the same user-facing truth: a payment that crosses networks should feel as seamless as breathing. The user should not care who runs the acquirer or which protocol handles the message. Nor should the user have to manage multiple apps or understand network boundaries. Simplicity at the edge requires sophistication at the core.

Yet the unresolved question remains sharp. If open standards and interoperability deliver resilience, competition, and dignity, why do so many providers resist them? The trade-off is rarely technical; it is strategic. Interoperability dilutes control. Shared rules level the playing field. Transparent governance subjects power to scrutiny. The real contest, therefore, is not about protocols but priorities. Should monetary systems privilege seamless handovers across domains, or preserve the moat-building strategies of dominant firms and national champions? And if we choose the former, who will guard the integrity of the shared rules when the next shock arrives?

About the Author

Jahan Vespari writes at the intersection of money, technology, and everyday life. Over a decade of interviewing builders, traders, and civil servants has shaped a worldview that treats money as a human design problem before it is a technical one. Jahan's work has appeared in independent publications and industry reports, and he has advised teams on clarity of communication rather than strategy or investment. Raised between market towns and megacities, he learned early how trust changes when prices, languages, and authorities shift. That sensibility runs through his writing: curious about systems, careful with claims, and grounded in lived use rather than hype. His mission is simple — give readers a sturdy way to judge new monetary ideas without fear or fervour.

www.ingramcontent.com/pod-product-compliance
Lightning Source LLC
Chambersburg PA
CBHW031339230926
51848CB00002B/310
9789374596722